Ajax
A Beginner's Guide

About the Author

Steven Holzner is an award-winning computer book author and web entrepreneur, with over 100 published books in 18 languages, with over 3 million copies sold. He's written extensively on Ajax, and uses it daily on his web sites. He's also been on the faculty of both Cornell University and MIT.

About the Technical Editor

Jim Keogh introduced PC programming nationally in his *Popular Electronics Magazine* column in 1982, and was a member of a team who built one of the first Windows applications by a Wall Street firm, featured by Bill Gates in 1986. He has spent almost two decades developing computer systems for Wall Street firms such as Salomon, Inc. and Bear Stearns, Inc. Keogh is presently on the faculty of New York University, and is the author of *J2EE: The Complete Reference* and *J2ME: The Complete Reference*, both published by McGraw-Hill, and more than 55 other titles.

Ajax
A Beginner's Guide

Steven Holzner

McGraw Hill

New York   Chicago   San Francisco
Lisbon   London   Madrid   Mexico City
Milan   New Delhi   San Juan
Seoul   Singapore   Sydney   Toronto

The **McGraw·Hill** Companies

Cataloging-in-Publication Data is on file with the Library of Congress

McGraw-Hill books are available at special quantity discounts to use as premiums and sales promotions, or for use in corporate training programs. To contact a special sales representative, please visit the Contact Us page at www.mhprofessional.com.

Ajax: A Beginner's Guide

1234567890 DOC DOC 0198

ISBN 978-0-07-149429-8
MHID   0-07-149429-4

Sponsoring Editor   Wendy Rinaldi
Editorial Supervisor   Janet Walden
Project Editor   Emilia Thiuri
Acquisitions Coordinator   Mandy Canales
Technical Editor   Jim Keogh
Copy Editor   Bill McManus
Proofreader   Paul Tyler
Indexer   Karin Arrigoni
Production Supervisor   Jean Bodeaux
Composition   International Typesetting and Composition
Illustration   International Typesetting and Composition
Art Director, Cover   Jeff Weeks

To Nancy

Contents at a Glance

Contents

Introduction

This book is dedicated to making web applications look and act like desktop applications that run on your computer. As we advance into the Internet Age, the difference between the desktop and the Internet is going to keep diminishing. One issue that up until now has divided desktop applications from browser-based applications is that in the browser, you usually have to wait for the whole page to refresh before you see any results. Want to buy a book online? Click the book and –*flash*– the shopping cart page appears. Want to check out? Click the checkout button and –*flash*– that page appears. Then it's on to –*flash*– the credit card information page.

All that flashing gives online applications a very different feel from that of applications on your computer. The idea behind Ajax is to get rid of all the flashing page refreshes that plague the online experience. With Ajax, you can connect to a web server behind the scenes, download data, and then display that data in the current page in a browser, all without refreshing the page.

That's the future of web development—creating a browsing experience that is no different from using a program on your own computer. Ajax enables you create that browsing experience.

This book gives you a complete introduction to Ajax—everything you need to know is here. We'll start with an overview of what Ajax can do, and how it's being used today. Then, you'll get an introduction to JavaScript, which is the foundation of Ajax on the browser side of the equation (later on, you'll see the web server side). After you have JavaScript under your belt, we'll dig into Ajax itself, showing you how to create Ajax-enabled applications. We'll also take a look at some special problems, such as how to keep two Ajax requests to the server from getting confused with each other.

There is even an easy way to create Ajax applications, in case you're utterly adverse to programming, and that's to use a package of prewritten code, called an *Ajax framework*, to do the programming for you. You'll see how to use some popular—and free—Ajax frameworks to make everything very easy to put together.

Often, the data you read from the server using Ajax is in XML form (it doesn't have to be—it can be simple text), so we're going to spend some time working with XML in the browser, seeing how to decode the XML that was downloaded from the server.

Another big part of Ajax involves updating web pages with the data you download behind the scenes unobtrusively, and we'll take a look at how to do that with dynamic HTML and Cascading Style Sheets (CSS).

In addition, we'll look at how to support Ajax on web servers. You can download static data files using Ajax, but that's not very exciting. Ajax usually involves some programming on the server, and the scripting language PHP is the language most commonly used on the server with Ajax, so you'll be introduced to PHP. You can send commands and data to the server using Ajax and, with PHP on the server, customize the data you send back to the browser.

All this and more is coming up in this book as you get a complete tour of the Ajax world.

Conventions Used in This Book

This book uses a number of conventions. For example, when a term is first introduced, it'll be shown in *italics*. When a new section of code is introduced, it'll appear in bold, such as this <div> HTML element:

```
<body>

  <h1>Appending Elements With the DOM and Ajax</h1>

  <form>
    <input type = "button" value = "Download the message"
      onclick = "getData()">
  </form>

  <div id="targetDiv" width =100 height=100>
    <p id="text"></p>
  </div>

</body>
```

You'll also find "Try This" elements, which invite you to give applications a try yourself, and "Ask the Expert" sections, which give you a little more techie insight into Ajax.

What You Need

To read this book, you should have a good knowledge of HTML. You don't have to be an HTML rock star, but you should know enough to put together a basic web page. If the level of HTML taken for granted in this book leaves you feeling lost, take a look at a good introductory HTML book before proceeding.

As far as the software side is concerned, you need a browser that can run JavaScript, such as Internet Explorer or Firefox. Ajax revolves around browsers, so you need to have access to an Internet browser to use this book profitably and follow along with the examples.

It's not totally necessary to do any server-side programming in this book, so you won't need to understand PHP as it's introduced in this book. However, I do recommend that you work with an Internet service provider (ISP) that will let you support PHP scripts online. If you don't do any server-side programming, your Ajax experience will be extremely limited and only let you download preexisting files from the server. When you use PHP on the server, you can send data from the browser to the server (for example, the ZIP code in which a prospective buyer is looking for houses) and use that data to tailor the response that you send back to the browser for display.

And that's all you need. Proceed to Chapter 1, which gives you a good overview of what Ajax has to offer.

Chapter 1

Essential Ajax

Key Skills & Concepts

- Introducing Ajax
- Live searches
- Auto-complete
- Drag and drop
- Ajax chat programs

Open your web browser, go to Google, www.google.com, type "Ajax" in the search text field, as shown in Figure 1-1, and click the Google Search button.

So what happens? The browser flickers and its display is refreshed, and you see the matches to your search term (according to Google, at the time of this writing, there are a healthy 66,700,000 matches), as shown in Figure 1-2.

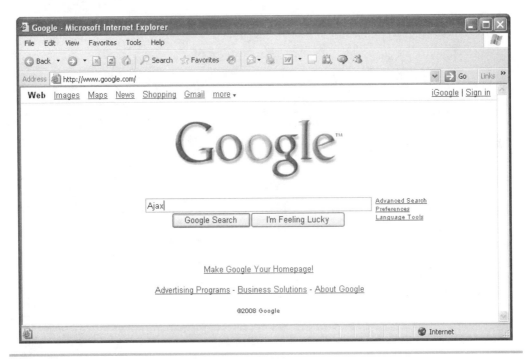

Figure 1-1 Searching for "Ajax" in Google

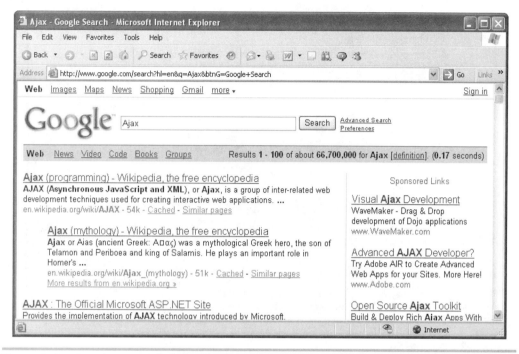

Figure 1-2   Google responds with search matches.

It's pretty clear you're working in a browser here—the display flickers as the browser downloads data from the Internet and shows you that data. In fact, the entire browser window flashed as it was updated, because the browser needed to download data from the Google web site.

What would it be like to have all of Google on your home computer, letting you avoid that flickering as the data was downloaded? In other words, what would it be like if Google were a *desktop* application instead of an Internet application?

You can get an idea how that would work by taking a look at Google Suggest, at www .google.com/webhp?complete=1&hl=en, which appears in Figure 1-3.

Now enter "Ajax" in the search text field. As you see in Figure 1-4, Google Suggest pops a drop-down list onto the screen, showing you matches to your search term in real time.

There was no flash, no flicker. Google Suggest just displayed the matches it found to the term you typed in. As you can see in Figure 1-4, Google Suggest doesn't just display the terms matching what you've entered—it also indicates the number of matches it has for each search term. No flash, no flicker, no screen update. Cool.

When you select a term from the drop-down list, the browser navigates to Google and looks up that term for you, displaying all the matches it found. Note that this time there *was* a page refresh in the browser, and its display flickered, because Ajax wasn't used when the browser navigated to Google.

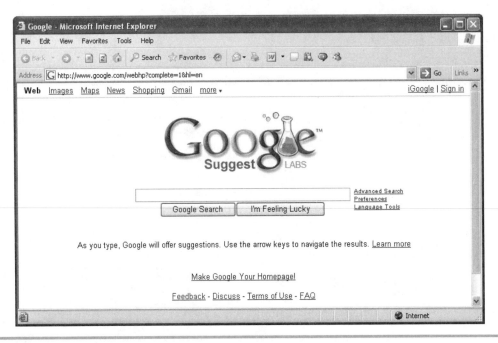

Figure 1-3 Google Suggest

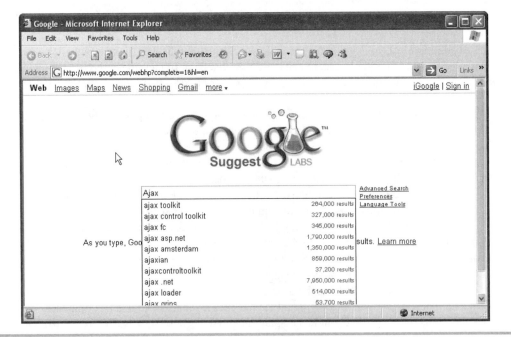

Figure 1-4 Google Suggest provides you with search matches.

As you can see, Google Suggest gives Google the feeling of a desktop application—at least partially: the screen still flickers when the browser navigates to Google to look up the term you've clicked in the drop-down list (and you'll see how to connect your own web site to Google Suggest later in this book). That's the main idea behind Ajax: taking interaction from the Internet and making it seem local, as if the application were right there on your computer.

Making Internet applications seem local is the basis of what has come to be called *Web 2.0*. That's the next step in software design: although the program you're using is really in San Francisco, it feels like it's on your computer in New York City, just as your word processor or spreadsheet program is.

In this chapter, you're going to get familiar with what Ajax is about and what it has to offer. There are thousands of Ajax-enabled web applications out there, and you're going to get a good sample of them in this chapter. We'll start this survey by determining just what Ajax is—and what it stands for.

What Is Ajax?

Ajax, which stands for *Asynchronous JavaScript and XML*, is a set of techniques for creating highly interactive web sites and web applications. The idea is to make what's on the Web appear to be local by giving you a rich user experience, offering you features that usually only appear in desktop applications.

The emphasis in Ajax applications is to update the web page, using data fetched from the Internet, without refreshing the web page in the browser. You saw an example of that with Google Suggest, where a drop-down list appears in the browser without a page refresh.

The term "Ajax" was created by Jesse James Garrett, president of Adaptive Path, in a February 18, 2005 article collecting the technologies that already existed, and which make up Ajax, under one umbrella term. That article, "Ajax: A New Approach to Web Applications," the most important one in the annals of Ajax, appears at www.adaptivepath.com/ideas/essays/archives/000385.php.

Jesse Garrett starts off his article this way:

If anything about current interaction design can be called "glamorous," it's creating Web applications. After all, when was the last time you heard someone rave about the interaction design of a product that wasn't on the Web? (Okay, besides the iPod.) All the cool, innovative new projects are online.

Despite this, Web interaction designers can't help but feel a little envious of our colleagues who create desktop software. Desktop applications have a richness and responsiveness that has seemed out of reach on the Web. The same simplicity that enabled the Web's rapid proliferation also creates a gap between the experiences we can provide and the experiences users can get from a desktop application.

That gap is closing.

And he goes on:

> The name is shorthand for Asynchronous JavaScript + XML, and it represents a fundamental shift in what's possible on the Web.

> Ajax isn't a technology. It's really several technologies, each flourishing in its own right, coming together in powerful new ways. Ajax incorporates:

> - standards-based presentation using XHTML and CSS;
> - dynamic display and interaction using the Document Object Model;
> - data interchange and manipulation using XML and XSLT;
> - asynchronous data retrieval using XMLHttpRequest;
> - and JavaScript binding everything together.

In other words, Ajax is an umbrella term for techniques you use to make web applications look like desktop applications. Here's how it works: In the browser, code written in a scripting language—most frequently, JavaScript, which Chapter 2 is all about—watches what information the user wants, such as what term they're searching for in Google Suggest. When, or even before, the user needs that information, the JavaScript code communicates with the web server *behind the scenes* to fetch that information without causing a page refresh in the browser.

That is, the way Ajax fetches data from the server is *invisible* to the user. The JavaScript code uses a special object built into the browser—an XMLHttpRequest object—to open a connection to the server and download data from the server. That data is often in XML format (the *x* in Ajax stands for XML), but it can be just plain text, as you're going to see.

When the data that the user needs has been downloaded behind the scenes, the JavaScript code uses that data to update the display in the browser. For example, in the earlier Google Suggest example, JavaScript was responsible for fetching, behind the scenes, the suggestions Google made and then displaying those suggestions in the drop-down list box after they were downloaded.

You're not restricted to using drop-down list boxes with Ajax. You can do just about anything to display or report on the downloaded data, using JavaScript, because browsers support *dynamic HTML*, which means changes you make in the page are updated instantly in the browser without having to refresh the page. You can update the text in the web page, for example, or change its size or color to bring the user's attention to new text. You can chat with friends and have their comments appear in the web page in real time. You can even use Ajax, together with dynamic HTML, to download and display images corresponding to the information the user wants. For example, you might draw graphs of business stock performance on the server and then download and display them using Ajax and dynamic HTML—all without a page refresh. Imagine how cool that looks: the user can select the stocks they want to chart, and the graph on the page changes to match, all with the feel of a desktop, not Internet, application.

Ajax is made up of several components—JavaScript, the XMLHttpRequest object, dynamic HTML, and so on—that have been around since 1998. And before Ajax had been formally introduced, it had already been used by a few applications (such as Microsoft's Outlook Web Access). But Ajax didn't really take off until 2005, with the introduction of new applications, such as Google Suggest, and Jesse Garrett's famous article collecting all the parts together into the single term Ajax.

Since then, Ajax has exploded. You can't be a web developer unless you know how to work with Ajax. Fortunately, Ajax is not hard to get to know, as you're going to see in this book.

Let's continue our guided tour of what Ajax has to offer us. Knowing what Ajax is capable of is very important when you set out to write your own Ajax-enabled applications.

We'll start off with a fun example: Tom Riddle's Diary.

An Example: Ajax-driven Tom Riddle's Diary

If you go to http://pandorabots.com/pandora/talk?botid=c96f911b3e35f9e1, shown in Figure 1-5, you'll see an online version of Tom Riddle's Diary (Tom is a character in the *Harry Potter* series).

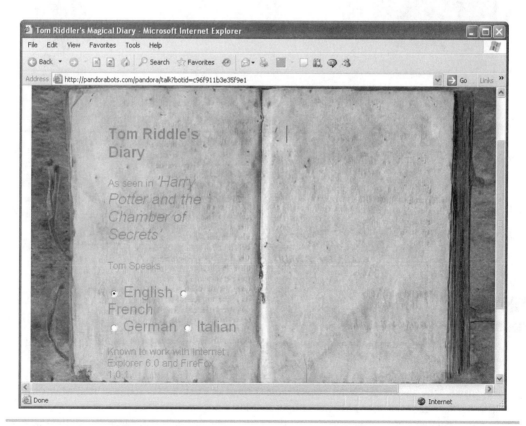

Figure 1-5   Tom Riddle's Diary

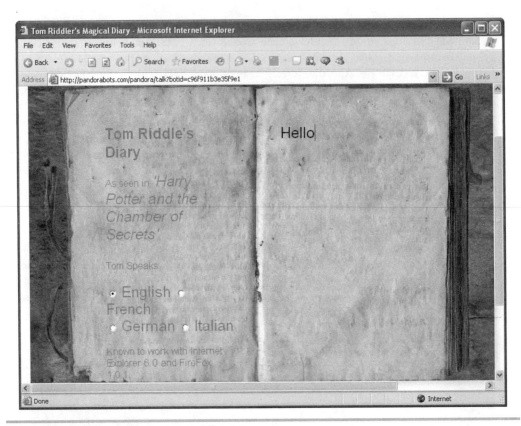

Figure 1-6 Saying Hello to Tom Riddle's Diary

The diary is actually an Ajax-enabled web application. If you type into it, it'll connect to its server using Ajax, and type a response back. For example, if you type "Hello," as shown in Figure 1-6, the diary will type back "Hi there!" as you see in Figure 1-7.

Behind the scenes, the web page connected to its server, sent what you typed to that server, and got a response back, which it displayed. Cool.

Try This   Tom Riddle's Diary

Open your browser and navigate to http://pandorabots.com/pandora/talk?botid=c96f911b3e35f9e1 to open Tom Riddle's diary.

Type something into the diary, such as the question, "What's your name?" You'll get an answer (the answer to "What's your name?" turns out to be: "My name is Tom Marvolo Riddle, also known as Lord Vol...eh, forget that last thing will you.").

You can ask detailed questions—the diary has been written to appear quite intelligent. Try "Where are you?", "How old are you?", and "What is the meaning of life?"

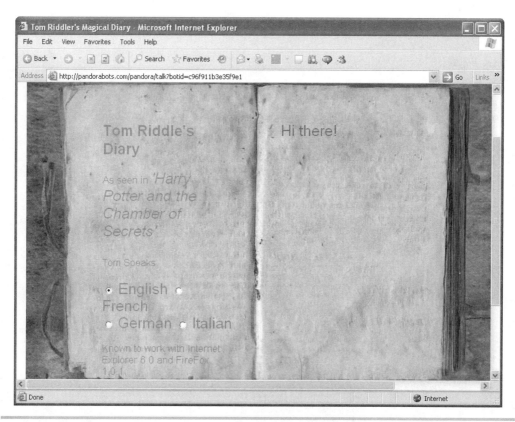

Figure 1-7   Getting a response from Tom Riddle's Diary

Updating Web Page Text with Ajax

Ajax is frequently used behind the scenes to fetch text from a web server and display that text in a web page without causing a page refresh. You can find a good example of that at http://demos.openrico.org/complex_ajax, which appears in Figure 1-8.

This page is made available by the Rico company, which sells a JavaScript framework for rich Internet applications. It is an Ajax demo that lets you create form letters—click a person's name on the left, and their name and information will appear in the body of the letter, as you can see in the figure, no page refresh needed.

The text that Ajax applications like this one fetch from the server can be in either XML or plain-text format—it's good to know that Ajax works with plain text, not just with XML (of course, "plain text" would make the acronym Ajapt, which doesn't sound nearly as good as Ajax).

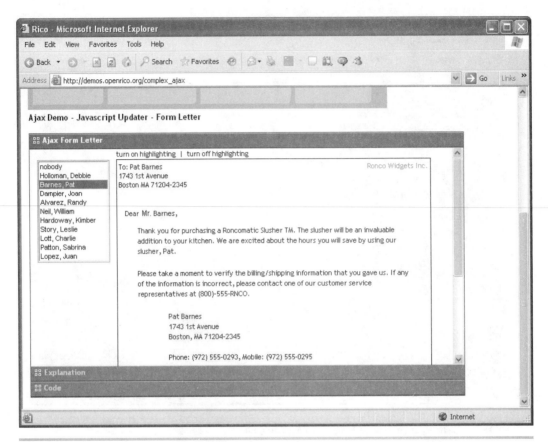

Figure 1-8 The Rico Ajax demo

Chatting in Real Time with Ajax

There are many, many Internet applications that would benefit by appearing as a desktop application, and some of those are chat applications that let you type interactively with other users on the Internet.

Ajax chat sessions operate by downloading what others have typed and uploading what you've typed, all behind the scenes—the page is updated in the browser without any flicker. One Ajax chat application appears at www.plasticshore.com/projects/chat/, which is shown in Figure 1-9.

To get started, all you have to do is enter text into the text field labeled "your message" and click the submit button. Your message will be added to the chat display seamlessly; you can see several people chatting back and forth in Figure 1-9.

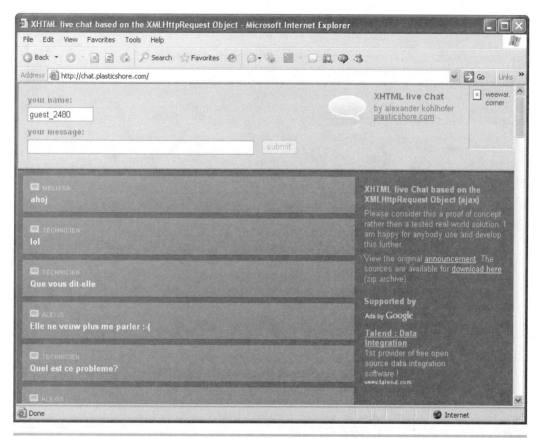

Figure 1-9   Chatting with Ajax

Dragging and Dropping with Ajax

In time, web applications are going to look more and more like desktop applications, and that means all types of desktop techniques will be available on the Web. For example, many desktop applications use drag-and-drop techniques—you can drag icons or objects around with the mouse and drop them. And now you can drag and drop on the Web as well, thanks to Ajax, which is used behind the scenes to inform the server where you dropped what you were dragging.

Figure 1-10 shows an Ajax-enabled drag-and-drop Internet application called Mosaic. The idea is that you and other people can drag and drop tiles to create a shared work of art. You can find Mosaic at www.thebroth.com/mosaic.

As you can see, you can do a lot with Ajax, just by sending text and XML back and forth to and from the server behind the scenes. It's just too bad you're limited to working with text and XML—wouldn't it be great if you could download images behind the scenes? As it turns out, you can.

Figure 1-10 Dragging and dropping Ajax

Downloading Images with Ajax (and Dynamic HTML)

Behind the scenes, Ajax communicates with the server using text (that includes XML, which is also text). So on the face of it, Ajax doesn't seem suited to downloading binary data, like images. However, with a little help from the dynamic HTML that's built into browsers these days, you can also download images.

You can download images using Ajax thanks to JavaScript. When you change the name of the image currently being displayed in an HTML <img> tag, the browser will automatically download the new image. That means that all you have to do with Ajax is download the *name* of the new image you want to display, and rely on JavaScript to do the rest.

You are going to create code for an example of this later in this book; the example appears in Figure 1-11. Simply click one of the two buttons to download a new image—completely behind the scenes—and display it, as shown in Figure 1-11. Very cool.

And, adapting this technique, you can download and use other binary data as well, using Ajax.

There are thousands of other Ajax applications. For example, take a look at Netflix's top 100 video list, at www.netflix.com/Top100, as shown in Figure 1-12. The information you see in the pop-up about the movie was downloaded using Ajax.

Figure 1-11   Downloading images with Ajax

Figure 1-12   The Netflix top 100

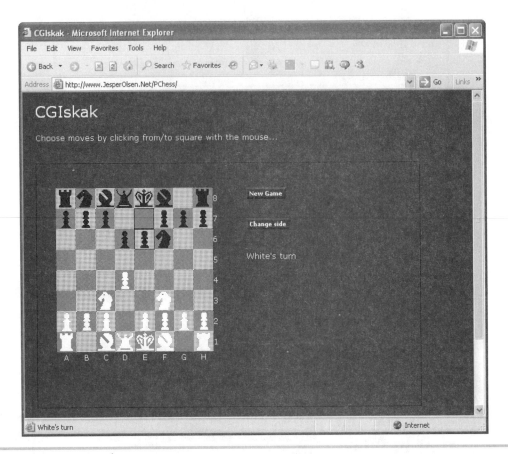

Figure 1-13 Ajax chess

How about a game of chess? Take a look at the Ajax-enabled chess site at www .JesperOlsen.Net/PChess/, which appears in Figure 1-13. Move a piece simply by clicking it and then clicking the square you want to move it to.

There are thousands and thousands of Ajax applications available, and by now you can see some of the potential. For example, imagine an online shopping site where you don't have to go through four or five flickering screens to add something to your shopping cart—you just drag the item to a shopping cart icon and, behind the scenes, Ajax informs the server of your purchase.

All this and more is coming up in this book. Turn now to Chapter 2, where you get JavaScript—the foundation of Ajax—under your belt.

Chapter 2

Getting to Know JavaScript

Key Skills & Concepts

- JavaScript properties and methods

- Storing your data in variables and arrays

- Making decisions with the if statement

- Looping with the for and while loops

- Connecting JavaScript to HTML buttons

We're going to start this chapter by jumping in with an Ajax example immediately. Take a look at Figure 2-1 to see this example, ajax.html, at work.

As shown in Figure 2-1, ajax.html displays a button with the caption "Fetch the message." When you click the button, the text in a file named data.txt is fetched from the server; here's what's in data.txt (note that this is simple text, which demonstrates that Ajax can download simple text in addition to XML):

```
Welcome to Ajax!
```

This text will be fetched from the server using Ajax, and displayed in the ajax.html page. All that happens when you click the button in ajax.html, as you can see in Figure 2-2.

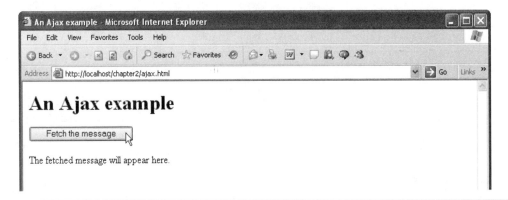

Figure 2-1 Ajax.html

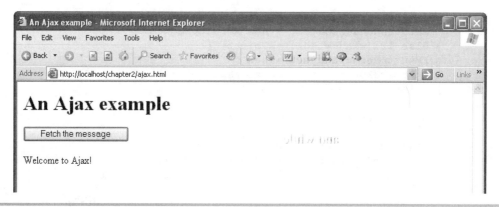

Figure 2-2   Ajax.html fetching data from the server

Try This   Test ajax.html

This is your first true example of an Ajax script written from scratch. To get this example working yourself, download the code for this book and unzip it, then copy ajax.html and data.txt from the chapter2 directory. Copy those files into a directory in a web server—for example, you might use your ISP's web server if you already host web pages there. If you don't have an ISP, you'll need to sign up for one at this point—ideally one that supports PHP, which we're going to use for programming later in this book. Ask your ISP staff how to upload files to the web server.

Copy ajax.html and data.txt to the same location on your web server (that is, they should be in the same directory). Then open your browser and navigate to ajax.html with a URL something like www.*your_isp*/*your_name*/ajax.html. When ajax.html appears in your browser, click the button to get the results shown in Figure 2-2.

If you have Windows XP Pro or Windows Vista Business or Ultimate, you may already have a functioning web server, Microsoft Internet Information Server (IIS), on your computer—if you have a directory named c:\inetpub, you have IIS. Open the directory c:\inetpub\wwwroot, and create a new directory, such as c:\inetpub\wwwroot\chapter2, and store ajax.html and data.txt in that directory. Then navigate to http://localhost/chapter2/ajax.html to see ajax.html at work.

So what does ajax.html actually look like? It is an example of the kind of code we're going to be developing throughout the book, and here it is:

```
<html>
  <head>
    <title>An Ajax example</title>

    <script language = "javascript">
      var XMLHttpRequestObject = false;
```

```
  if (window.XMLHttpRequest) {
    XMLHttpRequestObject = new XMLHttpRequest();
  } else if (window.ActiveXObject) {
    XMLHttpRequestObject = new
      ActiveXObject("Microsoft.XMLHTTP");
  }

  function getData(dataSource, divID)
  {
    if(XMLHttpRequestObject) {
      var obj = document.getElementById(divID);
      XMLHttpRequestObject.open("GET", dataSource);

      XMLHttpRequestObject.onreadystatechange = function()
      {
        if (XMLHttpRequestObject.readyState == 4 &&
          XMLHttpRequestObject.status == 200) {
            obj.innerHTML = XMLHttpRequestObject.responseText;
        }
      }

      XMLHttpRequestObject.send(null);
    }
  }
  </script>
</head>

<body>

  <H1>An Ajax example</H1>

  <form>
    <input type = "button" value = "Fetch the message"
      onclick = "getData('data.txt', 'targetDiv')">
  </form>

  <div id="targetDiv">
    <p>The fetched message will appear here.</p>
  </div>

</body>
</html>
```

The code above that's in bold is JavaScript, the heart of Ajax. To write Ajax applications, you need to know JavaScript—and that is what this chapter is all about.

Introducing JavaScript

JavaScript was first created and introduced to the world in 1995, by a developer named Brendan Eich at Netscape Communications Corporation. He named his programming language LiveScript, but the powers that were at Netscape renamed it JavaScript. The Java programming language was wildly popular at that time, and even though JavaScript is not related to Java, the name stuck. (In fact, the creators of the Java language, Sun Microsystems, had trademarked the name Java, and so the name "JavaScript" was made a trademark of Sun Microsystems.)

JavaScript was a hit. It was fun, it was powerful—in a word, it was cool. Programmers loved the things you could do with it in web pages. You could alter the text in web pages, respond to the mouse, change color schemes, and more. Web page writers ate this up.

And JavaScript inevitably caught the attention of Microsoft. At the time, the two dominant browsers were Netscape Navigator and Microsoft Internet Explorer. Microsoft didn't want to be left behind in the JavaScript wars, but it didn't want to simply license JavaScript from Netscape—so it created its own version, JScript.

JScript first appeared in 1996, in Internet Explorer 3.0, and over the years, JavaScript and JScript have become increasingly similar. However, there are a few differences that we'll come across in our guided tour of Ajax (for example, the way you create XMLHttpRequest objects, the fundamental programming construct of Ajax, differs in JavaScript and JScript), but it won't be anything we can't handle.

As an interesting historical note, both Netscape and Microsoft turned to a third party, the standards body European Computer Manufacturers Association (Ecma International, www.ecma-international.org) to standardize JavaScript so that it could be used in both browsers. What happened in fact was that a third language, ECMAScript, was born. And most browsers' versions of JavaScript are coming in line with ECMAScript these days.

Ask the Expert

Q: Are there any online references for JavaScript, JScript, and ECMAScript?

A: Yes indeed. You can find a reference for JavaScript at http://developer.mozilla.org/en/docs/Core_JavaScript_1.5_Reference, and a reference for JScript is at http://msdn2.microsoft.com/en-us/library/hbxc2t98(vs.71).aspx.

There is also a great deal of information about ECMAScript available online:

- The ECMAScript Language Specification, 3rd edition, is at www.ecma-international.org/publications/standards/Ecma-262.htm.

- The ECMAScript Components Specification is at www.ecma-international.org/publications/standards/Ecma-290.htm.

- The ECMAScript 3rd Edition Compact Profile Specification is at www.ecma-international.org/publications/standards/Ecma-327.htm.

Now let's start digging into JavaScript and seeing it work.

Getting Started with JavaScript

We're going to see JavaScript programming at once with a new example, javascript.html. This example appears in Figure 2-3.

In this first example, we're using JavaScript code to write the header "Welcome to JavaScript!" that appears in Figure 2-3; doing so will give us our start with JavaScript.

You embed your JavaScript in a web page. Say, for example, that javascript.html started off like this—just pure HTML:

```
<html>
  <head>
    <title>This is a first JavaScript example</title>
  </head>

  <body>
    This is a first JavaScript example.
  </body>
</html>
```

Now we're going to start adding JavaScript. You place your JavaScript code into an HTML <script> element, which goes inside the page's <head> element, like this:

```
<html>
  <head>
    <title>This is a first JavaScript example</title>

    <script language="javascript">
       .
       .
       .
    </script>
  </head>

  <body>
    This is a first JavaScript example.
  </body>
</html>
```

Figure 2-3   javascript.html

Note that the <script> element is an HTML element like any other. Its purpose is to tell the browser that there is JavaScript code present, and that the browser should run that code. Notice also the language attribute of the <script> element, which has been set to the value "javascript" here, indicating that the scripting language used inside the <script> element is JavaScript (there are other scripting languages, such as VBScript, which runs in Internet Explorer).

Now our job is to write the header "Welcome to JavaScript!" (see Figure 2-3) to the web page. In JavaScript, you interact with the browser through the use of built-in *objects*; these objects exist already, and can be accessed from your JavaScript code by name. Here are the four most commonly used objects:

- **document**   Represents the web page itself

- **history**   Represents the list of URLs that the browser has already been to

- **window**   Represents the browser itself

- **XMLHttpRequest**   The object that you use in Ajax to communicate with the server

In JavaScript, objects have methods and properties. A *method* is a chunk of code built into the object that performs some action—for example, you use the document object's write method, which you access as document.write, to write to the document (that is, the current web page). Here are some representative methods and what they do in JavaScript:

- **document.write**   Lets you write text to the current web page

- **history.go**   Moves the browser to a page in the browser's history

- **window.open**   Opens a new browser window

Properties, on the other hand, are just settings that you can place data into. For example, document.bgcolor lets you access the bgcolor value of the HTML <body> element—that is, the background color. (JavaScript properties often take their names from the attributes of HTML elements, such as the bgcolor attribute of the <body> element.) Here are a few of the useful properties that are available:

- **document.bgcolor**   Holds the background color of the current page

- **document.fgcolor**   Holds the foreground color of the current page

- **document.lastmodified**   Holds the date the page was last modified

- **document.title**   Holds the title of the page

- **location.hostname**   Holds the name of the page's host

- **navigator.appName**   Holds the type of the browser

We're going to use the document.write method to write to the current web page in the javascript.html example. You can send the text you want written to the web page by placing that text in parentheses, which passes that text to the document.write method, like this:

```html
<html>
  <head>
    <title>This is a first JavaScript example</title>

    <script language="javascript">
      document.write("<h1>Welcome to JavaScript!</h1>");
    </script>
  </head>

  <body>
    This is a first JavaScript example.
  </body>
</html>
```

Lines of code like this are called *statements* in JavaScript and, as you can see, they end with a semicolon. Note that we're actually passing HTML to the document.write method—that is, the text we're displaying in the current web page is "<h1>Welcome to JavaScript!</h1>", which displays the "Welcome to JavaScript!" text inside an <h1> header, just as if you added this HTML in a web page yourself:

```html
<h1>Welcome to JavaScript!</h1>
```

And you can see the results in Figure 2-3, where the new header appears. Not bad.

Note the placement of the text in Figure 2-3. The header, which we wrote with JavaScript, appears on top of the text in the <body> element. Why? That's because when the browser reads in javascript.html, it processes the page as it reads it, and it reads the <head> section (where our JavaScript is) first. So the JavaScript code gets executed before the browser sees the text in the <body> element, giving you the results you see in Figure 2-3. In general, the code in a <script> element is executed as soon as it is loaded, but that's not what you always want; you may want to wait to execute your JavaScript until the user clicks a button, for example. Later in this chapter, you'll see how to make sure JavaScript code is executed only when you want to execute it—not automatically when the page loads.

Try This Get javascript.html to Work

You're going to need a text editor of some kind to enter javascript.html and run it in a browser. (You could just get javascript.html from the chapter2 folder in the downloadable code for this book, but to follow along in this book, you have to know how to create your own files.)

For example, in Windows, Windows WordPad will work fine. Open WordPad and enter the text for javascript.html. To save javascript.html, choose File | Save As to open the Save As dialog box. Give the file the name **javascript.html** and—this is important—in the Save

As Type drop-down list box, choose Text Document, not the default Rich Text Format (RTF). If you save web pages in RTF format, browsers won't be able to read them.

And here's another note about WordPad: if you save a file with a filename extension that WordPad isn't familiar with, it'll append the suffix ".txt" to your file. That's not a problem with HTML files, because they have the extension .html, which WordPad understands. But it will be an issue when it comes to creating the PHP files we'll be using to perform programming on the web server toward the end of this book (PHP is a programming language you use on web servers, as you'll see starting in Chapter 9). For example, if you try to save a file as ajax.php with WordPad, WordPad saves the file as ajax.php.txt, which won't work on the server. Instead, you must enclose the name of the file in quotation marks in the File Name box in the Save As dialog box, like this: "ajax.php". Doing so tells WordPad that you don't want the name of the file you're saving to be changed, and thus it won't append the .txt extension.

You can save javascript.html to a web server or, if you like, simply to your hard disk— relying purely on JavaScript and not needing to interact with a server, javascript.html can be opened directly in your browser from disk. After saving javascript.html, open it in your browser and confirm the results by comparing it to what you see in Figure 2-3. You can navigate to javascript.html by entering the URL to access it on your web server, or by opening it directly from disk (in Internet Explorer, choose File | Open and browse to javascript.html; in Firefox, choose File | Open File).

Note also that some users may have JavaScript support turned off in their browsers, in which case they can't run javascript.html and can't run Ajax. (You might consider putting a note in your web page saying that if the user doesn't see the desired effect to make sure JavaScript support is turned on in their browser.)

Adding Comments to Your Code

Now that we've got some JavaScript running, it's worth noting that you can annotate your code with *comments*, text that is intended to be read by people, not by the computer (which ignores them). Using comments makes your JavaScript much more readable, and explains in plain language what your program does.

There are two forms of comments in JavaScript: single line and multiple line. A single-line comment starts with // (two forward slashes), like this:

```
<html>
  <head>
    <title>This is a first JavaScript example</title>

    <script language="javascript">
      //Write to the web page
      document.write("<h1>Welcome to JavaScript!</h1>");
    </script>
  </head>
```

```
  <body>
    This is a first JavaScript example.
  </body>
</html>
```

Everything that follows the // on a line is ignored by the browser. You can also put a single-line comment at the end of a line of code, like this:

```
<html>
  <head>
    <title>This is a first JavaScript example</title>

    <script language="javascript">
      document.write("<h1>Welcome to JavaScript!</h1>"); //Write to the page
    </script>
  </head>

  <body>
    This is a first JavaScript example.
  </body>
</html>
```

Multiple-line comments are surrounded by /* and */. When you use /*, the browser ignores everything that follows until it sees a */ to end the comment. Here's an example of a multiline comment:

```
<html>
  <head>
    <title>This is a first JavaScript example</title>

    <script language="javascript">
      /*
        Write
        to
        the
        web page.
      */
      document.write("<h1>Welcome to JavaScript!</h1>");
    </script>
  </head>

  <body>
    This is a first JavaScript example.
  </body>
</html>
```

Using External JavaScript Files

You'll often see Ajax-enabled web pages with this kind of syntax, and no JavaScript inside the web page itself (external.html):

```
<html>
  <head>
    <title>Using external JavaScript</title>

    <script language="javascript" src="script.js">
  </head>

  <body>
    <h1>Using external JavaScript</h1>
  </body>
</html>
```

What's going on here? In this case, the JavaScript code is being stored externally, in a file named script.js. So what's actually in script.js? Just the exact lines of JavaScript you want to execute, nothing else. For example, in this case, that would be

```
document.write("<h1>Welcome to JavaScript!</h1>");
```

This new example works much like the example you've already seen, javascript.html, except that the JavaScript is external to the web page. You'll see this often in Ajax—you can find large JavaScript libraries of prewritten code that can run to dozens of pages. Some of that code is written to support Ajax for you so that you only have to write minimal code, and in that case, those libraries are called Ajax frameworks (see Chapter 5). When you use such a framework, it would be awkward if you had to include its whole code—dozens of pages of it—in your own web pages. The solution is that Ajax frameworks package their JavaScript in external files, and you simply refer to that code as you see here, with the <script> element's src attribute. Problem solved.

Okay, up to this point, the JavaScript code you've seen was executed by the browser as soon as the page containing that JavaScript was loaded. But what if you want to run your JavaScript—for example, to display new text—only after the page is loaded and the user has clicked a button? That's coming up next.

Handling Events in the Browser

So far, your JavaScript has been run as soon as the page was loaded:

```
<html>
  <head>
    <title>This is a first JavaScript example</title>

    <script language="javascript">
      document.write("<h1>Welcome to JavaScript!</h1>");
    </script>
  </head>

  <body>
    This is a first JavaScript example.
  </body>
</html>
```

But you may want to execute some code only when something happens, such as a mouse click or when a character is typed. In that case, you can set up your JavaScript code to respond to browser *events* (like mouse clicks or key presses).

An event is just what it sounds like—something's happened; the user clicked a button, for example. What events are available? Here are some common ones that you might see in Ajax applications:

Event	Occurs when...
onabort	an action is aborted.
onblur	an element loses the input focus.
onchange	data changes in a control, such as a text field.
onclick	an element is clicked.
ondblclick	an element is double-clicked.
ondragdrop	a drag-and-drop operation is undertaken.
onerror	there's been a JavaScript error.
onfocus	an element gets the focus.
onkeydown	a key goes down.
onkeypress	a key is pressed and the key code is available.
onkeyup	a key goes up.
onload	the page loads.
onmousedown	a mouse button goes down.
onmousemove	the mouse moves.
onmouseout	the mouse leaves an element.
onmouseover	the mouse moves over an element.
onmouseup	a mouse button goes up.
onreset	the user clicks a Reset button.
onresize	an element or page is resized.
onsubmit	the user clicks a Submit button.
onunload	a page is unloaded.

To handle these events, you use attributes of the same name in HTML tags. Let's take a look at a simple example, click.html, that makes this more clear. In this case, we'll make the page respond when you click it, using *inline* JavaScript—that is, JavaScript code that is assigned to an event attribute in an HTML tag like this (click.html):

```
<html>
    <head>
        <title>
            Using browser events
```

```
            </title>
        </head>

        <body onmousedown="alert('You clicked the page.')">
            <h1>
                Click this page!
            </h1>
            Go ahead...
        </body>
</html>
```

What's happening here is that we're using the onmousedown event of the <body> element (which represents the whole web page) to respond to mouse down events (that is, the mouse button was pressed). When the user presses the mouse button while in the page, the onmousedown event "fires" (that's the technical term) and the JavaScript assigned to that event is executed.

In this case, that JavaScript is the statement alert('You clicked the page.'), which displays a JavaScript alert box (that is, a dialog box) with the text "You clicked the page." in it.

Ask the Expert

Q: Why did you use single quotation marks in the statement alert('You clicked the page.')? Should that be alert("You clicked the page.")?

A: You use single quotation marks to avoid confusing the browser. Note that inline JavaScript has to be totally enclosed in quotation marks, like this:

<body onmousedown="alert('You clicked the page.')">

If we didn't alternate between double and single quotation marks, the browser wouldn't know where the text to display started and stopped.

You can see this in action in Figure 2-4, where you see click.html.

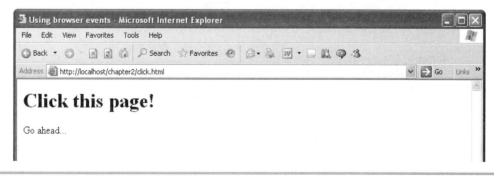

Figure 2-4   click.html

Figure 2-5 click.html at work

When you click the page, a dialog box appears indicating that the click was noticed, as you see in Figure 2-5. Cool. Now you've responded to a browser event.

Try This **Get click.html to Work**

Enter the code for click.html into a file using your text editor (or, if you want the easy way, just copy click.html from the chapter2 folder of the downloadable code from this book), and store that file either on a web server that is accessible to your browser or just on disk.

Now open your browser and navigate to click.html—and click the page. You should see the dialog box that appears in Figure 2-5. Good job!

Okay, that's one way to respond to browser events—with inline JavaScript code. But as your JavaScript code gets larger and larger, it's going to be impossible to store inline. So what can you do?

You can use JavaScript *functions*, coming up next.

Working with JavaScript Functions

You already know that you can write code in a <script> element that will be executed automatically when the page is loaded:

```
<html>
  <head>
    <title>This is a first JavaScript example</title>

    <script language="javascript">
      document.write("<h1>Welcome to JavaScript!</h1>");
    </script>
  </head>

  <body>
    This is a first JavaScript example.
  </body>
</html>
```

To execute code when you want to execute it, you need to place that code in a JavaScript *function* (functions are just like methods, except that methods are contained inside JavaScript objects, and functions are free-standing). For example, here's how you might create a function named display:

```html
<html>
  <head>
    <title>Using JavaScript functions</title>

    <script language="javascript">
      function display()
      {
         .
         .
         .
      }
    </script>
  </head>

  <body>
    <h1>Using JavaScript functions</h1>
  </body>
</html>
```

Note the syntax here—you use the keyword function, followed by the name of the new function, and a pair of parentheses. That's followed by the code of the function, enclosed in curly braces, { and }, which is where the code will go.

To run the code in the function, you have to *call* that function, and we'll do that when the user clicks a button, so add that button using the HTML <input> tag now, like this:

```html
<html>
    <head>
        <title>Using JavaScript functions</title>

        <script language="javascript">
            function display()
            {
               .
               .
               .
            }
        </script>

    </head>

    <body>
        <h1>Using JavaScript functions</h1>
```

```
<form>
  <input type="button" value="Click Here">
</form>
```

```
    </body>
</html>
```

Note that in HTML you have to enclose controls, like buttons, list boxes, checkboxes, and so on, in an HTML <form> element. The <input> element here creates a button with the caption "Click Here."

So how do we actually call the display function when the user clicks the button? You can use a little inline code for that. Just giving the name of the function, followed by parentheses, calls the function, so we can call the function when the user clicks the button by assigning the function call to the button's onclick event:

```
<html>
    <head>
        <title>Using JavaScript functions</title>

        <script language="javascript">
            function display()
            {
                  .
                  .
                  .

            }
        </script>

    </head>

    <body>
        <h1>Using JavaScript functions</h1>
        <form>
          <input type="button" onclick="display()"
            value="Click Here">
        </form>

    </body>
</html>
```

Now the display function will be called when the user clicks the button. In the display function, we can write a message—say, "You clicked the button."—to the web page. So, can we do that with the following code?

```
<html>
    <head>
        <title>Using JavaScript functions</title>

        <script language="javascript">
```

```
        function display()
        {
          document.write("You clicked the button.");
        }
    </script>

  </head>

  <body>
    <h1>Using JavaScript functions</h1>
    <form>
      <input type="button" onclick="display()"
        value="Click Here">
    </form>

  </body>
</html>
```

Unfortunately not. The display function will indeed be called after the body of the page loads—when the user clicks the button—and that's fine. But there's a catch. When the body of a page is loaded, you can no longer use the document.write method, because the document is considered *closed*. And opening it again to write to it clears any text in it, so that's no good here—all you'd see is the "You clicked the button." message because the "Using JavaScript functions" header will have been overwritten.

The way to display new text in a web page after that page has been loaded is to write to an existing HTML element, like a <div> element. For example, you might add a <div> element and give it the ID targetDiv:

```
<html>
  <head>
    <title>Using JavaScript functions</title>

    <script language="javascript">
      function display()
      {

            .
            .
            .

      }
    </script>

  </head>

  <body>
    <h1>Using JavaScript functions</h1>
    <form>
      <input type="button" onclick="display()"
        value="Click Here">
    </form>
```

```
        <div id="targetDiv">
        </div>
    </body>
</html>
```

So how can you address the targetDiv element in the JavaScript code in the display function? You have to tell JavaScript which HTML element you want to place text into in order to display that text, and to find an HTML element in the web page, you can use the JavaScript method document.getElementById.

You *pass* this method the ID of the element you want to find; to pass data to a method or function, you enclose that data in the parentheses (as you did with document.write: document .write("Here is the text")). So to find the targetDiv HTML element, you can call document .getElementById('targetDiv'). This method call *returns* an object corresponding to the targetDiv <div> element—when a method or function returns data, you get access to that data. For example, the object corresponding to the targetDiv <div> element supports various methods and properties of its own, and one of those properties, innerHTML, contains the text now in the element. That means you can store new text in the element by assigning that new text to the expression document.getElementById('targetDiv').innerHTML.

Here's the way you can store the text "You clicked the button." in the targetDiv <div> element:

```
<html>
    <head>
        <title>Using JavaScript functions</title>

        <script language="javascript">
            function display()
            {
              document.getElementById('targetDiv').innerHTML =
              "You clicked the button.";
            }
        </script>

    </head>

    <body>
        <h1>Using JavaScript functions</h1>
        <form>
          <input type="button" onclick="display()"
            value="Click Here">
        </form>

        <div id="targetDiv">
        </div>
    </body>
</html>
```

Great, we're ready to go; open functions.html in a browser, and click the button. When you do, you'll see the text "You clicked the button." displayed, as shown in Figure 2-6.

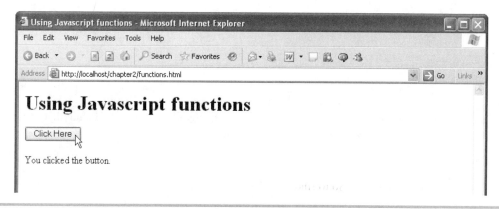

Figure 2-6   Using JavaScript functions and HTML buttons

Passing Data to Functions

Just as you can pass data to the methods already built into JavaScript, so too can you pass data to the functions you create. For example, say that you want to specify the message that you want to display by passing that message to the display function. You could pass that message to the display function by placing it inside the parentheses when you call display in a new web page, message.html, as we've seen with calls to methods:

```html
<html>
  <head>
    <title>Passing data to functions</title>

    <script language="javascript">
      function display()
      {
          .
          .
          .
      }
    </script>
  </head>

  <body>

    <h1>Passing data to functions</h1>

    <form>
      <input type="button" onclick=
      "display('You are seeing this thanks to JavaScript')" value=
      "Click Here">
    </form>
```

```
   <div id="targetDiv">
   </div>

</body>
</html>
```

So how do you read the message that was passed to the display function in code? It's simple—you just give a name to the data passed to the display function by listing that name in the parentheses when you create the display function:

```
<html>
  <head>
    <title>Passing data to functions</title>

    <script language="javascript">
      function display(message)
      {
             .
             .
             .
      }
    </script>
  </head>

  <body>

    <h1>Passing data to functions</h1>

    <form>
      <input type="button" onclick=
      "display('You are seeing this thanks to JavaScript')" value=
      "Click Here">
    </form>

    <div id="targetDiv">
    </div>

  </body>
</html>
```

Now you can refer to the data passed to the display function with the name you've given that data—message—in the body of the function. So, for example, to display that message in the web page, you could do this (message.html):

```
<html>
  <head>
    <title>Passing data to functions</title>
```

```
<script language="javascript">
  function display(message)
  {
    document.getElementById("targetDiv").innerHTML = message;
  }
</script>
</head>

<body>

  <h1>Passing data to functions</h1>

  <form>
    <input type="button" onclick=
    "display('You are seeing this thanks to JavaScript')" value=
    "Click Here">
  </form>

  <div id="targetDiv">
  </div>

</body>
</html>
```

You can see this at work in Figure 2-7. Click the Click Here button and your message will be passed to the display function, which grabs that message and displays it in the web page, as you see in Figure 2-7.

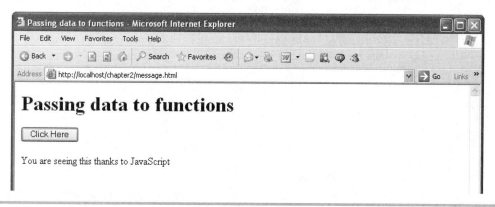

Figure 2-7   Passing data to JavaScript functions

Try This Pass Data to Functions

Enter the code for message.html into a file using your text editor, and store that file either on a web server that is accessible to your browser or just on disk. Change the message passed to the display function from 'You are seeing this thanks to JavaScript' to 'Hey, this works!'.

Now open your browser, navigate to message.html, and click the button. You should see your message displayed. Cool!

What if you want to pass multiple data items to a function? You can do that simply by passing those items, separated by commas, in the parentheses following the function's name. For example, say that you have two <div> elements in the page, targetDiv and targetDiv2:

```
<html>
  <head>
    <title>Passing data to functions</title>

    <script language="javascript">
      function display(message)
      {
        document.getElementById("targetDiv").innerHTML = message;
      }
    </script>
  </head>

  <body>

    <h1>Passing data to functions</h1>

      <input type="button" onclick=
      "display('You are seeing this thanks to JavaScript')" value=
      "Click Here">

    <div id="targetDiv">
    </div>
    <div id="targetDiv2">
    </div>

  </body>
</html>
```

How could you specify which <div> element to display your message in? You could pass the ID of that <div> element to the display function, and that would work like this:

```
<html>
  <head>
    <title>Passing data to functions</title>
```

```
<script language="javascript">
  function display(message)
  {
    document.getElementById("targetDiv").innerHTML = message;
  }
</script>
</head>

<body>

<h1>Passing data to functions</h1>

  <input type="button" onclick=
  "display('You are seeing this thanks to JavaScript', 'targetDiv')"
  value="Click Here">

<div id="targetDiv">
</div>
<div id="targetDiv2">
</div>

</body>
</html>
```

Next, in the display function, you could name the second data item that you pass something like elementID by writing the function like this:

```
function display(message, elementID)
{
  .
  .
  .
}
```

Now you're free to use the elementID data item in your code to place the message in the corresponding <div> element like this:

```
<html>
  <head>
    <title>Passing data to functions</title>

    <script language="javascript">
      function display(message, elementID)
      {
        document.getElementById(elementID).innerHTML = message;
      }
    </script>
  </head>
```

```
<body>

  <h1>Passing data to functions</h1>

    <input type="button" onclick=
    "display('You are seeing this thanks to JavaScript', 'targetDiv')"
    value="Click Here">

  <div id="targetDiv">
  </div>

  </body>
</html>
```

And that's all there is to it.

Returning Data from Functions

You can also return data from functions. In other words, a function can do its work and pass you a result of some kind back. For example, say that you have a clever function named adder, and you pass it two numbers to add—how can it send you back the answer from the adder function?

Say that adder looks like this:

```
function adder(operand1, operand2)
{
    .
    .
    .
}
```

You can return a value from a function with the return statement, which in adder's case looks like this:

```
function adder(operand1, operand2)
{
    return operand1 + operand2;
}
```

That is, we're adding operand1 and operand2, the two data items passed to adder, and returning the sum. That way, when you call, say, adder(6, 6), JavaScript will replace that call with the value returned from the adder function at run time. All of which means that here's how you can call adder from another function, display (this is adder.html):

```
<html>
  <head>
    <title>Returning data from functions</title>

    <script language="javascript">
      function display()
      {
        document.getElementById("targetDiv").innerHTML =
```

```
            "6 + 6 = " + adder(6, 6);
      }

      function adder(operand1, operand2)
      {
        return operand1 + operand2;
      }
    </script>
  </head>

  <body>
    <h1>Returning data from functions</h1>
      <input type="button" onclick="display()" value="Click to add 6 + 6">

    <div id="targetDiv">
    </div>

  </body>
</html>
```

Take a look at adder.html in Figure 2-8. When you click the button, presto, 6 is added to 6 and you can see the results.

What happened here was that 6 and 6 were passed to the adder function, which added them and returned the sum, 12. Nice.

Try This Return Data from Functions

Try your own version of the adder example, but instead of adding two numbers, multiply them! Write and put to work a function named multiplier instead of adder, and pass two values to multiplier—and then display the resulting product. In JavaScript code, you multiply using the * symbol; for example, 6 * 6 = 36.

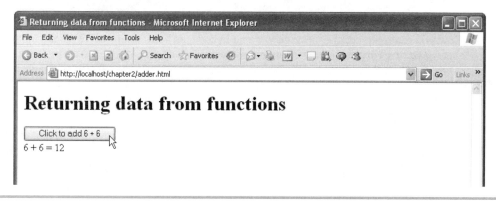

Figure 2-8   Returning data from JavaScript functions

Working with Variables

JavaScript lets you store your data in *variables*, which are placeholders in memory, set up to hold that data. When you store data in variables, that data hangs around, ready for you to use. You create variables with the JavaScript var statement; here's an example, which creates a variable named message, and stores the text "This text was stored in a variable." in it, in variable.html:

```
<html>
  <head>
    <title>Working with variables</title>

    <script language="javascript">

      var message = "This text was stored in a variable.";

      function display()
      {
          .
          .
          .
      }
    </script>
  </head>

  <body onload="showMessage()">
    <h1>Working with variables</h1>

    <input type="button" onclick="display()" value="Click Here">

    <div id="targetDiv">
    </div>

  </body>
</html>
```

Now you can reference the message variable in code, as here, where we're displaying the message's text in a <div> element (variable.html):

```
<html>
  <head>
    <title>Working with variables</title>

    <script language="javascript">

      var message = "This text was stored in a variable.";

      function display()
```

```
        {
          document.getElementById('targetDiv').innerHTML = message
        }
      </script>
  </head>

  <body onload="showMessage()">
    <h1>Working with variables</h1>

    <input type="button" onclick="display()" value="Click Here">

    <div id="targetDiv">
    </div>

  </body>
</html>
```

You can see variable.html at work in Figure 2-9. You just click the button and the message will be fetched from the message variable and popped into the web page.

Besides storing text in variables, you can also store numbers, as in this example, where we've modified the adder function to store the sum it calculates in a variable named sum, and then return that sum:

```
<html>
  <head>
    <title>Returning data from functions</title>

    <script language="javascript">
      function display()
      {
        document.getElementById("targetDiv").innerHTML =
          "6 + 6 = " + adder(6, 6);
      }
```

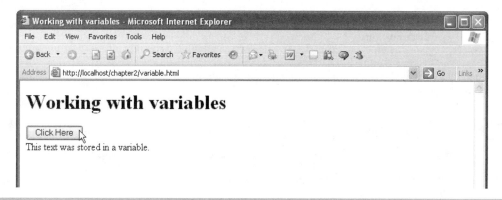

Figure 2-9   Storing data in variables

```
    function adder(operand1, operand2)
    {
      var sum = operand1 + operand2;
      return sum;
    }
  </script>
</head>

<body>
  <h1>Returning data from functions</h1>
  <input type="button" onclick="display()" value="Click to add 6 + 6">

  <div id="targetDiv">
  </div>

</body>
</html>
```

There's a difference between these two examples that you should know about. When you create a variable outside any function, like this:

```
<script language="javascript">

  var message = "This text was stored in a variable.";

  function display()
  {
    document.getElementById('targetDiv').innerHTML = message
  }
</script>
```

then that variable is called a *global* variable, and can be used anywhere in your code, inside functions or outside them. However, if you create a variable inside a function, like this:

```
function adder(operand1, operand2)
{
  var sum = operand1 + operand2;
  return sum;
}
```

then that variable is called a *local* variable, and it can only be used and accessed inside the same function.

Putting It All Together with Operators

You already know that you can add values using the + sign:

```
function adder(operand1, operand2)
{
  var sum = operand1 + operand2;
  return sum;
}
```

The plus sign, +, is the JavaScript addition operator. You can also subtract values with the subtraction operator, −:

```
var value = operand1 + operand2;
```

Or multiply values with the * operator:

```
var value = operand1 * operand2;
```

Or divide values with the division operator, /:

```
var value = operand1 / operand2;
```

There are many such operators already built into JavaScript. The whole list is provided in Table 2-1.

Operator	Description
Arithmetic Operators	
+	Adds two numbers.
++	Increments the value in a variable by one.
−	Subtracts one number from another. Also can change the sign of its operand like this: −variableName.
--	Decrements the value in a variable by one.
*	Multiplies two numbers.
/	Divides two numbers.
%	Evaluates to the remainder after dividing two numbers using integer division.
String Operators	
+	Joins (concatenates) two strings.
+=	Joins (concatenates) two strings and assigns the joined string to the first operand.
Logical Operators	
&&	Evaluates to true if both operands are true; otherwise, evaluates to false.
||	Evaluates to true if either operand is true. However, if both operands are false, evaluates to false.
!	Evaluates to false if its operand is true, and to true if its operand if false.
Bitwise Operators	
&	Sets a one in each bit position in which both operands' bits are ones.
^	Sets a one in a bit position if the bits of one operand, but not both operands, are one.
|	Sets a one in a bit if either operand has a one in that position.

Table 2-1   The JavaScript Operators

(continued)

Operator	Description
~	Flips each bit.
<<	Shifts the bits of the first operand to the left by the number of places specified by the second operand.
>>	Shifts the bits of the first operand to the right by the number of places specified by the second operand.
>>>	Shifts the bits of the first operand to the right by the number of places specified by the second operand, and shifts in zeros from the left.
Assignment Operators	
=	Assigns the value of the second operand to the first operand.
+=	Adds two operands and assigns the result to the first operand.
−=	Subtracts two operands and assigns the result to the first operand.
*=	Multiplies two operands and assigns the result to the first operand.
/=	Divides two operands and assigns the result to the first operand.
%=	Calculates the modulus of two operands and assigns the result to the first operand.
&=	Performs a bitwise AND operation on two operands and assigns the result to the first operand.
^=	Performs a bitwise exclusive OR operation on two operands and assigns the result to the first operand.
|=	Performs a bitwise OR operation on two operands and assigns the result to the first operand.
<<=	Performs a left-shift operation on two operands and assigns the result to the first operand.
>>=	Performs a sign-propagating right-shift operation on two operands and assigns the result to the first operand.
>>>=	Performs a zero-fill right-shift operation on two operands and assigns the result to the first operand.
Comparison Operators	
==	Evaluates to true if the two operands are equal to each other.
!=	Evaluates to true if the two operands are not equal to each other.
===	Evaluates to true if the two operands are both equal and of the same type.
!==	Evaluates to true if the two operands are either not equal or not of the same type.
>	Evaluates to true if the first operand's value is greater than the second operand's value.
>=	Evaluates to true if the first operand's value is greater than or equal to the second operand's value.

Table 2-1 The JavaScript Operators *(continued)*

Operator	Description
<	Evaluates to true if the first operand's value is less than the second operand's value.
<=	Evaluates to true if the first operand's value is less than or equal to the second operand's value.
Special Operators	
?:	Performs an "if...else" test.
,	Evaluates two expressions and returns the result of evaluating the second expression.
delete	Deletes an object and removes it from memory, or deletes an object's property, or deletes an element in an array.
function	Creates an anonymous function.
in	Evaluates to true if the property you're testing is supported by a specific object.
instanceof	Evaluates to true if the given object is an instance of the specified type.
new	Creates a new object from the specified object type.
typeof	Evaluates to the name of the type of the operand.
void	Allows evaluation of an expression without returning any value.

Table 2-1   The JavaScript Operators *(continued)*

Here's an example. Say that you have five apples and three oranges:

```
var apples = 5;
var oranges = 3;
```

If you want to add your apples and oranges, you can perform the addition like this:

```
var apples = 5;
var oranges = 3;
var fruit = apples + oranges;
```

Now the variable named fruit holds 8; the = sign is called the *assignment* operator, and you use it to assign values to variables. In fact, JavaScript gives you a shortcut with the *compound assignment operator* +=, which both adds two values and assigns the result to a variable. For example, if you want to add 3 to the value stored in a variable named temperature, you can do that like this:

```
var temperature = 72;
temperature = temperature + 3;
```

Or, you could use the += shortcut like this:

```
var temperature = 72;
temperature += 3;
```

Besides +=, there are also *=, −=, and other compound assignment operators, as you see in Table 2-1.

Note the operators like ==, <, and > in Table 2-1. What are they for? They're the comparison operators, and they let you make decisions in your code (Is the temperature less than 72? Yes? Time for a picnic!) with the if statement, coming up next.

Grooving with the if Statement

This if statement is the first statement we'll see that lets you execute code depending on whether or not a condition (that you set) is true. Here's what the if statement looks like formally (the parts in square brackets are optional, and you replace the parts in italics with your own JavaScript):

```
if (condition) {
    statements1
}
[else {
    statements2
}]
```

Let's see an example to make this clear. Do you have more than $1,000,000 in your bank account? If so, this next example will display the message "Time for a vacation!" (this is if.html):

```
<html>
  <head>
    <title>Using the if statement</title>

    <script language="javascript">

      function display()
      {
        var account = 2000000;
        if(account > 1000000) {
            document.getElementById('targetDiv').innerHTML =
                "Time for a vacation!";
        }
      }
    </script>

  </head>

  <body>

    <h1>Using the if statement</h1>

    <input type="button" onclick="display()" value="Click Here">
```

```
    <div id="targetDiv">
    </div>

    </body>
</html>
```

You can see the results in Figure 2-10, where it's time for a vacation.

How does this code work? You start off by putting the number two million into a variable named account:

```
    var account = 2000000;
```

And then you check to see if account holds more than $1 million by using the > (greater than) comparison operator:

```
    var account = 2000000;
    if(account > 1000000) {
        .
        .
        .
    }
```

If account is greater than one million (and it is), JavaScript executes the code in the curly braces, which displays the text "Time for a vacation!":

```
    var account = 2000000;
    if(account > 1000000) {
        document.getElementById('targetDiv').innerHTML =
            "Time for a vacation!";
    }
```

And that's the way if statements let you make decisions in your code, executing code or not, depending on whether or not a condition is true.

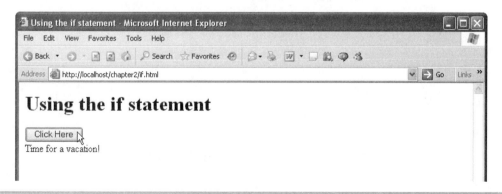

Figure 2-10   if.html

Try This Test the if Statement

Try your own version of the if.html example, creating a file named temperature.html. In your version, create a variable named temperature and assign it a value. Then test to see if that value is over 65, and if so, display the message "Time for a picnic!"

Using the else Statement

What if you don't happen to have more than $1 million in the bank? In other words, what if the condition you're checking (account > 1000000) is false? If you want to execute code when the if statement's condition is false, you can add an else statement. For example, if you don't have $1 million in the bank, you might want to display the (rather harsh) message "Get back to work!" You can do that by enclosing inside curly braces in an else statement (which must follow an if statement) the code that you want to run if the if statement's condition is false, like this (this is else.html):

```html
<html>
  <head>
    <title>Using the else statement</title>

    <script language="javascript">

      function display()
      {
        var account = 500000;
        if(account > 1000000) {
            document.getElementById('targetDiv').innerHTML =
                "Time for a vacation!";
        } else {
            document.getElementById('targetDiv').innerHTML =
                "Get back to work!";
        }
      }
    </script>

  </head>

  <body>

    <h1>Using the else statement</h1>

    <input type="button" onclick="display()" value="Click Here">

    <div id="targetDiv">
    </div>

    </body>
</html>
```

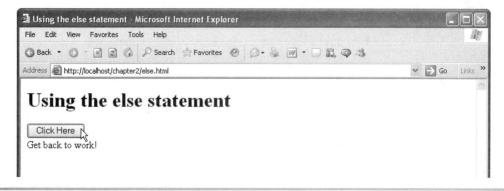

Figure 2-11   else.html

Note that we've changed the amount in the account variable (regretfully) to 500,000, so you get the results shown in Figure 2-11 when you run this code. Ah well.

Try This   Test the else Statement

Try modifying your temperature.html file so that it can handle the case where the temperature is less than 65 degrees. In that case, make your code display the message "Turn up the heat!"

Working with the Logical Operators

In this book, you're also going to see the JavaScript *logical operators* at work. These operators—you're going to see the && (And) and || (Or) operators in this book—connect two or more conditions together. For example, if you want to say that if you have more than $1 million in the bank and your debts are less than $500,000, then it's time for a vacation, you can put together the two conditions (account > 1000000 and debt < 500000) with the And operator, &&, like this (this is and.html):

```
<html>
  <head>
    <title>Using logical operators</title>

    <script language="javascript">

      function display()
      {
        var account = 2000000;
        var debt = 100000;
        if(account > 1000000 && debt < 500000) {
            document.getElementById('targetDiv').innerHTML =
```

```
                    "Time for a vacation!";
        } else {
            document.getElementById('targetDiv').innerHTML =
                "Get back to work!";
        }
    }
    </script>

</head>

<body>

    <h1>Using logical operators</h1>

    <input type="button" onclick="display()" value="Click Here">

    <div id="targetDiv">
    </div>

    </body>
</html>
```

You can see the results in Figure 2-12, where it's time for a vacation.

Try This | Test the Or Operator

The Or operator || (two upright bars) lets you check whether one of a number of conditions is true. For example, the expression a || b || c is true if any one of a or b or c is true.

Use the Or operator to check if the temperature is less than 65 *or* more than 85, and if so, display the message "Please adjust the temperature."

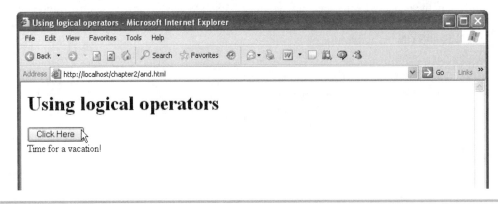

Figure 2-12   and.html

Now we're cooking with JavaScript; let's continue by taking a look at some looping constructs, starting with the for loop.

Over and Over with the for Loop

Computers are great at performing tasks over and over again (that's part of their charm—they can do the grunt work). One of the ways JavaScript lets you perform tasks over and over is with the *for* loop, which you can use to execute code multiple times (such as displaying "Happy Birthday!" 25 times for a 25-year-old). Here's what the for loop looks like formally speaking (as before, the parts in square brackets are optional, and you replace the parts in italics with your own JavaScript):

```
for ([initial-expression]; [condition]; [increment-expression]) {
    statements
}
```

You usually use a for loop with a loop index, also named a loop counter. A *loop index* is a variable that keeps track of the number of times the loop has been executed. In the initial-expression part, you usually set the loop index to a starting value; in the condition part, you test that value to see if you still want to keep on looping; and the increment-expression lets you increment the loop counter.

Here's an example, for.html. This example adds the numbers from 1 to 100—something you'd probably be pleased to let a computer do rather than add up all the numbers yourself. In this case, you want the computer to loop 100 times, which you can do with a for loop and a loop index variable like this:

```
var loopIndex;

for(loopIndex = 1; loopIndex <= 100; loopIndex++) {
    .
    .
    .
}
```

In this loop, the variable loopIndex starts at 1, and at the end of each time through the loop, 1 is added to loopIndex with the expression loopIndex++, because the JavaScript ++ operator increments the variable you apply it to by one (the -- operator decrements the variable you apply it to by 1). And the loop above stops when the value in loopIndex is greater than 100 (that is, the loop keeps looping while loopIndex <= 100).

So to add the numbers from 1 to 100, you just have to add this code:

```
var loopIndex;
var total = 0;

for(loopIndex = 1; loopIndex <= 100; loopIndex++) {
    total += loopIndex;
}
```

Here's what it looks like in a web page, for.html:

```html
<html>
  <head>
    <title>Using the for loop</title>

    <script language="javascript">

      function display()
      {
        var loopIndex;
        var total = 0;

        for(loopIndex = 1; loopIndex <= 100; loopIndex++) {
          total += loopIndex;
        }

        document.getElementById('targetDiv').innerHTML =
          "The total of 1 to 100 is " + total;

      }
    </script>

  </head>

  <body>

    <h1>Using the for loop</h1>

    <input type="button" onclick="display()" value="Click Here">

    <div id="targetDiv">
    </div>

  </body>
</html>
```

You can see the results in Figure 2-13, where we learn the numbers from 1 to 100 sum to 5050.

Try This Test the for Loop

The for loop is a great one, and the most essential of all the loops to know. Give this exercise a try: set a variable named age to a person's age, then have your code display "Happy Birthday!" once for each year of the person's age.

Figure 2-13 for.html

Keep on Looping with the while Loop

The while loop is like the for loop in many ways, but it is designed to simply keep looping while a condition is true:

```
while (condition) {
    statements
}
```

In other words, this loop keeps executing the statements in the loop's body while the loop's condition is true.

Here's an example. In this case, we're going to use a while loop together with an array of students to locate a specific student. An *array* is just like a collection of variables that you can index with a numerical index, and it's a handy construct to store multiple data elements. In fact, because you can address the elements in an array with a numerical index, arrays are perfect for use with loops, because you can increment a numerical index with a loop.

Let's get to the code to see how this works. In this case, we'll store the names of eight students, so we'll need to create an array that holds eight elements, which you do like this:

```
var students = new Array(8);
```

Now you're free to assign names to each element in the array. You address a particular element in the array by giving the array's name (students) followed by the numerical index of the element you want to reach, inside square brackets (like students[5]). The numerical index for arrays starts at 0, so you can assign names to all the elements in the array like this:

```
var students = new Array(8);

students[0] = "George";
students[1] = "Ed";
students[2] = "Stella";
```

```
students[3]  =  "Ted";
students[4]  =  "Liz";
students[5]  =  "Cary";
students[6]  =  "Nancy";
students[7]  =  "Zack";
```

Okay, now say that you want to see where Nancy is in the students array. You can do that with a while loop like this, where we keep looping until we find Nancy:

```
var loopIndex = 0;

while(students[loopIndex] != "Nancy" && loopIndex <
  students.length - 1){
  loopIndex++;
}
```

The expression students.length returns the number of total elements in the array, so setting up the while loop this way makes it loop until loopIndex is incremented to students.length – 1, or 7, unless Nancy is found at an earlier index.

If, at the end of this while loop, the variable loopIndex is less than or equal to the index of the last element in the array (which is students.length – 1), then we found Nancy, and we can report that fact this way (in while.html):

```
<html>
  <head>
    <title>Using the while loop</title>

    <script language="javascript">

      function display()
      {
        var loopIndex = 0, students = new Array(6);

        students[0]  =  "George";
        students[1]  =  "Ed";
        students[2]  =  "Stella";
        students[3]  =  "Ted";
        students[4]  =  "Liz";
        students[5]  =  "Cary";
        students[6]  =  "Nancy";
        students[7]  =  "Zack";

        while(students[loopIndex] != "Nancy" && loopIndex <
          students.length - 1){
          loopIndex++;
        }
```

```
      if(loopIndex <= students.length - 1){
        document.getElementById('targetDiv').innerHTML =
        "I found Nancy at student location " + loopIndex;
      }
      else {
        document.getElementById('targetDiv').innerHTML =
        "I did not find Nancy.";
      }
    }
  </script>

</head>

<body>

  <h1>Using the while loop</h1>

  <input type="button" onclick="display()" value="Click Here">

  <div id="targetDiv">
  </div>

</body>
</html>
```

NOTE

A shortcut was used to set up two variables here, loopIndex and the students array, which were declared like this, all in a single line: var loopIndex = 0, students = new Array(6);.

And you can see the results in Figure 2-14, where we found Nancy at index 6 in the students array.

Figure 2-14   while.html

Which Browser Does the User Have?

It can be very important for the Ajax programmer to know which browser the user has, because the browser is the way you communicate with the user, and different browsers have different capabilities (for example, Internet Explorer has a scrolling <marquee> element that Firefox doesn't have).

You can use JavaScript in your Ajax-enabled web pages to determine which browser the user has. To do that, you check the text string in the built-in navigator object's userAgent property (which you access in JavaScript as navigator.userAgent). In JavaScript, text strings are actually objects with their own properties and methods, and to search a text string, you can use the string's indexOf method, which returns the index of a substring you're searching for in the main string (that is, the position the substring starts at in the main string, where the first character is character 0). If the substring is not found in the main string, indexOf will return a negative value.

So, for example, to see if the browser identification string held in navigator.userAgent contains the text "Firefox" you could check the return value of the expression navigator .userAgent.indexOf("Firefox")—if it's non-negative, the string navigator.userAgent contains the word "Firefox".

Besides the navigator.userAgent string, there's also another string, navigator.appName, that this page, browser.html, uses. The navigtor.appName string lets browser.html make the first determination of the browser type—if it holds "Netscape", you're dealing with Firefox (or Netscape Navigator), and if it holds "MSIE", you're dealing with Microsoft Internet Explorer.

Here's what browser.html looks like (browser.html):

```
<html>
  <head>
    <title>
      What browser do you do have?
    </title>

    <script language="javascript">

    var begin, end

    function display()
    {
      if(navigator.appName == "Netscape") {
        if(navigator.userAgent.indexOf("Firefox") > 0) {
          begin = navigator.userAgent.indexOf("Firefox") +
          "Firefox".length + 1;
          end = navigator.userAgent.length;
          document.getElementById("targetDiv").innerHTML =
            "You are using Firefox " +
            navigator.userAgent.substring(begin, end);
        }
      }
```

```
    if (navigator.appName == "Microsoft Internet Explorer") {
      begin = navigator.userAgent.indexOf("MSIE ") +
      "MSIE ".length;
      if(navigator.userAgent.indexOf(";", begin) > 0) {
        end = navigator.userAgent.indexOf(";", begin);
      } else {
        end = navigator.userAgent.indexOf(")", begin)
          + 2;
      }
      document.getElementById("targetDiv").innerHTML =
        "You are using Internet Explorer " +
        navigator.userAgent.substring(begin, end);
    }
  }
  </script>
</head>

<body>
  <h1>Determining browser type and version</h1>

            <input type="button" onclick="display()" value="Click Here">

    <div ID="targetDiv"></div>
  </body>
</html>
```

And you can see the results in Figure 2-15, where browser.html is correctly identifying Internet Explorer. And in Figure 2-16, it's identifying Firefox.

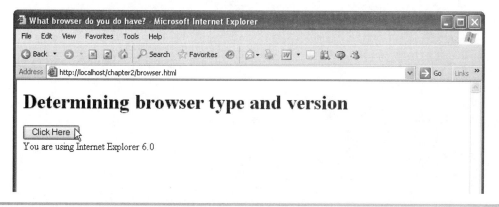

Figure 2-15   Determining browser type: Internet Explorer

Figure 2-16 Determining browser type: Firefox

Try This   Use browser.html

Make sure you understand how the JavaScript browser.html works. If you do, you've come far in a single chapter on JavaScript! Get browser.html to work in your own browser.

Chapter 3

Creating Ajax Applications

Key Skills & Concepts

- Creating XMLHttpRequest objects

- Configuring XMLHttpRequest objects

- Handling data downloads from the server using anonymous functions

- Fetching text data from the server

- Passing data to the server using Ajax and the GET and PUT HTTP methods

- Fetching XML data from the server and decoding that data

- Fetching XML data from the server by passing data to the server

I t's time to start talking Ajax, and we're going to do that by taking apart a working Ajax application piece by piece. You got a brief glimpse in Chapter 2 of the application we're going to examine in this chapter, ajax.html. You can see it at work in Figure 3-1.

When you click the button labeled "Fetch the message," ajax.html will fetch the contents of a file named data.txt from the server, shown here,

```
Welcome to Ajax!
```

and display that text in the web page, as you see in Figure 3-2.

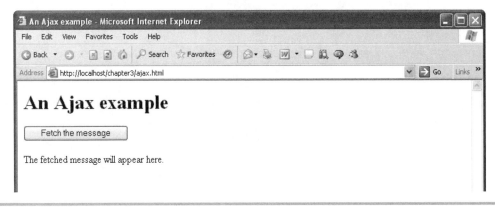

Figure 3-1 The ajax.html example

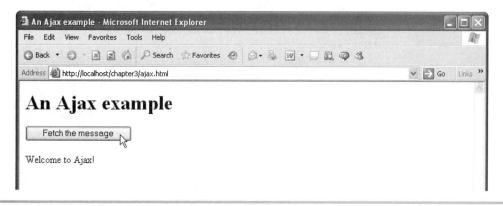

Figure 3-2   ajax.html fetching data from the server

This example is a true Ajax example—it fetches data from the server behind the scenes, using Ajax, and updates its web page in the browser without causing a page refresh.

Here's what ajax.html looks like—we're going to take this Ajax-enabled web page apart in this chapter, piece by piece:

```html
<html>
  <head>
    <title>An Ajax example</title>

    <script language = "javascript">
      var XMLHttpRequestObject = false;

      if (window.XMLHttpRequest) {
        XMLHttpRequestObject = new XMLHttpRequest();
      } else if (window.ActiveXObject) {
        XMLHttpRequestObject = new
          ActiveXObject("Microsoft.XMLHTTP");
      }

      function getData(dataSource, divID)
      {
        if(XMLHttpRequestObject) {
          var obj = document.getElementById(divID);
          XMLHttpRequestObject.open("GET", dataSource);

          XMLHttpRequestObject.onreadystatechange = function()
```

```
        {
          if (XMLHttpRequestObject.readyState == 4 &&
            XMLHttpRequestObject.status == 200) {
              obj.innerHTML = XMLHttpRequestObject.responseText;
          }
        }

        XMLHttpRequestObject.send(null);
      }
    }
  </script>
</head>

<body>

  <H1>An Ajax example</H1>

  <form>
    <input type = "button" value = "Fetch the message"
      onclick = "getData('data.txt', 'targetDiv')">
  </form>

  <div id="targetDiv">
    <p>The fetched message will appear here.</p>
  </div>

</body>
</html>
```

Try This   Get ajax.html to Work

To get anywhere in this chapter, it's important that you can get ajax.html to run. As mentioned in Chapter 2, you must place ajax.html and data.txt on a web server that you can access with your browser. Just putting those files onto your hard disk and then opening them with a browser isn't going to work, because Ajax has to interact with a true web server, one that can send data behind the scenes on request.

So make sure you can get ajax.html to run now. Copy ajax.html and data.txt from the chapter3 directory in the downloadable code for this book. Place those two files into a directory on a web server—for example, you might use your ISP's web server if you already host web pages there. Or you might even have a web server set up on your own computer. In either case, make sure you get the results you see in Figure 3-2.

Taking ajax.html Apart

It's time to see what makes ajax.html tick. You can recognize the outline of a basic web page in ajax.html by removing the Ajax parts, giving you this basic page with <head> and <body> parts, and a <div> element in the <body> to display the data fetched from the server:

```
<html>
  <head>
    <title>An Ajax example</title>
          .
          .
          .
  </head>

  <body>

    <H1>An Ajax example</H1>
          .
          .
          .
    <div id="targetDiv">
      <p>The fetched message will appear here.</p>
    </div>

  </body>
</html>
```

There's also a button in ajax.html, and when the user clicks that button, the browser calls the JavaScript function getData to get the Ajax part of the page rolling:

```
<html>
  <head>
    <title>An Ajax example</title>
          .
          .
          .
  </head>

  <body>

    <H1>An Ajax example</H1>

    <form>
      <input type = "button" value = "Fetch the message"
        onclick = "getData('data.txt', 'targetDiv')">
    </form>
```

```
<div id="targetDiv">
  <p>The fetched message will appear here.</p>
</div>

</body>
</html>
```

Creating the JavaScript

Two data items are passed to the JavaScript getData function: the name of the file to read on the server (data.txt), and the ID of the <div> element (targetDiv) in which to display the text fetched from the server. We can create the getData function to read both data items like this in a <script> element:

```
<html>
  <head>
    <title>An Ajax example</title>

    <script language = "javascript">
      function getData(dataSource, divID)
      {
           .
           .
           .
      }
    </script>
  </head>

  <body>
      .
      .
      .
  </body>
</html>
```

The first order of business in the JavaScript getData function is to check if we've been successful in creating the XMLHttpRequest object that ajax.html will use to communicate with the server. The XMLHttpRequest object that we're going to create is the basis of Ajax—it lets JavaScript code communicate with the server and download data from the server. This object will be stored in a global variable named XMLHttpRequestObject:

```
<html>
  <head>
    <title>An Ajax example</title>

    <script language = "javascript">
      var XMLHttpRequestObject = false;
           .
           .
```

```
        function getData(dataSource, divID)
        {
            .
            .
            .
        }
    </script>
  </head>

  <body>
    .
    .
    .
  </body>
</html>
```

In the getData function, we use an if statement to check if we've been successful in creating an XMLHttpRequest object—and if not, the if statement will fail, meaning that we don't attempt to use Ajax to contact the server (note that the variable XMLHttpRequestObject is initialized to false, meaning that unless we are successful in creating an XMLHttpRequest object, the if statement will fail):

```
<html>
  <head>
    <title>An Ajax example</title>

    <script language = "javascript">
      var XMLHttpRequestObject = false;
        .
        .
        .

      function getData(dataSource, divID)
      {
        if(XMLHttpRequestObject) {
          .
          .
          .
        }
      }
    </script>
  </head>

  <body>
    .
    .
    .
  </body>
</html>
```

So how do we create the XMLHttpRequest object?

Creating the XMLHttpRequest Object

We're going to add code to ajax.html to create the XMLHttpRequest object that we're going to use to communicate with the server as soon as ajax.html is loaded by the browser. That means placing that code outside the getData function, which is only called when the user clicks the button.

So how do you create an XMLHttpRequest object? That object is built into the browser, but you access it in different ways, depending on what browser ajax.html is running in. Netscape Navigator (version 7.0 and later), Apple Safari (version 1.2 and later), and Firefox let you create XMLHttpRequest objects directly with code like this:

```
XMLHttpRequestObject = new XMLHttpRequest();
```

In those browsers, the XMLHttpRequest object can be accessed through the browser window object, and you can check if the window object can be used in this way by checking if window.XMLHttpRequest exists. If it does, you're dealing with Netscape Navigator, Firefox, or Apple Safari, and can create an XMLHttpRequest object and store it in the variable XMLHttpRequestObject in this way:

```
<html>
  <head>
    <title>An Ajax example</title>

    <script language = "javascript">
      var XMLHttpRequestObject = false;

      if (window.XMLHttpRequest) {
        XMLHttpRequestObject = new XMLHttpRequest();
      }
          .
          .
          .

      function getData(dataSource, divID)
      {
        if(XMLHttpRequestObject) {
          .
          .

          .
        }
      }
    </script>
  </head>

  <body>
      .
      .

      .
  </body>
</html>
```

But what if you're dealing with Internet Explorer? In that case, you can create an XMLHttpRequest object by using this JavaScript:

```
XMLHttpRequestObject = new ActiveXObject("Microsoft.XMLHTTP");
```

And how does ajax.html determine that it is dealing with Internet Explorer? In that case, window.XMLHttpRequest doesn't exist—but window.ActiveXObject does, which means you can use this code to create an XMLHttpRequest object in Internet Explorer:

```html
<html>
  <head>
    <title>An Ajax example</title>

    <script language = "javascript">
      var XMLHttpRequestObject = false;

      if (window.XMLHttpRequest) {
        XMLHttpRequestObject = new XMLHttpRequest();
      } else if (window.ActiveXObject) {
        XMLHttpRequestObject = new
          ActiveXObject("Microsoft.XMLHTTP");
      }

      function getData(dataSource, divID)
      {
        if(XMLHttpRequestObject) {
          .
          .
          .
        }
      }
    </script>
  </head>

  <body>
    .
    .
    .
  </body>
</html>
```

Okay, that creates the XMLHttpRequest object we'll use to communicate with the server behind the scenes. Although the XMLHttpRequest object supported in different browsers differs, for nearly all Ajax work, you use the same basic properties and methods of this object—and thankfully, those basic properties and methods are the same in the different browsers.

You can see the properties of the Internet Explorer XMLHttpRequest object in Table 3-1, and its methods in Table 3-2. The properties of this object for Mozilla, Netscape Navigator, and Firefox appear in Table 3-3, and the methods in Table 3-4. Apple hasn't published a full version of the properties and methods for its XMLHttpRequest object yet, but it has published a set of commonly used properties, which appear in Table 3-5, and commonly used methods, which appear in Table 3-6.

Property	Description
onreadystatechange	Contains the name of the event handler that should be called when the value of the readyState property changes. Read/write.
readyState	Contains state of the request. Read-only.
responseBody	Contains a response body, which is one way HTTP responses can be returned. Read-only.
responseStream	Contains a response stream, a binary stream to the server. Read-only.
responseText	Contains the response body as a string. Read-only.
responseXML	Contains the response body as XML. Read-only.
status	Contains the HTTP status code returned by a request. Read-only.
statusText	Contains the HTTP response status text. Read-only.

Table 3-1 XMLHttpRequest Object Properties for Internet Explorer

Method	Description
abort	Aborts the HTTP request.
getAllResponseHeaders	Returns all the HTTP headers.
getResponseHeader	Returns the value of an HTTP header.
open	Opens a request to the server.
send	Sends an HTTP request to the server.
setRequestHeader	Sets the name and value of an HTTP header.

Table 3-2 XMLHttpRequest Object Methods for Internet Explorer

Property	Description
channel	Contains the channel used to perform the request. Read-only.
readyState	Contains the state of the request. Read-only.
responseText	Contains the response body as a string. Read-only.
responseXML	Contains the response body as XML. Read-only.
status	Contains the HTTP status code returned by a request. Read-only.
statusText	Contains the HTTP response status text. Read-only.

Table 3-3 XMLHttpRequest Object Properties for Mozilla, Firefox, and Netscape Navigator

Method	Description
abort	Aborts the HTTP request.
getAllResponseHeaders	Returns all the HTTP headers.
getResponseHeader	Returns the value of an HTTP header.
openRequest	Native (nonscript) method to open a request.
overrideMimeType	Overrides the MIME type the server returns.

Table 3-4   XMLHttpRequest Object Methods for Mozilla, Firefox, and Netscape Navigator

Property	Description
onreadystatechange	Contains the name of the event handler that should be called when the value of the readyState property changes. Read/write.
readyState	Contains state of the request. Read-only.
responseText	Contains the response body as a string. Read-only.
responseXML	Contains the response body as XML. Read-only.
status	Contains the HTTP status code returned by a request. Read-only.
statusText	Contains the HTTP response status text. Read-only.

Table 3-5   XMLHttpRequest Object Properties for Apple Safari

Method	Description
abort	Aborts the HTTP request.
getAllResponseHeaders	Returns all the HTTP headers.
getResponseHeader	Returns the value of an HTTP header.
open	Opens a request to the server.
send	Sends an HTTP request to the server.
setRequestHeader	Sets the name and value of an HTTP header.

Table 3-6   XMLHttpRequest Object Methods for Apple Safari

Now that we have an XMLHttpRequest object, what do we do with it? You can start by opening it, which lets you configure it in preparation for connecting to the server and downloading data.

Opening the XMLHttpRequest Object

When ajax.html first loads in the browser, it tries to create an XMLHttpRequest object. When the user clicks the button to fetch data from the server using Ajax, the getData function is called, and the first thing it does is check whether an XMLHttpRequest object was created successfully:

```
<script language = "javascript">
  var XMLHttpRequestObject = false;

  if (window.XMLHttpRequest) {
    XMLHttpRequestObject = new XMLHttpRequest();
  } else if (window.ActiveXObject) {
    XMLHttpRequestObject = new
      ActiveXObject("Microsoft.XMLHTTP");
  }

  function getData(dataSource, divID)
  {
    if(XMLHttpRequestObject) {
      .
      .
      .

    }
  }
</script>
```

In case an XMLHttpRequest object couldn't be created, you can add code to explain to the user that their browser can't do Ajax, as follows:

```
  function getData(dataSource, divID)
  {
    if(XMLHttpRequestObject) {
      .
      .
      .

    }
    else {
     var obj = document.getElementById(divID);
     obj.innerHTML = "Sorry, your browser is not Ajax-enabled.";
    }
  }
```

It's time to open the XMLHttpRequest object. Doing so lets you configure the XMLHttpRequest object with, for example, the URL that it is to contact when you connect to the server. Here's how you use the XMLHttpRequest object's open method in general (as always, items in square brackets are optional, and items in italics are placeholders that you fill in yourself):

```
open("method", "URL"[, asyncFlag[, "userName"[, "password"]]])
```

The following table explains what the various arguments mean:

method	The HTTP method used to open the connection, such as GET, POST, PUT, HEAD, or PROPFIND.
URL	The requested URL.
asyncFlag	A Boolean value indicating whether the call is asynchronous. The default is true.
userName	The username of your account.
password	The password used to connect to your account.

The following code shows how ajax.html uses the XMLHttpRequest object's open method. In this case, it uses the HTTP GET method to contact the server (that's the normal way of contacting servers—we'll see more about that later in this chapter, in the discussion of another option, the POST method), and passes the URL of the file it's looking for, which is passed to the getData function as the dataSource argument.

```
function getData(dataSource, divID)
{
    if(XMLHttpRequestObject) {

        XMLHttpRequestObject.open("GET", dataSource);
        .
        .
        .
    }
}
```

Using the open method like this configures the XMLHttpRequest object—it does *not* connect, or open, any connection to the server. The actual connection process is coming up in a few pages.

Note that the URL that the XMLHttpRequest object has been configured to access is simply the name of a file, data.txt, as you see here in the call made to getData when the button is clicked:

```
<body>

    <H1>An Ajax example</H1>

    <form>
        <input type = "button" value = "Fetch the message"
            onclick = "getData('data.txt', 'targetDiv')">
    </form>
```

```
<div id="targetDiv">
  <p>The fetched message will appear here.</p>
</div>

</body>
```

Referring to a file in this way will only work if the file (data.txt) is in the same directory as the web page (ajax.html) itself. In other words, if you simply give a filename, the browser will assume that file is to be found in the same directory as the web page the browser is currently displaying.

Now say that the data.txt file is in data, a subdirectory of the directory that contains ajax.html. In that case, you can refer to data.txt in a relative way as data/data.txt (you use a forward slash, /, on web servers, not the backward slash that you use in Windows to indicate subdirectories):

```
<body>

  <H1>An Ajax example</H1>

  <form>
    <input type = "button" value = "Fetch the message"
      onclick = "getData('data/data.txt', 'targetDiv')">
  </form>

  <div id="targetDiv">
    <p>The fetched message will appear here.</p>
  </div>

</body>
```

You can also give a complete URL for the data you want to fetch, like this:

```
<body>

  <H1>An Ajax example</H1>

  <form>
    <input type = "button" value = "Fetch the message"
      onclick = "getData('http://www.starpowder.com/data.txt',
      'targetDiv')">
  </form>

  <div id="targetDiv">
    <p>The fetched message will appear here.</p>
  </div>

</body>
```

And the URL need not be the URL of a file either—it could be any web resource, such as a PHP script (as you're going to see soon in this book, PHP is a programming language that runs on web servers and lets you take control of the HTML and data you send back to browsers):

```
<body>

  <H1>An Ajax example</H1>

  <form>
    <input type = "button" value = "Fetch the message"
      onclick = "getData('http://www.starpowder.com/data.php',
      'targetDiv')">
  </form>

  <div id="targetDiv">
    <p>The fetched message will appear here.</p>
  </div>

</body>
```

However, here's one thing to note: if the URL you connect to, such as http://www .starpowder.com/data.php, and the Ajax-enabled page (ajax.html here) that's attempting to download that URL are on different servers, you're going to have a security problem. If your Ajax-enabled page attempts to download data behind the scenes from a different server, your browser is going to suspect that something underhanded is going on, and will ask permission from the user, via a dialog box, before proceeding.

Making the user respond to a dialog box, however, is not exactly Ajax's idea of doing things unobtrusively, behind the scenes. We'll see how to get around this restriction in Chapter 4.

To keep it simple, the examples in this book mostly download data from the same web server directory that the Ajax-enabled HTML page itself is in.

Now you've configured the XMLHttpRequest object. The next step is to get ready for the data download.

Getting Ready for the Data Download

The *A* in Ajax stands for *asynchronous*, which means that you don't sit around waiting for the Ajax download to happen. While the download is going on, the browser can be doing other things—interacting with the user, for example. That means that Ajax needs to signal the browser when the data has been downloaded and is ready to be used, and that happens with a *callback* function. That's a function that Ajax calls when your data is downloading, or has been completely downloaded. How do you tell Ajax which function you want to call?

You tell the XMLHttpRequest object. That object has a property named onreadystatechange that you assign the callback function to. As an example of how it might work, suppose you have a callback function simply named callback. Here's how you could have the XMLHttpRequest object call that function, by assigning that function to the onreadystatechange property:

```
function getData(dataSource, divID)
{
  if(XMLHttpRequestObject) {

    XMLHttpRequestObject.open("GET", dataSource);

    XMLHttpRequestObject.onreadystatechange = callback()

  }
}
function callback()
{
    .
    .
    .
}
```

Now when there's a change in the status of the data you're downloading, such as when the downloading is complete, the callback function will be called.

This works, but in Ajax, you usually take a shortcut with an *anonymous* function—one without any name. You can create an anonymous function simply with the keyword function, followed by the arguments passed to that function enclosed in parentheses (there aren't any arguments here), followed by the body of the function, enclosed in curly braces. Here's what that looks like in ajax.html:

```
function getData(dataSource, divID)
{
  if(XMLHttpRequestObject) {

    XMLHttpRequestObject.open("GET", dataSource);

    XMLHttpRequestObject.onreadystatechange = function()
    {
        .
        .
        .
    }

  }
}
```

So what's going to happen here is that when there's a change in the status of the data the XMLHttpRequest object is downloading, the anonymous function is going to be called, which means that the code in the curly braces following the function keyword will be executed.

Inside the anonymous function, we need to check on the data that's been downloaded: Is the download complete? Are we ready to use that data? You can determine that with two properties of the XMLHttpRequest object: readyState and status.

The readyState property tells you how the data downloading is going. Here are the possible values for this property—a value of 4 is what you want to see, because that means the data has been fully downloaded:

0	Uninitialized
1	Loading
2	Loaded
3	Interactive
4	Complete

The status property is the property that contains the actual status of the download. This is actually the normal HTTP status code that you get when you try to download web pages. For example, if the data you're looking for wasn't found, you'll get a value of 404 in the status property. Here are some of the possible values—note that you'll want to see a value of 200 here, which means that the download completed normally:

200	OK
201	Created
204	No Content
205	Reset Content
206	Partial Content
400	Bad Request
401	Unauthorized
403	Forbidden
404	Not Found
405	Method Not Allowed
406	Not Acceptable
407	Proxy Authentication Required
408	Request Timeout
411	Length Required

413	Requested Entity Too Large
414	Requested URL Too Long
415	Unsupported Media Type
500	Internal Server Error
501	Not Implemented
502	Bad Gateway
503	Service Unavailable
504	Gateway Timeout
505	HTTP Version Not Supported

We'll start handling the downloaded data by checking the readyState property.

Using the readyState Property

The readyState property lets you know the state of the download, and we want to wait until the value of this property equals 4, which means the download is complete. Here's what that looks like in the anonymous function:

```
function getData(dataSource, divID)
{
  if(XMLHttpRequestObject) {

    XMLHttpRequestObject.open("GET", dataSource);

    XMLHttpRequestObject.onreadystatechange = function()
    {
      if (XMLHttpRequestObject.readyState == 4
        .
        .
        .
    }
  }

  }
}
```

Okay, if we're executing code inside this if statement, we know that the data download was completed. But was it completed successfully, or was there an error? To check that, you have to examine the status property.

Using the status Property

The status property holds the HTTP code that corresponds to the status of the data transfer. We want to see a value of 200, which means that the data transfer was OK. Here's how we make sure that the XMLHttpRequest object's status property holds a value of 200:

```
function getData(dataSource, divID)
{
  if(XMLHttpRequestObject) {

    XMLHttpRequestObject.open("GET", dataSource);

    XMLHttpRequestObject.onreadystatechange = function()
    {
      if (XMLHttpRequestObject.readyState == 4 &&
        XMLHttpRequestObject.status == 200) {
        .
        .
        .
      }
    }

  }
}
```

Now we've verified that the data we fetched from the server using Ajax was completed successfully. How do we display the fetched data?

Displaying the Fetched Data

The HTML ID of the <div> element we want to display the downloaded data in is passed to the getData function and named divID:

```
function getData(dataSource, divID)
{
  .
  .
  .
}
```

We can create an object named obj corresponding to that <div> element in this way:

```
function getData(dataSource, divID)
{
  if(XMLHttpRequestObject) {
    var obj = document.getElementById(divID);
    XMLHttpRequestObject.open("GET", dataSource);
```

```
XMLHttpRequestObject.onreadystatechange = function()
{
  if (XMLHttpRequestObject.readyState == 4 &&
    XMLHttpRequestObject.status == 200) {
      .
      .
      .
  }
}

    }
}
```

Now that we've downloaded the data to display successfully, how do we recover that data
from the XMLHttpRequest object and display that data in the <div> element? You can recover
the text that was downloaded from the XMLHttpRequest object's responseText property.
That property is where the XMLHttpRequest object stores downloaded plain text (if you're
downloading XML, as we will later in this chapter, the property you read that XML from is
named responseXML).

So here's how we display the text that we downloaded in the <div> element:

```
function getData(dataSource, divID)
{
  if(XMLHttpRequestObject) {
    var obj = document.getElementById(divID);
    XMLHttpRequestObject.open("GET", dataSource);

    XMLHttpRequestObject.onreadystatechange = function()
    {
      if (XMLHttpRequestObject.readyState == 4 &&
        XMLHttpRequestObject.status == 200) {
          obj.innerHTML = XMLHttpRequestObject.responseText;
      }
    }

  }
}
```

That's great—now we're ready to handle the data download from the server. Why just
"ready" to handle the data download? Because we haven't actually initiated the download,
that's why. How do we actually connect to the server to start the actual download process?

Connecting to the Server

It turns out that all we've done to this point is to get ready to connect to the server using Ajax.
We've created the XMLHttpRequest object, configured it with its open method, and set up a
callback function where we check on the download and display the downloaded text. But we
haven't actually connected to the server and gotten the whole download process started yet.

How do you connect to the server? That depends on the HTTP metho[c] connect. In this example, we're using the GET method, so you call the [X] object's send method, passing it a value of null, which is JavaScript's placeno. of nothing (you pass different arguments when you're using the POST HTTP metho[u] connect to the server). That looks like this in ajax.html:

```
function getData(dataSource, divID)
{
  if(XMLHttpRequestObject) {
    var obj = document.getElementById(divID);
    XMLHttpRequestObject.open("GET", dataSource);

    XMLHttpRequestObject.onreadystatechange = function()
    {
      if (XMLHttpRequestObject.readyState == 4 &&
        XMLHttpRequestObject.status == 200) {
          obj.innerHTML = XMLHttpRequestObject.responseText;
      }
    }

    XMLHttpRequestObject.send(null);
  }
}
```

And presto—you're done! Now you've completed ajax.html, and when you load it into your browser and click the button, the page uses Ajax to communicate with the server and download text data. Cool.

We've been able to download the text from a file, data.txt, and display it. On the other hand, just downloading the same file all the time might get a little boring. Why not have some data on the server that can change? That's where server-side programming comes in.

Adding Some Server-Side Programming

To do a little programming on the server, we're going to use PHP, the server-side language (that is, a language that runs on the web server, not on the user's machine) that has become the most popular choice with Ajax developers. Using PHP, which is formally introduced in Chapter 9, we'll get the server to send back data that varies, as opposed to just getting the contents of the same file, data.txt, all the time.

The PHP equivalent of data.txt is data.php, a PHP script that will send a message back to the browser. To follow along here, you're going to need a PHP-enabled server, as discussed in depth in Chapter 9. We start data.php with this markup, which indicates to the server that this is a PHP script, and should be executed as such:

```
<?php
   .
   .
   .
?>
```

Figure 3-3 data.php

To actually send text back to the browser, we can use the PHP echo statement:

```php
<?php
    echo 'This text comes to you thanks to PHP.';
?>
```

There you go—simple. You can see data.php at work in a browser (no Ajax involved yet) in Figure 3-3.

Now let's get the text that data.php sends back to the browser—this time using Ajax techniques. To do that, you simply have to change the accessed URL from data.txt to data.php like this (this is ajax2.html):

```html
<html>
  <head>
    <title>An Ajax example using PHP</title>

    <script language = "javascript">
    var XMLHttpRequestObject = false;

    if (window.XMLHttpRequest) {
      XMLHttpRequestObject = new XMLHttpRequest();
    } else if (window.ActiveXObject) {
      XMLHttpRequestObject = new
        ActiveXObject("Microsoft.XMLHTTP");
    }

    function getData(dataSource, divID)
    {
      if(XMLHttpRequestObject) {
        var obj = document.getElementById(divID);
        XMLHttpRequestObject.open("GET", dataSource);

        XMLHttpRequestObject.onreadystatechange = function()
        {
          if (XMLHttpRequestObject.readyState == 4 &&
            XMLHttpRequestObject.status == 200) {
```

```
                    obj.innerHTML = XMLHttpRequestObject.responseText;
                }
            }

            XMLHttpRequestObject.send(null);
        }
    }
    </script>
</head>

<body>

    <H1>An Ajax example using PHP</H1>

    <form>
        <input type = "button" value = "Fetch the message"
            onclick = "getData('data.php', 'targetDiv')">
    </form>

    <div id="targetDiv">
        <p>The fetched message will appear here.</p>
    </div>

    </body>
</html>
```

Is that it? Yep, that's it. Now you're accessing data.php using Ajax instead of accessing data.txt. You can see ajax2.html in Figure 3-4.

Now when you click the button, Ajax is used behind the scenes to fetch the data returned by data.php, as you can see in Figure 3-5.

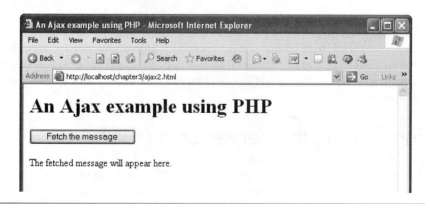

Figure 3-4   ajax2.html

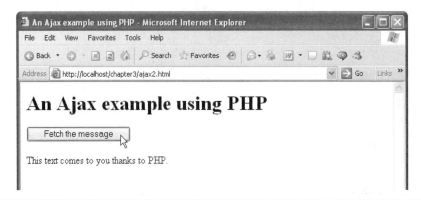

Figure 3-5 Accessing data.php with ajax2.html

Try This Get ajax2.html to Work

Got a server that can run PHP? There are plenty on the Internet, and you can download PHP to your own computer if you want, as discussed in Chapter 9. If you can execute PHP in a server, give ajax2.html a try.

To do that, put ajax2.html and data.php into the same directory (changing the protection of data.php so that it can be executed on your server, if needed), and navigate to ajax2.html in your browser. Hopefully, you'll see the page shown in Figures 3-4 and 3-5.

We're not going to use PHP in depth until Chapter 9, because we'll be working on the various skills involved in Ajax until then. But if you want to work with Ajax, it's important to be able to perform server-side programming—and the most common combination is Ajax and PHP.

Okay, now we've been successful in reading text from data.php, which is fun—but in time, it's going to get boring, because that text never changes. How about actually *interacting* with the server by sending data to it? In the next two sections, we are going to look at two means of communicating with the server, the HTTP GET method and the HTTP POST method, starting with the former.

Sending Data to the Server Using GET

Communicating with the server is at the heart of what Ajax does, and in order to make the server respond to what you've sent it, you need to be able to use some form of programming on the server. In this section, we'll create a PHP script named dataresponder.php that you can send data to.

If you send dataresponder.php a value of 1, it will send back the text "The server got a value of 1," and if you send a value of 2, the script will send back the text "The server got a value of 2."

Sending Data with URL Encoding

The GET method lets you send text data to the server by appending that text to the end of the URL you use to access the server. For example, if you want to send the name Steve to the server, you pass "Steve" as the value of an argument, just as with a JavaScript function. We might name that argument "name," and here is how you'd assign "Steve" to the argument "name" and send everything to the server using the HTTP GET method (note that you use a question mark to separate your data from the navigation part of the URL):

```
http://www.server.com/script.php?name=Steve
```

On the server, your PHP script can ask to get the value corresponding to the "name" argument, and it'll be passed the value "Steve."

What if you want to pass two or more data items to the server? You separate the data you want to pass into argument/value pairs (that is, as "argument=value") and separate those pairs with an ampersand, &. Here's an example:

```
http://www.server.com/script.php?firstname=Steve&lastname=Holzner
```

What if the data you want to send includes spaces? You can't include spaces in a URL. Instead, you replace the spaces with plus signs (+). Here's an example:

```
http://www.server.com/script.php?name=Steve+Holzner
```

Adding data to a URL like this is called *URL encoding*, and it lets you send your data to the server (as long as that data is text). However, note that the text you send is part of the (very public) URL you're accessing, so privacy is nonexistent with the GET method. The POST method, which encodes the data you're sending in the HTTP headers in the request sent to the server, does a better job of keeping things private (as discussed in "Sending Data to the Server Using POST" later in the chapter).

So this means that we can send a value of 1 to the dataresponder.php script like this, where we're naming the argument sent to the server data, and assigning data a value of 1:

```
http://www.server.com/dataresponder.php?data=1
```

To send a value of 2 to the server, you could do this:

```
http://www.server.com/dataresponder.php?data=2
```

Now we need to write our PHP script, dataresponder.php, to read the argument named "data," and respond by sending the right text back to the browser, "The server got a value of 1" or "The server got a value of 2."

Writing the PHP

We start dataresponder.php with the usual PHP markup, indicating that this is a PHP script that is meant to be executed by the server:

```php
<?php
    .
    .
    .
?>
```

Now we need to access the "data" argument sent to us via the GET method. PHP includes a special array named $_GET that lets you recover data sent to your PHP scripts via the GET method. All you have to do is to use the name of the argument whose value you want as the index in the $_GET array. In other words, to recover the value of the argument named "data" sent to dataresponder.php, you only have to use $_GET["data"].

Okay, now we have the data sent to us from the web page, and need to see if that data is a 1 or a 2. PHP's syntax is in many ways similar to JavaScript's, so we can use a PHP if statement to check if "data" holds 1 or 2 (note that == is the equality comparison operator in PHP, just as it is in JavaScript):

```php
<?php
    if ($_GET["data"] == "1") {
        .
        .
        .
    }
?>
```

At this point, then, we know that we were passed a value of 1, so we can send back the confirmation message "The server got a value of 1" to the browser with the PHP echo statement:

```php
<?php
    if ($_GET["data"] == "1") {
        echo 'The server got a value of 1';
    }
    .
    .
    .
?>
```

Conversely, if we were sent a value of 2,

```php
<?php
    if ($_GET["data"] == "1") {
        echo 'The server got a value of 1';
    }
    if ($_GET["data"] == "2") {
```

```
      .
      .
      .
  }
?>
```

then we can send back the message "The server got a value of 2" to the browser:

```php
<?php
  if ($_GET["data"] == "1") {
    echo 'The server got a value of 1';
  }
  if ($_GET["data"] == "2") {
    echo 'The server got a value of 2';
  }
?>
```

You can test dataresponder.php in a browser with a URL like this, sending it a value of 1:

```
http://www.server.com/dataresponder.php?data=1
```

And you can see the results in Figure 3-6, where dataresponder.php correctly identified the value sent to it.

Swell, we are all set with dataresponder.php. Now we've got to write the Ajax-enabled page that will interact with it.

Interacting with dataresponder.php

Let's write the Ajax-enabled page, ajax3.html, that interacts with dataresponder.php. We're going to need two buttons here: one to send a value of 1 to dataresponder.php, and the other to send a value of 2. Here's what the first button—the button we use to send a value of 1 to dataresponder.php—looks like in HTML:

```html
<form>
  <input type = "button" value = "Fetch message 1"
    .
    .
    .
</form>
```

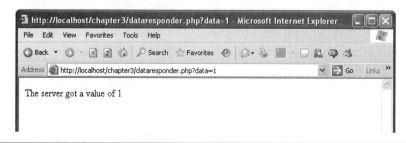

Figure 3-6 Testing dataresponder.php

We can use this button to call the getData function that we've already seen in ajax.html. You pass two arguments to getData—the URL to download data from, and the ID of the <div> element to display the results in, so we can add this to the button:

```
<form>
  <input type = "button" value = "Fetch message 1"
    onclick = "getData('dataresponder.php', 'targetDiv')">
    .
    .
    .
</form>
```

That's not complete, though—we need to pass a value of 1 to dataresponder.php, and we can use URL encoding to do that by changing the URL to dataresponder.php?data=1:

```
<form>
  <input type = "button" value = "Fetch message 1"
    onclick = "getData('dataresponder.php?data=1', 'targetDiv')">
    .
    .
    .
</form>
```

That takes care of the first button. The second button is similar except for the caption and the URL it calls, dataresponder.php?data=2 (this is ajax3.html):

```
<html>
  <head>
    <title>Sending Data to the Server</title>

    <script language = "javascript">
      var XMLHttpRequestObject = false;

      if (window.XMLHttpRequest) {
        XMLHttpRequestObject = new XMLHttpRequest();
      } else if (window.ActiveXObject) {
        XMLHttpRequestObject = new
          ActiveXObject("Microsoft.XMLHTTP");
      }

      function getData(dataSource, divID)
      {
        if(XMLHttpRequestObject) {
          var obj = document.getElementById(divID);
          XMLHttpRequestObject.open("GET", dataSource);

          XMLHttpRequestObject.onreadystatechange = function()
          {
            if (XMLHttpRequestObject.readyState == 4 &&
```

```
            XMLHttpRequestObject.status == 200) {
                obj.innerHTML = XMLHttpRequestObject.responseText;
            }
        }

        XMLHttpRequestObject.send(null);
    }
}
    </script>
</head>

<body>

  <h1>Sending Data to the Server</h1>

  <form>
    <input type = "button" value = "Fetch message 1"
      onclick = "getData('dataresponder.php?data=1', 'targetDiv')">
    <input type = "button" value = "Fetch message 2"
      onclick = "getData('dataresponder.php?data=2', 'targetDiv')">
  </form>

  <div id="targetDiv">
    <p>The fetched message will appear here.</p>
  </div>

</body>
</html>
```

You can see ajax3.html at work in Figure 3-7, where the user has clicked the first button, and the server responded correctly.

Figure 3-7   ajax3.html sending 1 to the server

Figure 3-8   ajax3.html sending 2 to the server

If the user clicks the second button, a value of 2 is sent to the server, and the appropriate message comes back, as you see in Figure 3-8. Cool.

Sending Data to the Server Using POST

The GET method is only one way to send data to the server—there are other methods, including the POST method, which we'll take a look at now. The POST method offers more security, because the data you send to the server is not URL-encoded, out there for everyone to see.

Writing the PHP

Now that we've created the PHP script dataresponder.php, creating a PHP script that you can POST to is easy. All you have to do is to change the $_GET array in dataresponder.php,

```php
<?php
  if ($_GET["data"] == "1") {
    echo 'You sent the server a value of 1';
  }
  if ($_GET["data"] == "2") {
    echo 'You sent the server a value of 2';
  }
?>
```

to the $_POST array in a new PHP script, dataresponderpost.php:

```php
<?php
  if ($_POST["data"] == "1") {
    echo 'You sent the server a value of 1';
  }
  if ($_POST["data"] == "2") {
    echo 'You sent the server a value of 2';
  }
?>
```

As you may have guessed, the $_POST array lets you read data that was sent to your PHP script using the POST method, instead of the GET method. Let's take a look at the Ajax-enabled page, ajax4.html, that interacts with dataresponderpost.php on the server. Starting from the Ajax-enabled web pages that we've already created in this chapter, how do you set things up to send data via POST to the server?

Interacting with dataresponderpost.php

The first step seems clear—you have to change this line in the getData function,

```
function getData(dataSource, divID)
{
  if(XMLHttpRequestObject) {
    var obj = document.getElementById(divID);
    XMLHttpRequestObject.open("GET", dataSource);
      .
      .
      .

}
```

to this, where we're using the POST method:

```
function getData(dataSource, divID)
{
  if(XMLHttpRequestObject) {
    var obj = document.getElementById(divID);
    XMLHttpRequestObject.open("POST", dataSource);
      .
      .
      .

  }
```

Next, to enable sending data via POST, you also have to set an HTTP request header, Content-Type, to "application/x-www-form-urlencoded". Even if you don't know what that means, just make sure you include this code:

```
function getData(dataSource, divID)
{
  if(XMLHttpRequestObject) {
    var obj = document.getElementById(divID);
    XMLHttpRequestObject.open("POST", dataSource);
    XMLHttpRequestObject.setRequestHeader('Content-Type',
      'application/x-www-form-urlencoded');
      .
      .
      .

  }
```

So far so good. Now we can handle the data we want to send to dataresponderpost.php. When we used the GET method, we just URL-encoded the data like this in the calls to getData:

```
<body>

  <h1>Sending Data to the Server</h1>

  <form>
    <input type = "button" value = "Fetch message 1"
      onclick = "getData('dataresponder.php?data=1', 'targetDiv')">
    <input type = "button" value = "Fetch message 2"
      onclick = "getData('dataresponder.php?data=2', 'targetDiv')">
  </form>

  <div id="targetDiv">
    <p>The fetched message will appear here.</p>
  </div>

</body>
```

With the POST method, you can't do URL encoding directly like this. But we still need to pass a 1 or a 2 to the getData function, so let's add a third argument to the getData call—an argument named data. In the getData function, the data argument will hold 1 or 2, depending on which button was clicked:

```
<script language = "javascript">
  var XMLHttpRequestObject = false;

  if (window.XMLHttpRequest) {
    XMLHttpRequestObject = new XMLHttpRequest();
  } else if (window.ActiveXObject) {
    XMLHttpRequestObject = new ActiveXObject("Microsoft.XMLHTTP");
  }

  function getData(dataSource, divID, data)
  {
    if(XMLHttpRequestObject) {
      var obj = document.getElementById(divID);
      XMLHttpRequestObject.open("POST", dataSource);
      XMLHttpRequestObject.setRequestHeader('Content-Type',
        'application/x-www-form-urlencoded');
          .
          .
          .
    }
  }
</script>
</head>
```

```
<body>

  <H1>Sending Data to the Server With POST</H1>

  <form>
    <input type = "button" value = "Fetch message 1"
      onclick = "getData('dataresponderpost.php', 'targetDiv', 1)">
    <input type = "button" value = "Fetch message 2"
      onclick = "getData('dataresponderpost.php', 'targetDiv', 2)">
  </form>

  <div id="targetDiv">
    <p>The fetched message will appear here.</p>
  </div>

</body>
```

Now we have to send the data using POST in the getData function. We first add the standard callback function so the data that's downloaded from the server can be handled correctly:

```
function getData(dataSource, divID, data)
{
  if(XMLHttpRequestObject) {
    var obj = document.getElementById(divID);
    XMLHttpRequestObject.open("POST", dataSource);
    XMLHttpRequestObject.setRequestHeader('Content-Type',
      'application/x-www-form-urlencoded');

    XMLHttpRequestObject.onreadystatechange = function()
    {
      if (XMLHttpRequestObject.readyState == 4 &&
        XMLHttpRequestObject.status == 200) {
          obj.innerHTML = XMLHttpRequestObject.responseText;
      }
    }
     .
     .
     .

  }
}
```

And we're ready to send the data via the POST method. To do that, you use the XMLHttpRequest object's send method. In the other Ajax web pages in this chapter, which used the GET method, this line is how we connected to the server using the send method:

```
function getData(dataSource, divID)
{
  if(XMLHttpRequestObject) {
    var obj = document.getElementById(divID);
    XMLHttpRequestObject.open("GET", dataSource);
```

```
XMLHttpRequestObject.onreadystatechange = function()
{
  if (XMLHttpRequestObject.readyState == 4 &&
    XMLHttpRequestObject.status == 200) {
      obj.innerHTML = XMLHttpRequestObject.responseText;
  }
}

XMLHttpRequestObject.send(null);
  }
}
```

Now, however, instead of sending a value of null, you send the data you want to send via POST in a URL-encoded string. In this case, that string is "data=1" or "data=2" depending on what the getData function's data argument holds. So we can send our data to the server in this way, using the XMLHttpRequest object's send method:

```
function getData(dataSource, divID, data)
{
  if(XMLHttpRequestObject) {
    var obj = document.getElementById(divID);
    XMLHttpRequestObject.open("POST", dataSource);
    XMLHttpRequestObject.setRequestHeader('Content-Type',
      'application/x-www-form-urlencoded');

    XMLHttpRequestObject.onreadystatechange = function()
    {
      if (XMLHttpRequestObject.readyState == 4 &&
        XMLHttpRequestObject.status == 200) {
          obj.innerHTML = XMLHttpRequestObject.responseText;
      }
    }

    XMLHttpRequestObject.send("data=" + data);
  }
}
```

Here's all of ajax4.html for reference:

```
<html>
  <head>
    <title>Sending Data to the Server With POST</title>

    <script language = "javascript">
      var XMLHttpRequestObject = false;

      if (window.XMLHttpRequest) {
        XMLHttpRequestObject = new XMLHttpRequest();
      } else if (window.ActiveXObject) {
```

```
        XMLHttpRequestObject = new ActiveXObject("Microsoft.XMLHTTP");
      }

      function getData(dataSource, divID, data)
      {
        if(XMLHttpRequestObject) {
          var obj = document.getElementById(divID);
          XMLHttpRequestObject.open("POST", dataSource);
          XMLHttpRequestObject.setRequestHeader('Content-Type',
            'application/x-www-form-urlencoded');

          XMLHttpRequestObject.onreadystatechange = function()
          {
            if (XMLHttpRequestObject.readyState == 4 &&
              XMLHttpRequestObject.status == 200) {
                obj.innerHTML = XMLHttpRequestObject.responseText;
            }
          }

          XMLHttpRequestObject.send("data=" + data);
        }
      }
    </script>
  </head>

<body>

  <H1>Sending Data to the Server With POST</H1>

  <form>
    <input type = "button" value = "Fetch message 1"
      onclick = "getData('dataresponderpost.php', 'targetDiv', 1)">
    <input type = "button" value = "Fetch message 2"
      onclick = "getData('dataresponderpost.php', 'targetDiv', 2)">
  </form>

  <div id="targetDiv">
    <p>The fetched message will appear here.</p>
  </div>

</body>
</html>
```

And you can see ajax4.html at work in Figures 3-9 and 3-10, where it's able to communicate with the server via POST.

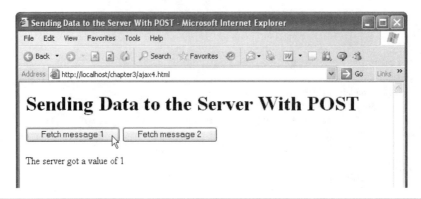

Figure 3-9 ajax4.html sending 1 to the server

Figure 3-10 ajax4.html sending 2 to the server

Now we've seen how to work with asynchronous downloads, the *A* in Ajax. So far, we've only dealt with plain text sent from the server, but Ajax can also handle XML, the *X* in Ajax. It'll take a little more work, as it turns out, to handle that XML in JavaScript (that's the topic of Chapter 6), but we can get an introduction right now.

Using Ajax Together with XML

Say that you have a very important XML document, colors.xml (which lists the colors red, green, and blue), that you want to download. As with any XML document, colors.xml starts with an XML declaration (more on this in Chapter 6):

```
<?xml version = "1.0" ?>
    .
    .
    .
```

All XML documents need a *document element*—that is, a single element that contains all the other elements in the document. In this case, let's call the document element <colors>:

```
<?xml version = "1.0" ?>
<colors>
        .
        .
        .
</colors>
```

The <colors> element will contain three <color> elements, each with a color in it, red, green, and blue:

```
<?xml version = "1.0" ?>
<colors>
  <color>red</color>
  <color>green</color>
  <color>blue</color>
</colors>
```

That's the XML document, colors.xml, we want to fetch and decode using Ajax in a new example, colors.html, which appears in Figure 3-11. When you click the Fetch the Colors button in colors.html, colors.xml is downloaded, decoded, and the colors—red, green, and blue—are displayed.

The colors.html document starts off much like the other Ajax examples you've seen in this chapter, with a button that calls a JavaScript function named getData and a <div> element in which to display the results:

```
<body>

    <h1>Using Ajax with XML</h1>
```

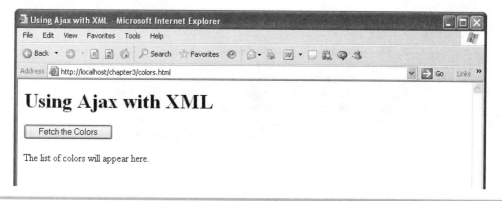

Figure 3-11   colors.html

```
<form>
  <input type = "button" value = "Fetch the Colors"
    onclick = "getData('colors.xml', 'targetDiv')">
</form>

<div id="targetDiv" width =100 height=100>
The list of colors will appear here.</div>

</body>
```

In the <script> element, we start by creating the XMLHttpRequest object we'll use:

```
<script language = "javascript">

  var colors;

  var XMLHttpRequestObject = false;

  if (window.XMLHttpRequest) {
    XMLHttpRequestObject = new XMLHttpRequest();
  } else if (window.ActiveXObject) {
    XMLHttpRequestObject = new ActiveXObject("Microsoft.XMLHTTP");
  }
        .
        .
        .
</script>
```

In the Firefox/Mozilla brand of browsers, you also have to specify that you're going to be downloading XML, not plain text. To do that, you use this line of code, which sets the MIME type of the download to text/xml (there's a MIME type for every major data format):

```
<script language = "javascript">

  var colors;

  var XMLHttpRequestObject = false;

  if (window.XMLHttpRequest) {
    XMLHttpRequestObject = new XMLHttpRequest();
    XMLHttpRequestObject.overrideMimeType("text/xml");
  } else if (window.ActiveXObject) {
    XMLHttpRequestObject = new ActiveXObject("Microsoft.XMLHTTP");
  }
        .
        .
        .
</script>
```

Now we can write the getData function. In this function, we check if the XMLHttpRequest object was created, and if so, open it:

```
function getData(dataSource, divID)
{
  if(XMLHttpRequestObject) {
    XMLHttpRequestObject.open("GET", dataSource);
      .
      .
      .
  }
}
```

Next, we can add the anonymous callback function, and check the status and readyState properties of the download:

```
function getData(dataSource, divID)
{
  if(XMLHttpRequestObject) {
    XMLHttpRequestObject.open("GET", dataSource);
    var obj = document.getElementById(divID);

    XMLHttpRequestObject.onreadystatechange = function()
    {
      if (XMLHttpRequestObject.readyState == 4 &&
        XMLHttpRequestObject.status == 200) {
          .
          .
          .
      }
    }

  }
}
```

If we're executing code inside this if statement, the download went okay. So how do we get our XML data? Do we use the XMLHttpRequest object's responseText property? Nope—we use the XMLHttpRequest object's responseXML property, which holds a JavaScript XML document object (that's the subject of Chapter 6):

```
function getData(dataSource, divID)
{
  if(XMLHttpRequestObject) {
    XMLHttpRequestObject.open("GET", dataSource);

    XMLHttpRequestObject.onreadystatechange = function()
```

```
        {
          if (XMLHttpRequestObject.readyState == 4 &&
            XMLHttpRequestObject.status == 200) {
            var xmlDocument = XMLHttpRequestObject.responseXML;
              .
              .
              .
          }
        }

      }
    }
```

You'll see more about handling XML document objects in Chapter 6, but we can dissect the object passed to us here with a little code. To start, you can get an array of the <color> elements from the XML document with the document's getElementsByTagName method. We'll create an array named colors that way:

```
function getData(dataSource, divID)
{
  if(XMLHttpRequestObject) {
    XMLHttpRequestObject.open("GET", dataSource);

    XMLHttpRequestObject.onreadystatechange = function()
    {
      if (XMLHttpRequestObject.readyState == 4 &&
        XMLHttpRequestObject.status == 200) {
        var xmlDocument = XMLHttpRequestObject.responseXML;
        colors = xmlDocument.getElementsByTagName("color");
          .
          .
          .
      }
    }

  }
}
```

Now we can prepare to list the fetched colors by displaying a message "Here are the fetched colors:" in the target <div> element; we'll also start an unordered list with a <ul> HTML tag so the colors appear in a bulleted list:

```
function getData(dataSource, divID)
{
  if(XMLHttpRequestObject) {
    XMLHttpRequestObject.open("GET", dataSource);
    var obj = document.getElementById(divID);

    XMLHttpRequestObject.onreadystatechange = function()
```

```
        {
          if (XMLHttpRequestObject.readyState == 4 &&
            XMLHttpRequestObject.status == 200) {
            var xmlDocument = XMLHttpRequestObject.responseXML;
            colors = xmlDocument.getElementsByTagName("color");
            obj.innerHTML = "Here are the fetched colors:<ul>";
              .
              .
              .
          }
        }
      }
    }
```

Now we can loop over the colors array to extract the three colors:

```
    function getData(dataSource, divID)
    {
      if(XMLHttpRequestObject) {
        XMLHttpRequestObject.open("GET", dataSource);
        var obj = document.getElementById(divID);

        XMLHttpRequestObject.onreadystatechange = function()
        {
          if (XMLHttpRequestObject.readyState == 4 &&
            XMLHttpRequestObject.status == 200) {
            var xmlDocument = XMLHttpRequestObject.responseXML;
            colors = xmlDocument.getElementsByTagName("color");
            obj.innerHTML = "Here are the fetched colors:<ul>";
            for (loopIndex =0; loopIndex < colors.length; loopIndex++)
            {
                .
                .
                .
            }
          }
        }
      }
    }
```

We can refer to the current <color> element in this for loop as colors[loopIndex]. Does that mean we can simply display colors[loopIndex] to display the current color every time through the loop? Nope, we have to extract the colors from the <color> elements specifically. Here's what the <color> elements look like:

```
<?xml version = "1.0" ?>
<colors>
  <color>red</color>
```

```
<color>green</color>
<color>blue</color>
</colors>
```

The text inside each <color> element is considered a *text node* in XML. And we can access that text node as colors[loopIndex].firstChild, because the text node is the first child of each <color> element.

Great, does that mean we can display each color as colors[loopIndex].firstChild? Nope, because in JavaScript, a text node is an object, not just text. To actually extract the text from the text node, you have to use the text node's data property like this: colors[loopIndex] .firstChild.data. So we can add each color to the bulleted list using a list item HTML tag, <li>, and then end the bulleted list with </ul> like this:

```
function getData(dataSource, divID)
{
  if(XMLHttpRequestObject) {
    XMLHttpRequestObject.open("GET", dataSource);
    var obj = document.getElementById(divID);

    XMLHttpRequestObject.onreadystatechange = function()
    {
      if (XMLHttpRequestObject.readyState == 4 &&
        XMLHttpRequestObject.status == 200) {
        var xmlDocument = XMLHttpRequestObject.responseXML;
        colors = xmlDocument.getElementsByTagName("color");
        obj.innerHTML = "Here are the fetched colors:<ul>";
        for (loopIndex =0; loopIndex < colors.length; loopIndex++)
        {
            obj.innerHTML += "<li>" +
            colors[loopIndex].firstChild.data + "</li>";
        }
        obj.innerHTML += "</ul>";
      }
    }

  }
}
```

We're finally ready to connect to the server using the XMLHttpRequest object's send method. Since we're using the GET method, we can just pass a value of null to that method:

```
function getData(dataSource, divID)
{
  if(XMLHttpRequestObject) {
    XMLHttpRequestObject.open("GET", dataSource);
    var obj = document.getElementById(divID);

    XMLHttpRequestObject.onreadystatechange = function()
    {
      if (XMLHttpRequestObject.readyState == 4 &&
```

```
        XMLHttpRequestObject.status == 200) {
        var xmlDocument = XMLHttpRequestObject.responseXML;
        colors = xmlDocument.getElementsByTagName("color");
        obj.innerHTML = "Here are the fetched colors:<ul>";
        for (loopIndex =0; loopIndex < colors.length; loopIndex++)
        {
            obj.innerHTML += "<li>" +
              colors[loopIndex].firstChild.data + "</li>";
        }
        obj.innerHTML += "</ul>";
      }
    }

    XMLHttpRequestObject.send(null);
  }
}
```

And that completes colors.html, which you can see here for reference:

```
<html>
  <head>

    <title>Using Ajax with XML</title>

    <script language = "javascript">

      var colors;

      var XMLHttpRequestObject = false;

      if (window.XMLHttpRequest) {
        XMLHttpRequestObject = new XMLHttpRequest();
        XMLHttpRequestObject.overrideMimeType("text/xml");
      } else if (window.ActiveXObject) {
        XMLHttpRequestObject = new ActiveXObject("Microsoft.XMLHTTP");
      }

      function getData(dataSource, divID)
      {
        if(XMLHttpRequestObject) {
          XMLHttpRequestObject.open("GET", dataSource);
          var obj = document.getElementById(divID);

          XMLHttpRequestObject.onreadystatechange = function()
          {
            if (XMLHttpRequestObject.readyState == 4 &&
              XMLHttpRequestObject.status == 200) {
              var xmlDocument = XMLHttpRequestObject.responseXML;
              colors = xmlDocument.getElementsByTagName("color");
              obj.innerHTML = "Here are the fetched colors:<ul>";
              for (loopIndex =0; loopIndex < colors.length; loopIndex++)
```

```
                        {
                            obj.innerHTML += "<li>" +
                            colors[loopIndex].firstChild.data + "</li>";
                        }
                        obj.innerHTML += "</ul>";
                    }
                }

                XMLHttpRequestObject.send(null);
            }
        }

    </script>
</head>

<body>

    <h1>Using Ajax with XML</h1>

    <form>
        <input type = "button" value = "Fetch the Colors"
            onclick = "getData('colors.xml', 'targetDiv')">
    </form>

    <div id="targetDiv" width =100 height=100>
    The list of colors will appear here.</div>

</body>

</html>
```

And you can see the results in Figure 3-12, which shows that clicking the button fetches the XML in the colors.xml document, decodes it, and displays the colors in a bulleted list.

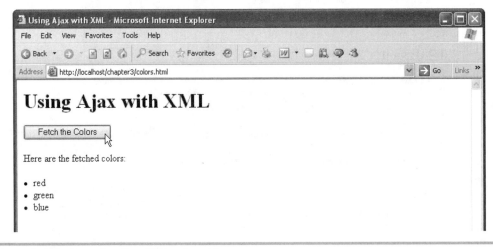

Figure 3-12 Downloading XML using Ajax

Chapter 4

Full Throttle Ajax

Key Skills & Concepts

- Handling multiple XMLHttpRequest requests

- Using two XMLHttpRequest requests

- Using an array of XMLHttpRequest requests

- Using inner functions and multiple XMLHttpRequest requests

- Handling JavaScript sent from the server

- Overcoming browser caching

This chapter gets us into some serious Ajax. Chapter 3 gave us our start with Ajax, and this chapter takes it from there, delving deep into the topic. One of the primary topics we'll take a look at in this chapter is how to work with multiple XMLHttp requests in the same page— that is, if you have multiple buttons that use Ajax to connect to the server, what happens if one request isn't finished before the user clicks another button? When Ajax returns, which request is returning the data? We'll handle how to work with multiple XMLHttp requests in the same page here.

We'll also see that besides downloading plain text and XML, you can also download other character-based data, such as JavaScript, which turns out to be a common thing to download using Ajax. For example, connecting to some Google applications yourself in code, such as Google Suggest (see Chapter 1), involves downloading JavaScript.

And there's more Ajax in this chapter as well—how to overcome browser caching, handling the HTTP headers you can download with Ajax, and more. We'll start by looking at the case where having multiple XMLHttpRequest objects in the same page creates the possibility of a mix-up.

Handling Multiple XMLHttpRequest Objects in the Same Page

Perhaps you recall the example from Chapter 3 in which we communicated with a PHP script on the server, dataresponder.php. When you clicked button 1, a value of 1 was sent to the server, which sent that value back, as you see in Figure 4-1.

When you clicked button 2, a value of 2 was sent to the server, which sent that value back. So far so good.

But now say that the user gets impatient, and clicks buttons at random. The problem is that the application uses only one XMLHttpRequest object, but now that object is being asked

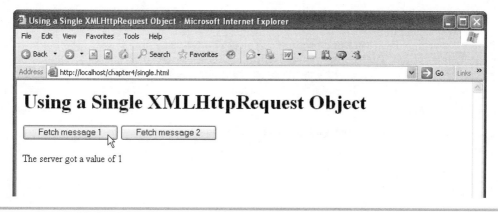

Figure 4-1   single.html at work

to send multiple requests to the server. And depending on how fast or slow the server is, the responses could get mixed up—the user could even click button 1, and then button 2, and see the response from clicking button 1 if the server returned the responses out of order.

That out-of-order possibility comes about because the application uses only one XMLHttpRequest object, even though the user might make multiple requests. You can see the problem in the code, which just uses one XMLHttpRequest object (this is single.html, which has been renamed ajax3.html from the previous chapter):

```html
<html>
  <head>
    <title>Sending Data to the Server</title>

    <script language = "javascript">
      var XMLHttpRequestObject = false;

      if (window.XMLHttpRequest) {
        XMLHttpRequestObject = new XMLHttpRequest();
      } else if (window.ActiveXObject) {
        XMLHttpRequestObject = new
          ActiveXObject("Microsoft.XMLHTTP");
      }

      function getData(dataSource, divID)
      {
        if(XMLHttpRequestObject) {
          var obj = document.getElementById(divID);
          XMLHttpRequestObject.open("GET", dataSource);
```

```
XMLHttpRequestObject.onreadystatechange = function()
{
  if (XMLHttpRequestObject.readyState == 4 &&
    XMLHttpRequestObject.status == 200) {
      obj.innerHTML = XMLHttpRequestObject.responseText;
  }
}

XMLHttpRequestObject.send(null);
    }
  }
</script>
</head>

<body>

  <h1>Sending Data to the Server</h1>

  <form>
    <input type = "button" value = "Fetch message 1"
      onclick = "getData('dataresponder.php?data=1', 'targetDiv')">
    <input type = "button" value = "Fetch message 2"
      onclick = "getData('dataresponder.php?data=2', 'targetDiv')">
  </form>

  <div id="targetDiv">
    <p>The fetched message will appear here.</p>
  </div>

</body>
</html>
```

And here's the server-side code, dataresponder.php:

```
<?php
  if ($_GET["data"] == "1") {
    echo 'The server got a value of 1';
  }
  if ($_GET["data"] == "2") {
    echo 'The server got a value of 2';
  }
?>
```

Okay, so the question becomes, how do you handle multiple XMLHttpRequest requests at more or less the same time? Our first solution is the obvious one—use two XMLHttpRequest objects.

Using Two XMLHttpRequest Objects

There are two buttons in single.html, but only one XMLHttpRequest object, which can lead to getting the responses mixed up. How about we create two XMLHttpRequest objects, one for each button?

That's just what we'll do in a new example, double.html. First, we create one XMLHttpRequest object, XMLHttpRequest1:

```
<html>
  <head>
    <title>Using Two XMLHttpRequest Objects</title>

    <script language = "javascript">
      var XMLHttpRequestObject1 = false;

      if (window.XMLHttpRequest) {
        XMLHttpRequestObject1 = new XMLHttpRequest();
      } else if (window.ActiveXObject) {
        XMLHttpRequestObject1 = new
          ActiveXObject("Microsoft.XMLHTTP");
      }
            .
            .
            .
```

Next, we create a new version of the getData function, getData1, that uses this XMLHttpRequest object:

```
<html>
  <head>
    <title>Using Two XMLHttpRequest Objects</title>

    <script language = "javascript">
      var XMLHttpRequestObject1 = false;

      if (window.XMLHttpRequest) {
        XMLHttpRequestObject1 = new XMLHttpRequest();
      } else if (window.ActiveXObject) {
        XMLHttpRequestObject1 = new
          ActiveXObject("Microsoft.XMLHTTP");
      }

      function getData1(dataSource, divID)
      {
        if(XMLHttpRequestObject1) {
          var obj = document.getElementById(divID);
          XMLHttpRequestObject1.open("GET", dataSource);

          XMLHttpRequestObject1.onreadystatechange = function()
```

```
       {
         if (XMLHttpRequestObject1.readyState == 4 &&
           XMLHttpRequestObject1.status == 200) {
             obj.innerHTML = XMLHttpRequestObject1.responseText;
         }
       }

       XMLHttpRequestObject1.send(null);
     }
   }
     .
     .
     .
```

Next, we create a second new XMLHttpRequest object, XMLHttpRequest2:

```
<html>
  <head>
    <title>Using Two XMLHttpRequest Objects</title>

    <script language = "javascript">
      var XMLHttpRequestObject1 = false;

      if (window.XMLHttpRequest) {
        XMLHttpRequestObject1 = new XMLHttpRequest();
      } else if (window.ActiveXObject) {
        XMLHttpRequestObject1 = new
          ActiveXObject("Microsoft.XMLHTTP");
      }

      var XMLHttpRequestObject2 = false;

      if (window.XMLHttpRequest) {
        XMLHttpRequestObject2 = new XMLHttpRequest();
      } else if (window.ActiveXObject) {
        XMLHttpRequestObject2 = new
          ActiveXObject("Microsoft.XMLHTTP");
      }

      function getData1(dataSource, divID)
      {
        if(XMLHttpRequestObject1) {
          var obj = document.getElementById(divID);
          XMLHttpRequestObject1.open("GET", dataSource);

          XMLHttpRequestObject1.onreadystatechange = function()
          {
            if (XMLHttpRequestObject1.readyState == 4 &&
```

```
                XMLHttpRequestObject1.status == 200) {
                    obj.innerHTML = XMLHttpRequestObject1.responseText;
                }
            }

            XMLHttpRequestObject1.send(null);
        }
    }
        .
        .
        .
```

Then, we add another version of the getData function, getData2, which uses
XMLHttpRequest2:

```
<html>
  <head>
    <title>Using Two XMLHttpRequest Objects</title>

    <script language = "javascript">
      var XMLHttpRequestObject1 = false;

      if (window.XMLHttpRequest) {
        XMLHttpRequestObject1 = new XMLHttpRequest();
      } else if (window.ActiveXObject) {
        XMLHttpRequestObject1 = new
          ActiveXObject("Microsoft.XMLHTTP");
      }

      var XMLHttpRequestObject2 = false;

      if (window.XMLHttpRequest) {
        XMLHttpRequestObject2 = new XMLHttpRequest();
      } else if (window.ActiveXObject) {
        XMLHttpRequestObject2 = new
          ActiveXObject("Microsoft.XMLHTTP");
      }

      function getData1(dataSource, divID)
      {
        if(XMLHttpRequestObject1) {
          var obj = document.getElementById(divID);
          XMLHttpRequestObject1.open("GET", dataSource);

          XMLHttpRequestObject1.onreadystatechange = function()
          {
            if (XMLHttpRequestObject1.readyState == 4 &&
              XMLHttpRequestObject1.status == 200) {
```

```
            obj.innerHTML = XMLHttpRequestObject1.responseText;
        }
    }

    XMLHttpRequestObject1.send(null);
  }
}

function getData2(dataSource, divID)
{
  if(XMLHttpRequestObject2) {
    var obj = document.getElementById(divID);
    XMLHttpRequestObject2.open("GET", dataSource);

    XMLHttpRequestObject2.onreadystatechange = function()
    {
      if (XMLHttpRequestObject2.readyState == 4 &&
        XMLHttpRequestObject2.status == 200) {
          obj.innerHTML = XMLHttpRequestObject2.responseText;
      }
    }

    XMLHttpRequestObject2.send(null);
  }
}
        .
        .
        .
```

That's fine—now we've created two XMLHttpRequest objects and two getData functions to handle them. All that remains is to connect one button to getData1 and the other button to getData2 (this is double.html):

```
<body>

  <h1>Using Two XMLHttpRequest Objects</h1>

  <form>
    <input type = "button" value = "Fetch message 1"
      onclick = "getData1('dataresponder.php?data=1', 'targetDiv')">
    <input type = "button" value = "Fetch message 2"
      onclick = "getData2('dataresponder.php?data=2', 'targetDiv')">
  </form>

  <div id="targetDiv">
    <p>The fetched message will appear here.</p>
  </div>

</body>
</html>
```

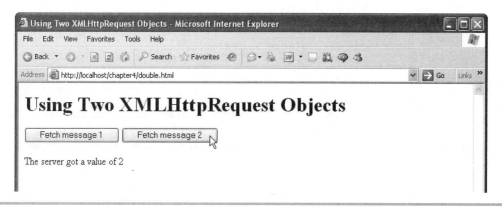

Figure 4-2   double.html

And we're done. You can test double.html. Clicking either button will download the correct message, as you see in Figure 4-2.

Get double.html to Work

Create double.html now, or get it from the downloadable code for this book, and get it working. This application is our first attempt at working with multiple XMLHttpRequest objects, so make sure you understand how it works and what it does.

Okay, using two XMLHttpRequest objects addressed the problem. But what if there are three buttons in the application? Do you write code for three XMLHttpRequest objects? What if there are a hundred buttons? What if the user clicked the two buttons a dozen times? Clearly, we need a better solution.

Using an Array of XMLHttpRequest Objects

A better solution might be to use an array of XMLHttpRequest objects. We could create a new XMLHttpRequest for each new request, and keep them separate easily using an array.

Here's how that works in a new example, array.html. We can start by creating for the XMLHttpRequest objects a new array named XMLHttpRequestObjects, using the JavaScript Array function:

```
<html>
  <head>
    <title>Using an Array of XMLHttpRequest Objects</title>
```

```
<script language = "javascript">

  var XMLHttpRequestObjects = new Array();
     .
     .
     .
```

An easy way to add items to the end of an array in JavaScript is to use the push function. We can use the push function to store new XMLHttpRequest objects in the XMLHttpRequestObjects array, like this in getData1, the function connected to button 1:

```
<html>
  <head>
    <title>Using an Array of XMLHttpRequest Objects</title>

    <script language = "javascript">

    var XMLHttpRequestObjects = new Array();

    function getData1(dataSource, divID)
    {
      if (window.XMLHttpRequest) {
        XMLHttpRequestObjects.push(new XMLHttpRequest());
      } else if (window.ActiveXObject) {
        XMLHttpRequestObjects.push(new ActiveXObject("Microsoft.XMLHTTP"));
      .
      .
      .
```

The index in the array at which the newest XMLHttpRequest object is stored is XMLHttpRequestObjects.length −1, and we assign that value to a variable named index so that we can keep track of the newest XMLHttpRequest object:

```
<html>
  <head>
    <title>Using an Array of XMLHttpRequest Objects</title>

    <script language = "javascript">
      var index = 0;

    var XMLHttpRequestObjects = new Array();

    function getData1(dataSource, divID)
    {
      if (window.XMLHttpRequest) {
        XMLHttpRequestObjects.push(new XMLHttpRequest());
      } else if (window.ActiveXObject) {
        XMLHttpRequestObjects.push(new ActiveXObject("Microsoft.XMLHTTP"));
      }
```

```
      index = XMLHttpRequestObjects.length - 1;
         .
         .
         .
```

Now we can refer to the most current XMLHttpRequest object as XMLHttpRequestObjects
[index] like this in the remainder of getData1:

```
<html>
  <head>
    <title>Using an Array of XMLHttpRequest Objects</title>

    <script language = "javascript">
      var index = 0;

      var XMLHttpRequestObjects = new Array();

      function getData1(dataSource, divID)
      {
        if (window.XMLHttpRequest) {
          XMLHttpRequestObjects.push(new XMLHttpRequest());
        } else if (window.ActiveXObject) {
          XMLHttpRequestObjects.push(new ActiveXObject("Microsoft.XMLHTTP"));
        }

        index = XMLHttpRequestObjects.length - 1;

        if(XMLHttpRequestObjects[index]) {
          XMLHttpRequestObjects[index].open("GET", dataSource);
          var obj = document.getElementById(divID);

          XMLHttpRequestObjects[index].onreadystatechange = function()
          {
            if (XMLHttpRequestObjects[index].readyState == 4 &&
              XMLHttpRequestObjects[index].status == 200) {
                obj.innerHTML = XMLHttpRequestObjects[index].responseText;
            }
          }

          XMLHttpRequestObjects[index].send(null);
        }
      }
         .
         .
         .
```

And getData2, the function tied to button 2, works in a similar fashion:

```
      function getData2(dataSource, divID)
      {
        if (window.XMLHttpRequest) {
          XMLHttpRequestObjects.push(new XMLHttpRequest());
```

```
    } else if (window.ActiveXObject) {
    XMLHttpRequestObjects.push(new ActiveXObject("Microsoft.XMLHTTP"));
    }

    index = XMLHttpRequestObjects.length - 1;

    if(XMLHttpRequestObjects[index]) {
      XMLHttpRequestObjects[index].open("GET", dataSource);
      var obj = document.getElementById(divID);

      XMLHttpRequestObjects[index].onreadystatechange = function()
      {
        if (XMLHttpRequestObjects[index].readyState == 4 &&
          XMLHttpRequestObjects[index].status == 200) {
            obj.innerHTML = XMLHttpRequestObjects[index].responseText;
        }
      }

      XMLHttpRequestObjects[index].send(null);
    }
  }
```

Finally, we tie getData1 and getData2 to the two buttons:

```
<html>
  <head>
    <title>Using an Array of XMLHttpRequest Objects</title>

    <script language = "javascript">
      var index = 0;

      var XMLHttpRequestObjects = new Array();

      function getData1(dataSource, divID)
      {
        if (window.XMLHttpRequest) {
          XMLHttpRequestObjects.push(new XMLHttpRequest());
        } else if (window.ActiveXObject) {
        XMLHttpRequestObjects.push(new ActiveXObject("Microsoft.XMLHTTP"));
        }

        index = XMLHttpRequestObjects.length - 1;

        if(XMLHttpRequestObjects[index]) {
          XMLHttpRequestObjects[index].open("GET", dataSource);
          var obj = document.getElementById(divID);

          XMLHttpRequestObjects[index].onreadystatechange = function()
          {
            if (XMLHttpRequestObjects[index].readyState == 4 &&
              XMLHttpRequestObjects[index].status == 200) {
                obj.innerHTML = XMLHttpRequestObjects[index].responseText;
            }
          }
```

```
      XMLHttpRequestObjects[index].send(null);
    }
  }

  function getData2(dataSource, divID)
  {
    if (window.XMLHttpRequest) {
      XMLHttpRequestObjects.push(new XMLHttpRequest());
    } else if (window.ActiveXObject) {
    XMLHttpRequestObjects.push(new ActiveXObject("Microsoft.XMLHTTP"));
    }

    index = XMLHttpRequestObjects.length - 1;

    if(XMLHttpRequestObjects[index]) {
      XMLHttpRequestObjects[index].open("GET", dataSource);
      var obj = document.getElementById(divID);

      XMLHttpRequestObjects[index].onreadystatechange = function()
      {
        if (XMLHttpRequestObjects[index].readyState == 4 &&
          XMLHttpRequestObjects[index].status == 200) {
            obj.innerHTML = XMLHttpRequestObjects[index].responseText;
        }
      }

      XMLHttpRequestObjects[index].send(null);
    }
  }
    </script>
  </head>

<body>

  <h1>Using an Array of XMLHttpRequest Objects</h1>

  <form>
    <input type = "button" value = "Fetch message 1"
      onclick = "getData1('dataresponder.php?data=1', 'targetDiv')">
    <input type = "button" value = "Fetch message 2"
      onclick = "getData2('dataresponder.php?data=2', 'targetDiv')">
  </form>

  <div id="targetDiv">
    <p>The fetched message will appear here.</p>
  </div>

  </body>
</html>
```

You can see this new application, array.html, at work in Figure 4-3. Cool.
Clicking either button will download the correct message, as you see in Figure 4-3.

Figure 4-3 array.html

Try This Get array.html to Work

Create array.html now, or get it from the downloadable code for this book, and get it working. This application is a better option for working with multiple XMLHttpRequest requests, so make sure you understand how it works.

So array.html works by creating a new XMLHttpRequest object for each Ajax request. But isn't it a little wasteful? After all, all those old XMLHttpRequest objects keep hanging around in the array, even after their request is completed. And that clutters up memory. Worse, it could halt your application if the user clicks the buttons several hundred or thousand times, as in an Ajax-enabled game.

Isn't there some way to easily get rid of XMLHttpRequest objects that you don't need any more?

Using Inner Functions

It turns out that the way you usually handle multiple XMLHttpRequest requests in Ajax is with *inner functions*, not with arrays of XMLHttpRequest objects.

What are inner functions? Those are functions contained inside another function, like this:

```
function outer(value)
{
  var item1 = value;

  function inner(item2)
  {
    return (item1 + item2)
  }
}
```

As you can see, the inner function is contained inside the outer function. What's so special about that? If you call the outer function with a value that is used to set the variable item1, item1 preserves its value when you call the inner function. So, for example, if you call outer and pass it a value of 1, and then call inner, passing it a value of 2, inner will return 1 + 2. If you then call inner with a value of 4, it will return 1 + 4.

Suppose you then call outer with a new value, 2, and then call inner with a value of 3. In this case, item1 is 2 and item2 is 3, so inner returns 3 + 2 = 5.

What does this buy you? Here's the key: every time you call outer, a new copy of the outer function is created, which includes a new copy of the inner function inside it. Make the transition from thinking in terms of item1 to thinking in terms of an XMLHttpRequest object, and you can see the point: you can work this so that every time the getData function is called, a new XMLHttpRequest object is created, and the anonymous function that uses it—the inner function—will always have a fresh XMLHttpRequest object to work with.

Here's what our code looks like in general now—note that the XMLHttpRequest object creation is outside the getData function:

```
var XMLHttpRequestObject = false;

if (window.XMLHttpRequest) {
  XMLHttpRequestObject = new XMLHttpRequest();
} else if (window.ActiveXObject) {
  XMLHttpRequestObject = new
    ActiveXObject("Microsoft.XMLHTTP");
}

function getData(dataSource, divID)
{
  if(XMLHttpRequestObject) {
    var obj = document.getElementById(divID);
    XMLHttpRequestObject.open("GET", dataSource);

    XMLHttpRequestObject.onreadystatechange = function()
    {
      if (XMLHttpRequestObject.readyState == 4 &&
        XMLHttpRequestObject.status == 200) {
          obj.innerHTML = XMLHttpRequestObject.responseText;
      }
    }

    XMLHttpRequestObject.send(null);
  }
}
```

To make sure there's a new XMLHttpRequest object for each Ajax request, you just move the XMLHttpRequest object creation code inside the getData function. That makes getData into the outer function that encloses the inner, anonymous function that actually works with the XMLHttpRequest object. Each time you call getData, a new copy of that function will be created, which in turn will create a new XMLHttpRequest object that will be used by the inner function when the Ajax request returns from the server.

Here's what it looks like in code:

```
function getData(dataSource, divID)
{
  var XMLHttpRequestObject = false;

  if (window.XMLHttpRequest) {
    XMLHttpRequestObject = new XMLHttpRequest();
  } else if (window.ActiveXObject) {
    XMLHttpRequestObject = new
      ActiveXObject("Microsoft.XMLHTTP");
  }

  if(XMLHttpRequestObject) {
    var obj = document.getElementById(divID);
    XMLHttpRequestObject.open("GET", dataSource);

    XMLHttpRequestObject.onreadystatechange = function()
    {
      if (XMLHttpRequestObject.readyState == 4 &&
        XMLHttpRequestObject.status == 200) {
          obj.innerHTML = XMLHttpRequestObject.responseText;
      }
    }

    XMLHttpRequestObject.send(null);
  }
}
```

So instead of creating multiple XMLHttpRequest objects and two functions, getData1 and getData2, like this,

```
var XMLHttpRequestObject1 = false;

if (window.XMLHttpRequest) {
  XMLHttpRequestObject1 = new XMLHttpRequest();
} else if (window.ActiveXObject) {
  XMLHttpRequestObject1 = new
    ActiveXObject("Microsoft.XMLHTTP");
}

var XMLHttpRequestObject2 = false;
```

```
if (window.XMLHttpRequest) {
  XMLHttpRequestObject2 = new XMLHttpRequest();
} else if (window.ActiveXObject) {
  XMLHttpRequestObject2 = new
    ActiveXObject("Microsoft.XMLHTTP");
}

function getData1(dataSource, divID)
{
  if(XMLHttpRequestObject1) {
    var obj = document.getElementById(divID);
    XMLHttpRequestObject1.open("GET", dataSource);

    XMLHttpRequestObject1.onreadystatechange = function()
    {
      if (XMLHttpRequestObject1.readyState == 4 &&
        XMLHttpRequestObject1.status == 200) {
          obj.innerHTML = XMLHttpRequestObject1.responseText;
      }
    }

    XMLHttpRequestObject1.send(null);
  }
}

function getData2(dataSource, divID)
{
  if(XMLHttpRequestObject2) {
    var obj = document.getElementById(divID);
    XMLHttpRequestObject2.open("GET", dataSource);

    XMLHttpRequestObject2.onreadystatechange = function()
    {
      if (XMLHttpRequestObject2.readyState == 4 &&
        XMLHttpRequestObject2.status == 200) {
          obj.innerHTML = XMLHttpRequestObject2.responseText;
      }
    }

    XMLHttpRequestObject2.send(null);
  }
}
  .
  .
  .
```

you need only one getData function, and can simply move the XMLHttpRequest object creation code into that function, like this in inner.html:

```html
<html>
  <head>
    <title>Using Inner Functions and Multiple XMLHttpRequest Objects</title>

    <script language = "javascript">
      function getData(dataSource, divID)
      {
        var XMLHttpRequestObject = false;

        if (window.XMLHttpRequest) {
          XMLHttpRequestObject = new XMLHttpRequest();
        } else if (window.ActiveXObject) {
          XMLHttpRequestObject = new
            ActiveXObject("Microsoft.XMLHTTP");
        }

        if(XMLHttpRequestObject) {
          var obj = document.getElementById(divID);
          XMLHttpRequestObject.open("GET", dataSource);

          XMLHttpRequestObject.onreadystatechange = function()
          {
            if (XMLHttpRequestObject.readyState == 4 &&
              XMLHttpRequestObject.status == 200) {
                obj.innerHTML = XMLHttpRequestObject.responseText;
            }
          }

          XMLHttpRequestObject.send(null);
        }
      }
    </script>
  </head>

  <body>

    <h1>Using Inner Functions and Multiple XMLHttpRequest Objects</h1>

    <form>
      <input type = "button" value = "Fetch message 1"
        onclick = "getData('dataresponder.php?data=1', 'targetDiv')">
      <input type = "button" value = "Fetch message 2"
        onclick = "getData('dataresponder.php?data=2', 'targetDiv')">
    </form>

    <div id="targetDiv">
      <p>The fetched message will appear here.</p>
    </div>

  </body>
</html>
```

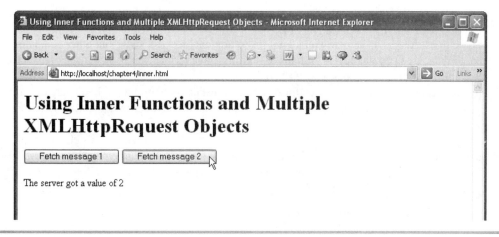

Figure 4-4 inner.html

You can see inner.html at work in Figure 4-4. Go ahead, click the buttons as often as you like; there won't be any conflict between Ajax requests.

The inner.html example shows how to avoid potential conflicts between Ajax requests—just place the XMLHttpRequest creation code inside the getData function (or whatever you call that function in your own code).

That's it. Now you can handle multiple XMLHttpRequest requests with ease.

Try This   Get Inner Functions to Work

Confirm that inner functions work as advertised by checking out this chunk of code:

```
function outer(value)
{
  var item1 = value;

  function inner(item2)
  {
    return (item1 + item2)
  }
}
```

Put it into a page and call outer(1), then inner(2). Do you get a result of 3? Then try calling outer(2) and inner(2) again. Did you get 4?

Downloading JavaScript

Sometimes, Ajax is used to download not just plain text, not just XML, but other character-based data. One popular choice is, believe it or not, JavaScript. That choice makes sense, for example, if your web site has a dozen JavaScript functions and code that determines which function is appropriate to call now; for example, a restaurant web site might display different menus depending on the time of day. Or you could read the JavaScript that calls a function with particular data.

In fact, that's how we'll be able to connect to Google Suggest later in this chapter to download the matches it found to the search term the user typed. What you actually download from Google is text that is JavaScript, and that JavaScript is a function call. For example, if you type the letter "a," you'd be able to download this JavaScript from Google Suggest:

```
window.google.ac.Suggest_apply(frameElement, "a", new Array(2,
"amazon", "855,000,000 results", "argos", "12,500,000 results",
"aol", "278,000,000 results", "autotrader", "5,820,000 results",
"apple", "436,000,000 results", "amazon.com", "461,000,000 results",
"aol.com", "87,200,000 results", "american airlines",
"14,600,000 results", "australian open", "12,300,000 results",
"ask.com", "39,600,000 results"), new Array(""));
```

This is JavaScript that's a call to a function with the odd name window.google.ac.Suggest_apply (it's odd because that's a completely illegal JavaScript function name—the browser window object does not have a built-in method named google.ac.Suggest_apply), and you can see the matches Google Suggest found for the character "a" in the function call, which we'll decode later in this chapter.

We'll start by taking a look at an example that downloads JavaScript, javascript.html. This Ajax application will read text from a PHP script, javascript.php, and that text is just a call to a function named show (bear in mind that you're going to read all about PHP in Chapter 9):

```
<?php
    echo 'show()';
?>
```

When we download the text from javascript.php, we can execute that text as JavaScript, which will cause the browser to look for a JavaScript function we've written named show and call that function.

Here's how we start javascript.html—note that we create a button in HTML and connect it to a JavaScript function named getData:

```
<html>
  <head>
    <title>Downloading JavaScript with Ajax</title>

    <script language = "javascript">
      var XMLHttpRequestObject = false;
```

```
      if (window.XMLHttpRequest) {
        XMLHttpRequestObject = new XMLHttpRequest();
      } else if (window.ActiveXObject) {
        XMLHttpRequestObject = new ActiveXObject("Microsoft.XMLHTTP");
      }

      function getData(dataSource)
      {
        if(XMLHttpRequestObject) {

          XMLHttpRequestObject.open("GET", dataSource);

          XMLHttpRequestObject.onreadystatechange = function()
          {
            if (XMLHttpRequestObject.readyState == 4 &&
              XMLHttpRequestObject.status == 200) {

                  .
                  .
                  .

            }
          }

          XMLHttpRequestObject.send(null);
        }
      }
    </script>
  </head>

  <body>

    <H1>Downloading JavaScript with Ajax</H1>

    <form>
      <input type = "button" value = "Get the JavaScript"
        onclick = "getData('javascript.php')">
    </form>

    <div id="targetDiv">
      <p>The data will go here.</p>
    </div>

  </body>
</html>
```

When you download the text (which reads, "show( )") from javascript.php, you can execute that text with the JavaScript eval function. That's what the eval function does—you pass it text and it executes that text as JavaScript.

The downloaded text will be in XMLHttpRequestObject.responseText, and you can execute that text as JavaScript in this way in getData:

```
function getData(dataSource)
{
  if(XMLHttpRequestObject) {

    XMLHttpRequestObject.open("GET", dataSource);

    XMLHttpRequestObject.onreadystatechange = function()
    {
      if (XMLHttpRequestObject.readyState == 4 &&
        XMLHttpRequestObject.status == 200) {

        eval(XMLHttpRequestObject.responseText);
      }
    }

    XMLHttpRequestObject.send(null);
  }
}
```

Of course, this means that we'll need a JavaScript function named show. In that function, we might just display the text "Yep, it worked!" in the web page. Here's what that looks like in the final form of javascript.html:

```
<html>
  <head>
    <title>Downloading JavaScript with Ajax</title>

    <script language = "javascript">
      var XMLHttpRequestObject = false;

      if (window.XMLHttpRequest) {
        XMLHttpRequestObject = new XMLHttpRequest();
      } else if (window.ActiveXObject) {
        XMLHttpRequestObject = new ActiveXObject("Microsoft.XMLHTTP");
      }

      function getData(dataSource)
      {
        if(XMLHttpRequestObject) {

          XMLHttpRequestObject.open("GET", dataSource);

          XMLHttpRequestObject.onreadystatechange = function()
```

```
        {
          if (XMLHttpRequestObject.readyState == 4 &&
            XMLHttpRequestObject.status == 200) {

              eval(XMLHttpRequestObject.responseText);
          }
        }

        XMLHttpRequestObject.send(null);
      }
    }

    function show()
    {
      var targetDiv = document.getElementById("targetDiv");

      targetDiv.innerHTML = "Yep, it worked!";
    }
  </script>
</head>

<body>

  <H1>Downloading JavaScript with Ajax</H1>

  <form>
    <input type = "button" value = "Get the JavaScript"
      onclick = "getData('javascript.php')">
  </form>

  <div id="targetDiv">
    <p>The data will go here.</p>
  </div>

</body>
</html>
```

So when the user clicks the button, the application reads the text returned by javascript.php and executes that text as JavaScript, calling the show function, which displays the message you see in Figure 4-5.

This example demonstrates that you can download and execute JavaScript almost as easily as you can download text. And that prepares you for working with Google Suggest, coming up next.

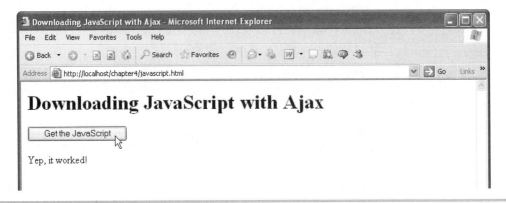

Figure 4-5 javascript.html

Download JavaScript

Try creating a new Ajax-enabled web page that includes a JavaScript function named adder, which adds two values and returns the sum:

```
function adder(value1, value2)
{
  return (item1 + item2)
}
```

Then download the text adder(2, 3) from the server, execute it, and confirm that you get an answer of 5.

Now that we've seen how to download and execute JavaScript using Ajax, we're ready for the major example of this chapter—connecting to Google Suggest.

Connecting to Google Suggest

Behold Google Suggest in Figure 4-6. When you start typing a search term, Google Suggest suggests, in a drop-down list, matches to what you've typed. You then can select a term from that list, which saves you from having to type the whole search term.

You can connect to Google Suggest yourself by using Ajax, and we'll take a look at how to do that now. Among other things, this example will let you learn how to use Ajax to respond to single keystrokes typed by the user.

Let's get our version of the Google Suggest page going now.

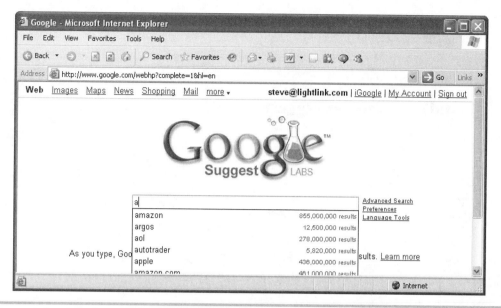

Figure 4-6 Google Suggest

Creating the Search Term Field

We're going to connect to Google Suggest ourselves using Ajax. First, we'll need a text field that lets the user enter their search term, and that might look like this in the body of the page:

```
<body>

  <H1>Handling Google Suggest</H1>

  Search for <input id = "textField" type = "text">
      .
      .
      .
</body>
```

You can see what this web page looks like so far in Figure 4-7.

We're going to need to check what the user has entered each time they press a key, and display the matches found to what they've typed. We can respond to keystrokes by using the text field's onkeyup event, which occurs when the user releases a key. We can handle that event by calling a function named, say, askGoogleSuggest:

```
<body>

  <H1>Handling Google Suggest</H1>
```

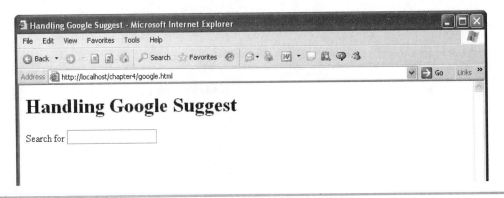

Figure 4-7 Our version of Google Suggest

```
Search for <input id = "textField" type = "text"
  name = "textField" onkeyup = "askGoogleSuggest()">
        .
        .
        .

</body>
```

So far so good. Now we'll need an element to display our drop-down menu (of the kind you see in Figure 4-6) that shows the user the matches to their partial search term. We'll display that drop-down list—which will actually be an HTML table—using a <div> element with the ID targetDiv like this:

```
<body>

  <H1>Handling Google Suggest</H1>

  Search for <input id = "textField" type = "text"
    name = "textField" onkeyup = "askGoogleSuggest()">

  <div id = "targetDiv"><div></div></div>

</body>
```

That completes the body of the web page. Let's turn to the JavaScript next, which is where the real action is.

Writing the JavaScript

Let's create the askGoogleSuggest function now:

```
<script language = "javascript">
  function askGoogleSuggest()
```

```
    {
        .
        .
        .
    }
  </script>
```

This function is called when the user presses a key, and we can read that key using the value property of the text field. First, we get an object corresponding to the text field (the text field has the ID textField):

```
  <script language = "javascript">
    function askGoogleSuggest()
    {
      var input = document.getElementById("textField");
        .
        .
        .
    }
  </script>
```

If there is a partial search term in the text field, we can send it to Google Suggest to get its suggestions; here's how you check if there is a partial search term already entered:

```
  <script language = "javascript">
    function askGoogleSuggest()
    {
      var input = document.getElementById("textField");

      if (input.value) {
        .
        .
        .
      }
    }
  </script>
```

If there is a search term waiting, we can send it to Google Suggest. We'll do that via a PHP script, google.php, using the GET method, which means we have to URL-encode our data. We'll send the partial search term to google.php (which will forward that term on to Google Suggest) using the argument name qu (short for query). Here's how we send the partial search term to google.php, by calling a function we've named getData:

```
  <script language = "javascript">
    function askGoogleSuggest()
    {
      var input = document.getElementById("textField");

      if (input.value) {
        getData("google.php?qu=" + input.value);
      }
    }
  </script>
```

Why do we communicate with Google Suggest via a PHP script? Why can't we just contact Google Suggest directly, from this web page? These are important questions. The answer is that this is an issue of security. If a web browser sees that your Ajax script is trying to contact a server that's not the same server on which your web page resides, it will get suspicious. That's the case here—the server on which Google Suggest resides is not the same as our server.

In cases like this, the browser puts up an (annoying) dialog box, asking the user if it should proceed. That kind of thing destroys the utility of Ajax, which is supposed to operate seamlessly, behind the scenes. To get around this problem, you can use server-side programming, on your own server, to connect to the foreign server. That's what we're doing here—we're connecting to Google Suggest via google.php to avoid security issues (and we'll write google.php a bit later).

Okay, we're nearly done with the askGoogleSuggest function. The last step is to clear the drop-down list box if the user has erased the text in the search text field, which we do like this:

```
<script language = "javascript">
  function askGoogleSuggest()
  {
    var input = document.getElementById("textField");

    if (input.value) {
      getData("google.php?qu=" + input.value);
    }
    else {
      var targetDiv = document.getElementById("targetDiv");

      targetDiv.innerHTML = "<div></div>";
    }
  }
</script>
```

The getData function in this example just takes a URL argument, named dataSource:

```
<script language = "javascript">
  function getData(dataSource)
  {
    .
    .
    .
  }
</script>
```

The dataSource argument will hold the URL of google.php, along with the URL-encoded search term the user has typed. We're going to connect to google.php using Ajax in the getData function, and we'll start by creating an XMLHttpRequest object:

```
<script language = "javascript">
  function getData(dataSource)
  {
    var XMLHttpRequestObject = false;

    if (window.XMLHttpRequest) {
      XMLHttpRequestObject = new XMLHttpRequest();
    } else if (window.ActiveXObject) {
      XMLHttpRequestObject = new ActiveXObject("Microsoft.XMLHTTP");
    }
        .
        .
        .

  }
</script>
```

Now we can connect to google.php in the usual way—using an anonymous function:

```
<script language = "javascript">
  function getData(dataSource)
  {
    var XMLHttpRequestObject = false;

    if (window.XMLHttpRequest) {
      XMLHttpRequestObject = new XMLHttpRequest();
    } else if (window.ActiveXObject) {
      XMLHttpRequestObject = new ActiveXObject("Microsoft.XMLHTTP");
    }

    if(XMLHttpRequestObject) {
      XMLHttpRequestObject.open("GET", dataSource);

      XMLHttpRequestObject.onreadystatechange = function()
      {
        if (XMLHttpRequestObject.readyState == 4 &&
          XMLHttpRequestObject.status == 200) {
            .
            .
            .
        }
      }


    }
  }
</script>
```

What kind of return text will we get from Google Suggest? If your search term is "a," for example, this is the text you'll get back from Google Suggest using Ajax:

```
window.google.ac.Suggest_apply(frameElement, "a", new Array(2,
"amazon", "855,000,000 results", "argos", "12,500,000 results",
"aol", "278,000,000 results", "autotrader", "5,820,000 results",
```

```
"apple", "436,000,000 results", "amazon.com", "461,000,000 results",
"aol.com", "87,200,000 results", "american airlines",
"14,600,000 results", "australian open", "12,300,000 results",
"ask.com", "39,600,000 results"), new Array(""));
```

This is JavaScript; Google Suggest returns a JavaScript function call (in text form, of course) that is built so that you can call a function of the same name in your Ajax application. But that introduces a problem: if you try to create a function of this name, window.google .ac.Suggest_apply, Firefox and Internet Explorer will both have errors and tell you that their built-in window object does not contain a "google" property or method. How can you fix that? You can rename the function in the JavaScript returned from Google Suggest into something legal, such as "callback":

```
callback(frameElement, "a", new Array(2, "amazon",
"855,000,000 results", "argos", "12,500,000 results",
"aol", "278,000,000 results", "autotrader", "5,820,000 results",
"apple", "436,000,000 results", "amazon.com",
"461,000,000 results", "aol.com", "87,200,000 results",
"american airlines", "14,600,000 results", "australian open",
"12,300,000 results", "ask.com", "39,600,000 results"),
new Array(""));
```

How do you rename "window.google.ac.Suggest_apply" as "callback" in the text you get back from Google Suggest? You can use the handy JavaScript replace function, which is built to do just this—replace text inside strings. The text we get from Google Suggest (via google .php) will be accessible in the responseText property of the XMLHttpRequest object, and we can use the replace method as follows to convert the call "window.google.ac.Suggest_apply" to "callback" and store the resulting, edited text in a variable named text:

```
<script language = "javascript">
  function getData(dataSource)
  {
    var XMLHttpRequestObject = false;

    if (window.XMLHttpRequest) {
      XMLHttpRequestObject = new XMLHttpRequest();
    } else if (window.ActiveXObject) {
      XMLHttpRequestObject = new ActiveXObject("Microsoft.XMLHTTP");
    }

    if(XMLHttpRequestObject) {
      XMLHttpRequestObject.open("GET", dataSource);

      XMLHttpRequestObject.onreadystatechange = function()
      {
        if (XMLHttpRequestObject.readyState == 4 &&
          XMLHttpRequestObject.status == 200) {
            var text =
```

```
XMLHttpRequestObject.responseText.replace(
"window.google.ac.Suggest_apply", "callback");
.
.
.
              }
            }
          }
        }
      }
    </script>
```

Excellent; now the JavaScript stored in the text variable can be treated as workable JavaScript (as soon as we create the function named callback). Here's how to execute that JavaScript with the eval function—note that we also connect to the server with the XMLHttpRequest object's send method:

```
<script language = "javascript">
  function getData(dataSource)
  {
    var XMLHttpRequestObject = false;

    if (window.XMLHttpRequest) {
      XMLHttpRequestObject = new XMLHttpRequest();
    } else if (window.ActiveXObject) {
      XMLHttpRequestObject = new ActiveXObject("Microsoft.XMLHTTP");
    }

    if(XMLHttpRequestObject) {
      XMLHttpRequestObject.open("GET", dataSource);

      XMLHttpRequestObject.onreadystatechange = function()
      {
        if (XMLHttpRequestObject.readyState == 4 &&
          XMLHttpRequestObject.status == 200) {
            var text =
            XMLHttpRequestObject.responseText.replace(
            "window.google.ac.Suggest_apply", "callback");
            eval(text);
        }
      }

      XMLHttpRequestObject.send(null);
    }
  }
</script>
```

That completes the getData function, which calls the JavaScript downloaded from Google Suggest. We've edited that JavaScript so that it calls a function named callback, and now we have to write the callback function.

Displaying the Matches

Here's the JavaScript downloaded, edited, and executed by the getData function:

```
callback(frameElement, "a", new Array(2, "amazon", "855,000,000 results",
"argos", "12,500,000 results", "aol", "278,000,000 results", "autotrader",
"5,820,000 results", "apple", "436,000,000 results", "amazon.com",
"461,000,000 results", "aol.com", "87,200,000 results",
"american airlines", "14,600,000 results", "australian open",
"12,300,000 results", "ask.com", "39,600,000 results"), new Array(""));
```

Our callback function should accept these arguments, so here's how to create that function:

```
<script language = "javascript">
  function callback(unusedVariable, searchTerm, arrayTerm,
    unusedArray)
  {
    .
    .
    .
  }
</script>
```

We're going to display the drop-down list of suggestions as an HTML table, and we're going to store that HTML in a variable named data. Here's how we create the data variable and set up a loop to add all the suggestions we get from Google Suggest:

```
<script language = "javascript">
  function callback(unusedVariable, searchTerm, arrayTerm,
    unusedArray)
  {
    var data = "<table>";
    var loopIndex;

    for (loopIndex = 1; loopIndex < arrayTerm.length;
      loopIndex++) {
      .
      .
      .
    }

    data += "</table>";
  }
</script>
```

And here's the actual loop that loops over the suggestions from Google Suggest—note that we make the search terms into hyperlinks (pointing the user to Google), just as in the real Google Suggest page:

```
<script language = "javascript">
  function callback(unusedVariable, searchTerm, arrayTerm,
```

```
      unusedArray)
  {
    var data = "<table>";
    var loopIndex;

    for (loopIndex = 1; loopIndex < arrayTerm.length;
      loopIndex++) {
      data += "<tr><td>" +
      "<a href='http://www.google.com/search?q=" +
      arrayTerm[loopIndex] + "'>" + arrayTerm[loopIndex] +
      '</a></td><td>' + arrayTerm[++loopIndex] + "</td></tr>";
    }

    data += "</table>";
  }
</script>
```

Ask the Expert

Q: What does the term ++loopIndex do in the above code? Is it different from loopIndex++?

A: Putting the JavaScript increment operator (introduced in Chapter 2) in front of a variable name (++loopIndex) adds 1 to the value of the variable before the rest of the JavaScript statement is executed, whereas putting the increment operator at the end of a variable name (loopIndex++) means that 1 will be added to the value in the variable after the rest of the statement has been executed. It doesn't usually matter which one you choose, but here it does, because we needed to increment loopIndex before using it to reach the next suggestion in the array of suggestions.

At the end of the code in the callback function, the data variable holds the HTML table we're going to use to display the suggestions we got from Google Suggest, and we display that table by assigning data to the innerHTML property of the <div> element that will show the drop-down list:

```
<script language = "javascript">
  function callback(unusedVariable, searchTerm, arrayTerm,
    unusedArray)
  {
    var data = "<table>";
    var loopIndex;

    for (loopIndex = 1; loopIndex < arrayTerm.length;
      loopIndex++) {
```

```
        data += "<tr><td>" +
        "<a href='http://www.google.com/search?q=" +
        arrayTerm[loopIndex] + "'>" + arrayTerm[loopIndex] +
        '</a></td><td>' + arrayTerm[++loopIndex] + "</td></tr>";
    }

    data += "</table>";

    var targetDiv = document.getElementById("targetDiv");

    targetDiv.innerHTML = data;
    }
  </script>
```

There's one last step here. We can style the <div> element that displays the Google Suggest suggestions, giving it the appearance of a drop-down list. Here's how we give HTML that appears in the <div> element a light-pink background, using a <style> element in the google.html application:

```
<html>
  <head>

    <title>Handling Google Suggest</title>

    <style>
    #targetDiv {
      background-color: #FFAAAA;
      width: 40%;
    }
    </style>

    <script language = "javascript">
      function getData(dataSource)
        .
        .
        .
```

And that finishes google.html—here it is in all its glory:

```
<html>
  <head>

    <title>Handling Google Suggest</title>

    <style>
    #targetDiv {
      background-color: #FFAAAA;
      width: 40%;
    }
```

```
</style>

<script language = "javascript">
  function getData(dataSource)
  {
    var XMLHttpRequestObject = false;

    if (window.XMLHttpRequest) {
      XMLHttpRequestObject = new XMLHttpRequest();
    } else if (window.ActiveXObject) {
      XMLHttpRequestObject = new ActiveXObject("Microsoft.XMLHTTP");
    }

    if(XMLHttpRequestObject) {
      XMLHttpRequestObject.open("GET", dataSource);

      XMLHttpRequestObject.onreadystatechange = function()
      {
        if (XMLHttpRequestObject.readyState == 4 &&
          XMLHttpRequestObject.status == 200) {
            var text = XMLHttpRequestObject.responseText.replace(
            "window.google.ac.Suggest_apply", "callback");
            eval(text);
        }
      }

      XMLHttpRequestObject.send(null);
    }
  }

  function askGoogleSuggest()
  {
    var input = document.getElementById("textField");

    if (input.value) {
      getData("google.php?qu=" + input.value);
    }
    else {
      var targetDiv = document.getElementById("targetDiv");

      targetDiv.innerHTML = "<div></div>";
    }
  }


  function callback(unusedVariable, searchTerm, arrayTerm,
    unusedArray)
  {
    var data = "<table>";
    var loopIndex;
```

```
        for (loopIndex = 1; loopIndex < arrayTerm.length;
          loopIndex++) {
          data += "<tr><td>" +
          "<a href='http://www.google.com/search?q=" +
          arrayTerm[loopIndex] + "'>" + arrayTerm[loopIndex] +
          '</a></td><td>' + arrayTerm[++loopIndex] + "</td></tr>";
        }

        data += "</table>";

        var targetDiv = document.getElementById("targetDiv");

        targetDiv.innerHTML = data;
      }
    </script>

  </head>

  <body>

    <H1>Handling Google Suggest</H1>

    Search for <input id = "textField" type = "text"
      name = "textField" onkeyup = "askGoogleSuggest()">

      <div id = "targetDiv"><div></div></div>

  </body>

</html>
```

Great, that takes care of google.html. The last step is to create the PHP script that it communicates with, google.php.

Creating google.php

As you know, google.html relies on a PHP script, google.php, to connect to Google Suggest. The google.html application connects to Google Suggest in this way to avoid the security issues that are raised when you use Ajax to connect to a server other than the one your page is hosted on.

So we're going to use google.php to connect to Google Suggest. The URL of Google Suggest is "http://www.google.com/complete/search?hl=en&js=true&qu=", where you add the partial search term that the user has typed to the end of this URL—for example, if the search term is "ajax," the URL you access is "http://www.google.com/complete/search?hl=en&js=tru e&qu=ajax".

How do you use a PHP script to access a URL like that? You'll see more about PHP later in the book, but it turns out that you can treat URLs much as you would treat filenames in PHP, and you can "open" a URL with the fopen (file open) function, which returns a *file handle*, which you store in a variable (we're not going to make much use of file handles or file handling in PHP in this book, but it's useful for this example). You can then use the file handle to refer to the URL, including reading data from that URL. Here's how to "open" Google Suggest with the partial search string passed to google.php (you recover the partial search term from the $_GET array and then add that term to the URL with the PHP string concatenation operator, which is a dot, .):

```php
<?php
  $filehandle =
    fopen("http://www.google.com/complete/search?hl=en&js=true&qu=" .
    $_GET["qu"], "r");
        .
        .
        .

?>
```

The "r" here indicates that we want to open the Google Suggest URL for reading (as opposed to trying to write to it).

Now you're ready to read the suggestions that Google Suggest will pass back to you. You can do that in a while loop in PHP, which works just like a while loop in JavaScript. In this while loop, we'll be reading from the file handle, and can use the feof (File End of File) PHP function to determine when we're at the end of the "file" (and the while loop should terminate):

```php
<?php
  $filehandle =
    fopen("http://www.google.com/complete/search?hl=en&js=true&qu=" .
    $_GET["qu"], "r");
  while (!feof($filehandle)){
        .
        .
        .

  }
?>
```

Note the while loop's condition here—!feof($filehandle). What's the ! for? It's an operator (in both PHP and JavaScript; see Table 2-1) that reverses the logical sense of an expression. So while feof($filehandle) is true when we're at the end of a file, !feof($filehandle) is true while we're *not* at the end of the file—just what we want, to make sure the while loop keeps looping until we reach the end of the file.

Now google.php reads individual lines of text from Google Suggest and echoes them back to google.html using the PHP fgets (File Get String) and echo functions:

```php
<?php
  $filehandle =
    fopen("http://www.google.com/complete/search?hl=en&js=true&qu=" .
    $_GET["qu"], "r");
  while (!feof($filehandle)){
```

```
    $download = fgets($filehandle);
    echo $download;
  }
?>
```

And we're almost done. All that's left at the end of google.php is to close the URL that we've been reading from, and we can use the PHP fclose (File Close) function to do that in this way:

```
<?php
  $filehandle =
    fopen("http://www.google.com/complete/search?hl=en&js=true&qu=" .
    $_GET["qu"], "r");
  while (!feof($filehandle)){
    $download = fgets($filehandle);
    echo $download;
  }
  fclose($filehandle);
?>
```

Whew. All done. This example—google.html and google.php—is ready to roll. This example reads what the user types as they type it, relays what they've typed to Google Suggest through google.php, downloads the Google Suggest suggestions, and displays them.

You can see this example at work in Figure 4-8, where the user has typed "a," and the application has downloaded the suggestions Google Suggest made and is displaying them. Very cool.

And that completes google.html.

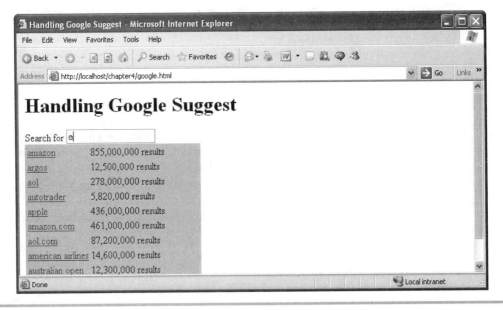

Figure 4-8 google.html at work

Downloading from Other Domains with Ajax

As you saw when you built google.html, accessing a web server other than the one your web page is hosted on is a little tricky with Ajax. Say your Ajax page is at www.myserver.com/ hamster_fan.html, but you want to download the page at www.theirserver.com/hamster_data .html—that is, on a different server. You can access that page directly in Ajax from your current page, but the browser is going to display a warning dialog box to the user, asking their permission to proceed.

Not the most ultra-cool thing that can happen.

The common solution is to communicate with the other server (www.theirserver.com) via server-side code, and you saw an example of that in google.php. With google.php, we were able to relay our request to Google Suggest, and then download Google Suggest's response.

Here's a general PHP script that lets you redirect Ajax requests in this way—replace *URL* with the URL of the web resource you want to reach:

```php
<?php
  $filehandle =
    fopen(URL, "r");
  while (!feof($filehandle)){
    $download = fgets($filehandle);
    echo $download;
  }
  fclose($filehandle);
?>
```

Try This Contact Another Server Using Ajax

After you get google.html and google.php to work, try the same technique with another server. For example, you might download and display the HTML of the *USA Today* site, www .usatoday.com. Here's how that would work in a PHP script:

```php
<?php
  $filehandle =
    fopen("www.usatoday.com", "r");
  while (!feof($filehandle)){
    $download = fgets($filehandle);
    echo $download;
  }
  fclose($filehandle);
?>
```

If you like, you can even change google.php to download from www.usatoday.com and use google.html as it stands to connect and display the HTML of *USA Today*'s site.

Now it's time to turn to another topic—requesting HTML header info with Ajax.

Getting More Info: HTML Header Requests and Ajax

You not only can download the contents of files with Ajax, you can get information *about* those files. To do that, you can use the XMLHttpRequest object's getAllResponseHeaders method, which gives you the text corresponding to all the HTML headers received about the file from the server.

HTTP headers are given names like Server, Date, and so on, and are assigned text about the resource you're accessing. You can use this kind of information before you even try to download a web resource, to find out about that resource's size, type, last-modified date, and so on, which allows you to better prepare for the download. And if the user asks you to download a resource that doesn't exist, you can let them know without having your application suffer some kind of error when needed data doesn't show up.

Let's give this a try and see what kind of HTTP headers we can download for the google.html file. Here's head.html, which just uses the XMLHttpRequest object's getAllResponseHeaders method to get all the HTTP headers available from the server about google.html. We start by using the "HEAD" method in the call to the open function, as opposed to "GET" or "POST":

```
<html>
  <head>
    <title>Getting head data</title>

    <script language = "javascript">
      function getData(dataSource, divID)
      {
        var XMLHttpRequestObject = false;

        if (window.XMLHttpRequest) {
          XMLHttpRequestObject = new XMLHttpRequest();
        } else if (window.ActiveXObject) {
          XMLHttpRequestObject = new ActiveXObject("Microsoft.XMLHTTP");
        }

        if(XMLHttpRequestObject) {
          var obj = document.getElementById(divID);
          XMLHttpRequestObject.open("HEAD", dataSource);
          .
          .
          .
```

Then we use getAllResponseHeaders to read all the HTTP headers:

```
<html>
  <head>
    <title>Getting head data</title>

    <script language = "javascript">
      function getData(dataSource, divID)
```

```
      {
        var XMLHttpRequestObject = false;

        if (window.XMLHttpRequest) {
          XMLHttpRequestObject = new XMLHttpRequest();
        } else if (window.ActiveXObject) {
          XMLHttpRequestObject = new ActiveXObject("Microsoft.XMLHTTP");
        }

        if(XMLHttpRequestObject) {
          var obj = document.getElementById(divID);
          XMLHttpRequestObject.open("HEAD", dataSource);

          XMLHttpRequestObject.onreadystatechange = function()
          {
            if (XMLHttpRequestObject.readyState == 4 &&
              XMLHttpRequestObject.status == 200) {
                obj.innerHTML =
                XMLHttpRequestObject.getAllResponseHeaders();
            }
          }

          XMLHttpRequestObject.send(null);
        }
      }
    </script>
  </head>

  <body>

    <H1>Getting header data</H1>

    <form>
      <input type = "button" value = "Get info on google.html"
        onclick = "getData('google.html', 'targetDiv')">
    </form>

    <div id="targetDiv">
      <p>The fetched data will go here.</p>
    </div>

  </body>
</html>
```

You can see head.html at work in Figure 4-9, where the user has clicked the button and the application fetched information about google.html.

Here's the data the application got:

```
Server: Microsoft-IIS/5.1 Date: Fri, 22 Feb 2008 17:15:09 GMT
Content-Type: text/html Accept-Ranges: bytes Last-Modified:
Thu, 21 Feb 2008 18:26:23 GMT ETag: "82283a43b774c81:a57"
Content-Length: 2304
```

Figure 4-9 Getting header information about google.html

You can see the individual HTTP headers here: Server: Microsoft-IIS/5.1, for example, tells you what software the server is running. Content-Length: 2304 tells you the length of google.html. Content-Type: text/html tells you that it's an HTML file, and so on.

Try This Get a Specific HTML Header

You can also request just one specific HTTP header at a time if you use getResponseHeader. Try this technique of getting the "Last-Modified" header of google.html:

```
function getData(dataSource, divID)
{
  if(XMLHttpRequestObject) {
    var obj = document.getElementById(divID);
    XMLHttpRequestObject.open("HEAD", dataSource);

    XMLHttpRequestObject.onreadystatechange = function()
    {
      if (XMLHttpRequestObject.readyState == 4 &&
        XMLHttpRequestObject.status == 200) {
          obj.innerHTML =
            "The file google.html was last modified on " +
            XMLHttpRequestObject.getResponseHeader(
              "Last-Modified");
      }
    }

    XMLHttpRequestObject.send(null);
  }
}
```

Defeating Caching

One frustrating aspect of developing Ajax applications is browser caching, especially in Internet Explorer. Caching happens when the browser visits a URL—it stores a copy of the response from the server and doesn't actually access the URL again directly, even when you ask it to.

That's a problem if you are modifying a web resource—as when you're developing an application—or if the web resource gives you different data at different times. For example, say that you are debugging important_data.php and are downloading text from that PHP file like this when the user clicks a button:

```
<body>

  <H1>Reading JavaScript with Ajax</H1>

  <form>
    <input type = "button" value = "Get the JavaScript"
      onclick = "getData('important_data.php)">
  </form>

  <div id="targetDiv">
    <p>The data will go here.</p>
  </div>

</body>
```

When you make changes to important_data.php, you want the new data it sends back to the browser to be used, but when the browser caches that data, you just keep seeing the old data. To get around that caching, you can change the URL you access slightly by adding a little URL encoding (which will be ignored by important_data.php). When the browser sees that you're accessing a different URL, one that it doesn't have cached, it will download a fresh copy of the data from that URL. Here's what it looks like—note the dummy "?a=5" URL encoding added to the end of the URL:

```
<body>

  <H1>Reading JavaScript with Ajax</H1>

  <form>
    <input type = "button" value = "Get the JavaScript"
      onclick = "getData('important_data.php?a=5')">
  </form>

  <div id="targetDiv">
    <p>The data will go here.</p>
  </div>

</body>
```

The problem with this technique is that once you use the new URL, important_data .php?a=5, the browser caches that URL too, and you can't use it again. A better solution is to use something that will always change, such as the current time, in your URL-encoded text. Here's how to do that, using the JavaScript getTime function:

```
<body>

  <H1>Reading JavaScript with Ajax</H1>

  <form>
    <input type = "button" value = "Get the JavaScript"
      onclick = "getData('important_data.php?a=' +
        new Date().getTime())">
  </form>

  <div id="targetDiv">
    <p>The data will go here.</p>
  </div>

</body>
```

This code will overcome caching in browsers.

Chapter 5

Using Ajax Frameworks

Key Skills & Concepts

- Building the Ajax Framework library

- Creating the downloadText function

- Creating the downloadXml function

- Creating the postDataDownloadText function

- Creating the postDataDownloadXml function

- Using the libXmlRequest Ajax framework

- Using the AJAXLib Ajax framework

As you have seen in the previous chapters, programming Ajax can get a little tricky. And for that reason, you'll run across dozens of Ajax *frameworks* online. An Ajax framework is prewritten code, often JavaScript, that makes using Ajax a snap. All the Ajax programming is done for you—for example, all you have to do to use Ajax to download text from the server is to call a function named, say, downloadText. You don't have to concern yourself with the details.

We'll build our own Ajax framework in this chapter, ajaxframework.js (available for free in the downloadable code for this book), ready for you to plug in and use. The Ajax framework developed here will use good coding techniques and support multiple XMLHttpRequest requests. And we'll also take a look in this chapter at a few of the Ajax frameworks that are already out there.

Let's begin by creating ajaxframework.js.

Creating ajaxframework.js

As you can tell from the .js extension, ajaxframework.js is a JavaScript library of functions. There are four functions, and they support the four Ajax operations—downloading text with GET, downloading XML with GET, downloading text with POST, and downloading XML with POST. Here's an overview of the four functions you can call in our Ajax framework:

- **downloadText(url, callbackFunction)**   Uses the GET method to get text from the server.

- **downloadXml(url, callbackFunction)**   Uses the GET method to get XML from the server.

- **postDataDownloadText(url, dataToSend, callbackFunction)**   Uses the POST method to send dataToSend to the server, and gets text back. You pass the data to send in parameter/value pairs, like this: "value=100".

- **postDataDownloadXml(url, dataToSend, callbackFunction)**   Uses the POST method
to send dataToSend to the server, and gets XML back. You pass the data to send in
parameter/value pairs like this: "value=100".

Note that for each function, you pass an URL to call—that's the URL for the data you want
to download. You also pass a callback function, and our Ajax framework will call that function
with the downloaded data. If you're going to use POST, you can also send data to the server.

Let's start this chapter by seeing how to create the downloadText function.

Downloading Text with the downloadText Function

The first function we'll build in our Ajax framework is the downloadText function, which uses the
GET method to download text from a server. You pass this function the URL from which to fetch
the data using Ajax, and a callback function that it should call back with the downloaded data:

```
function downloadText(url, callbackFunction)
{
        .
        .
        .

}
```

The first order of business is to create an XMLHttpRequest object to use to communicate
with the server behind the scenes—note that we're creating it inside the downloadText
function, so the upcoming anonymous function will be an inner function. Here's how we create
an XMLHttpRequest object for Firefox-type browsers (such as Firefox, Netscape, and Safari):

```
function downloadText(url, callbackFunction)
{
  var XMLHttpRequestObject = false;

  if (window.XMLHttpRequest) {
    XMLHttpRequestObject = new XMLHttpRequest();
  }
    .
    .
    .
}
```

And here's how we create an XMLHttpRequest object for Internet Explorer:

```
function downloadText(url, callbackFunction)
{
  var XMLHttpRequestObject = false;

  if (window.XMLHttpRequest) {
    XMLHttpRequestObject = new XMLHttpRequest();
  } else if (window.ActiveXObject) {
```

```
XMLHttpRequestObject = new
  ActiveXObject("Microsoft.XMLHTTP");
}

      .
      .
      .

}
```

Next, we check if we were successful in creating the needed XMLHttpRequest object:

```
function downloadText(url, callbackFunction)
{
  var XMLHttpRequestObject = false;

  if (window.XMLHttpRequest) {
    XMLHttpRequestObject = new XMLHttpRequest();
  } else if (window.ActiveXObject) {
    XMLHttpRequestObject = new
      ActiveXObject("Microsoft.XMLHTTP");
  }

  if(XMLHttpRequestObject) {
      .
      .
      .

  }
}
```

If the XMLHttpRequest object exists, we can open it to configure that object as follows, passing the open method the HTTP method ("GET") and the URL to access (which was passed in the url argument to the downloadText function):

```
function downloadText(url, callbackFunction)
{
  var XMLHttpRequestObject = false;

  if (window.XMLHttpRequest) {
    XMLHttpRequestObject = new XMLHttpRequest();
  } else if (window.ActiveXObject) {
    XMLHttpRequestObject = new
      ActiveXObject("Microsoft.XMLHTTP");
  }

  if(XMLHttpRequestObject) {
    XMLHttpRequestObject.open("GET", url);
      .
      .
      .


  }
}
```

Next we can set up the anonymous function that will handle the downloaded text:

```
function downloadText(url, callbackFunction)
{
  var XMLHttpRequestObject = false;

  if (window.XMLHttpRequest) {
    XMLHttpRequestObject = new XMLHttpRequest();
  } else if (window.ActiveXObject) {
    XMLHttpRequestObject = new
     ActiveXObject("Microsoft.XMLHTTP");
  }

  if(XMLHttpRequestObject) {
    XMLHttpRequestObject.open("GET", url);

    XMLHttpRequestObject.onreadystatechange = function()
    {
        .
        .
        .
    }

  }
}
```

And then we check if the download was okay:

```
function downloadText(url, callbackFunction)
{
  var XMLHttpRequestObject = false;

  if (window.XMLHttpRequest) {
    XMLHttpRequestObject = new XMLHttpRequest();
  } else if (window.ActiveXObject) {
    XMLHttpRequestObject = new
     ActiveXObject("Microsoft.XMLHTTP");
  }

  if(XMLHttpRequestObject) {
    XMLHttpRequestObject.open("GET", url);

    XMLHttpRequestObject.onreadystatechange = function()
    {
      if (XMLHttpRequestObject.readyState == 4 &&
        XMLHttpRequestObject.status == 200) {
          .
          .
          .
      }
    }

  }
}
```

At this point, we know the data was downloaded safely. How do we handle that data? We have to send that data to the callback function that was passed to the downloadText function (as the callbackFunction argument). Here's how we pass the downloaded text to the callback function:

```
function downloadText(url, callbackFunction)
{
  var XMLHttpRequestObject = false;

  if (window.XMLHttpRequest) {
    XMLHttpRequestObject = new XMLHttpRequest();
  } else if (window.ActiveXObject) {
    XMLHttpRequestObject = new
      ActiveXObject("Microsoft.XMLHTTP");
  }

  if(XMLHttpRequestObject) {
    XMLHttpRequestObject.open("GET", url);

    XMLHttpRequestObject.onreadystatechange = function()
    {
      if (XMLHttpRequestObject.readyState == 4 &&
        XMLHttpRequestObject.status == 200) {
          callbackFunction(XMLHttpRequestObject.responseText);
             .
             .
             .
      }
    }

  }
}
```

Now that we're done with the XMLHttpRequest object, we can explicitly delete it if we like. That looks like this, where we delete the object and set the variable XMLHttpRequestObject to null:

```
function downloadText(url, callbackFunction)
{
  var XMLHttpRequestObject = false;

  if (window.XMLHttpRequest) {
    XMLHttpRequestObject = new XMLHttpRequest();
  } else if (window.ActiveXObject) {
    XMLHttpRequestObject = new
      ActiveXObject("Microsoft.XMLHTTP");
  }
```

```
  if(XMLHttpRequestObject) {
    XMLHttpRequestObject.open("GET", url);

    XMLHttpRequestObject.onreadystatechange = function()
    {
      if (XMLHttpRequestObject.readyState == 4 &&
        XMLHttpRequestObject.status == 200) {
          callbackFunction(XMLHttpRequestObject.responseText);
          delete XMLHttpRequestObject;
          XMLHttpRequestObject = null;
      }
    }
  }
}
```

And finally, all that remains is to connect to the server with the XMLHttpRequest object's send method:

```
function downloadText(url, callbackFunction)
{
  var XMLHttpRequestObject = false;

  if (window.XMLHttpRequest) {
    XMLHttpRequestObject = new XMLHttpRequest();
  } else if (window.ActiveXObject) {
    XMLHttpRequestObject = new
      ActiveXObject("Microsoft.XMLHTTP");
  }

  if(XMLHttpRequestObject) {
    XMLHttpRequestObject.open("GET", url);

    XMLHttpRequestObject.onreadystatechange = function()
    {
      if (XMLHttpRequestObject.readyState == 4 &&
        XMLHttpRequestObject.status == 200) {
          callbackFunction(XMLHttpRequestObject.responseText);
          delete XMLHttpRequestObject;
          XMLHttpRequestObject = null;
      }
    }

    XMLHttpRequestObject.send(null);
  }
}
```

Let's test the downloadText function now by creating an Ajax-enabled page that uses it. This page will have two buttons, one of which will download the contents of data.txt:

```
This text was downloaded with Ajax.
```

And the other button will download the contents of data2.txt:

```
This text was also downloaded with Ajax.
```

We'll name this page, which tests the downloadText function, downloadText.html. We start by including ajaxframework.js, which makes the downloadText function accessible to our JavaScript:

```
<html>
  <head>
    <title>Downloading Text With the Ajax Framework Library Pack</title>

    <script type = "text/javascript" src = "ajaxframework.js"></script>

        .
        .
        .
```

Now we can add the two buttons to the test web page:

```
<form>
  <input type = "button" value = "Get message 1"
    onclick = "downloadText('data.txt', callbackMessage1)">
  <input type = "button" value = "Get message 2"
    onclick = "downloadText('data2.txt', callbackMessage2)">
</form>
```

Note what we're doing here: we're passing the downloadText function the URL of the data to get (which is just "data.txt" or "data2.txt"—we're making the assumption that data .txt and data2.txt are in the same directory and on the same server as ajaxframework.js and downloadText.html, so we can use a relative URL here) and the callback function.

The callback function is named callbackMessage1 for button 1 and callbackMessage2 for button 2. In these callback functions, we just want to display the downloaded text in a <div> element that has the ID "targetDiv":

```
<body>

  <H1>Downloading Text With the Ajax Framework Library Pack</H1>

  <form>
    <input type = "button" value = "Get message 1"
      onclick = "downloadText('data.txt', callbackMessage1)">
```

```
      <input type = "button" value = "Get message 2"
        onclick = "downloadText('data2.txt', callbackMessage2)">
    </form>

    <div id="targetDiv">
      <p>The fetched data will go here.</p>
    </div>

  </body>
```

Here's what the callback function callbackMessage1 looks like:

```
    <script language = "javascript">
      function callbackMessage1(text)
      {
        document.getElementById("targetDiv").innerHTML = text;
      }
        .
        .
        .
    </script>
```

And here's what the callback function callbackMessage2 looks like:

```
    <script language = "javascript">
      function callbackMessage1(text)
      {
        document.getElementById("targetDiv").innerHTML = text;
      }

      function callbackMessage2(text)
      {
        document.getElementById("targetDiv").innerHTML = text;
      }
    </script>
```

Great; that does it. Here's the whole page, downloadText.html, that tests the downloadText function:

```
<html>
  <head>
    <title>Downloading Text With the Ajax Framework Library Pack</title>

    <script type = "text/javascript" src = "ajaxframework.js"></script>

    <script language = "javascript">
      function callbackMessage1(text)
```

```
        {
          document.getElementById("targetDiv").innerHTML = text;
        }

        function callbackMessage2(text)
        {
          document.getElementById("targetDiv").innerHTML = text;
        }
    </script>

  </head>

  <body>

    <H1>Downloading Text With the Ajax Framework Library Pack</H1>

    <form>
      <input type = "button" value = "Get message 1"
        onclick = "downloadText('data.txt', callbackMessage1)">
      <input type = "button" value = "Get message 2"
        onclick = "downloadText('data2.txt', callbackMessage2)">
    </form>

    <div id="targetDiv">
      <p>The fetched data will go here.</p>
    </div>

  </body>
</html>
```

You can see this page at work in Figure 5-1.

When you click button 1, the correct data is indeed downloaded and displayed. We're in business—so far so good.

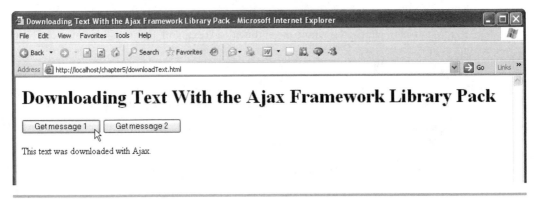

Figure 5-1 downloadText.html at work

Try This   Get downloadText.html to Work

Note that if you want to send data to the server with the HTTP GET method, you have to URL-encode that data. That works with the downloadText function as well. Here's a way to test whether you have access to a server that supports PHP, using the dataresponder.php script developed in Chapter 3:

```php
<?php
  if ($_GET["data"] == "1") {
    echo 'The server got a value of 1';
  }
  if ($_GET["data"] == "2") {
    echo 'The server got a value of 2';
  }
?>
```

Connect to this PHP script and send it data by using URL encoding, something like this:

```
<form>
  <input type = "button" value = "Get message 1"
    onclick = "downloadText('dataresponder.php?data=1',
      callbackMessage1)">
  <input type = "button" value = "Get message 2"
    onclick = "downloadText('dataresponder.php?data=2',
      callbackMessage2)">
</form>
```

When you click the first button, you should see "The server got a value of 1," and when you click the second button, you should see "The server got a value of 2."

Downloading XML with the downloadXml Function

You can also use the GET method to download XML, using ajaxframework.js's downloadXml function (bear in mind that you'll read all about creating XML in Chapter 6). You pass that function the URL of your XML on the server, and a callback function that it will pass a JavaScript XML document to:

```
function downloadXml(url, callbackFunction)
{
    .
    .
    .
}
```

As you might expect, we begin the downloadXml function by creating an XMLHttpRequest object—note that we set the MIME type to text/xml for Firefox-type browsers:

```
function downloadXml(url, callbackFunction)
{
  var XMLHttpRequestObject = false;

  if (window.XMLHttpRequest) {
    XMLHttpRequestObject = new XMLHttpRequest();
    XMLHttpRequestObject.overrideMimeType("text/xml");
  } else if (window.ActiveXObject) {
    XMLHttpRequestObject = new
     ActiveXObject("Microsoft.XMLHTTP");
  }
      .
      .
      .


}
```

Then we put that XMLHttpRequest object to work, downloading the requested XML from the URL passed to the downloadXml function:

```
function downloadXml(url, callbackFunction)
{
  var XMLHttpRequestObject = false;

  if (window.XMLHttpRequest) {
    XMLHttpRequestObject = new XMLHttpRequest();
    XMLHttpRequestObject.overrideMimeType("text/xml");
  } else if (window.ActiveXObject) {
    XMLHttpRequestObject = new
     ActiveXObject("Microsoft.XMLHTTP");
  }

  if(XMLHttpRequestObject) {
    XMLHttpRequestObject.open("GET", url);

    XMLHttpRequestObject.onreadystatechange = function()
    {
      if (XMLHttpRequestObject.readyState == 4 &&
        XMLHttpRequestObject.status == 200) {
          .
          .
          .
      }
    }
  }
}
```

After the download is complete, we want to pass the downloaded XML—in the form of a JavaScript XML document object (as given to us by the XMLHttpRequest object's responseXML property)—to the callback function. Here's how that works—note that we also connect to the server using the XMLHttpRequest object's send method:

```
function downloadXml(url, callbackFunction)
{
  var XMLHttpRequestObject = false;

  if (window.XMLHttpRequest) {
    XMLHttpRequestObject = new XMLHttpRequest();
    XMLHttpRequestObject.overrideMimeType("text/xml");
  } else if (window.ActiveXObject) {
    XMLHttpRequestObject = new
     ActiveXObject("Microsoft.XMLHTTP");
  }

  if(XMLHttpRequestObject) {
    XMLHttpRequestObject.open("GET", url);

    XMLHttpRequestObject.onreadystatechange = function()
    {
      if (XMLHttpRequestObject.readyState == 4 &&
        XMLHttpRequestObject.status == 200) {
          callbackFunction(XMLHttpRequestObject.responseXML);
          delete XMLHttpRequestObject;
          XMLHttpRequestObject = null;
      }
    }

    XMLHttpRequestObject.send(null);
  }
}
```

Okay, that completes the downloadXml function. Let's test it out with a new web page, downloadXml.html, which will use the downloadXml function to download and display the data in Chapter 3's colors.xml:

```
<?xml version = "1.0" ?>
<colors>
  <color>red</color>
  <color>green</color>
  <color>blue</color>
</colors>
```

We'll start downloadXml.html by including the Ajax framework, ajaxframework.js:

```
<html>
  <head>

    <title>Downloading XML With the Ajax Framework Library Pack</title>
```

```
<script type = "text/javascript" src = "ajaxframework.js"></script>
        .
        .
        .
```

Next, we'll provide a button in downloadXml.html to allow the user to download colors.xml:

```
<form>
  <input type = "button" value = "Get the colors"
    onclick = "downloadXml('colors.xml', callback)">
</form>
```

Note that this button calls the downloadXml function, passing the URL of the XML file to download, and a callback function simply named callback. When the user clicks this button, we'll download colors.xml, decipher it, and display the colors in a <div> element whose ID is targetDiv:

```
<body>

  <h1>Downloading XML With the Ajax Framework Library Pack</h1>

  <form>
    <input type = "button" value = "Get the colors"
      onclick = "downloadXml('colors.xml', callback)">
  </form>

  <div id="targetDiv">The colors will appear here.</div>

</body>
```

The callback function will be called by the code in ajaxframework.js with a JavaScript XML document object:

```
<script language = "javascript">

  function callback(xmlDocument)
  {
      .
      .
      .
  }

</script>
```

Now we have a JavaScript XML document object to work with, and we have to extract the <color> elements. We start by getting an array of those elements, which we'll name colors, with the getElementsByTagName method:

```
<script language = "javascript">

  function callback(xmlDocument)
  {
      colors = xmlDocument.getElementsByTagName("color");
          .
          .
          .
  }

</script>
```

Now we can set up the text and begin the bulleted list we'll use to display the colors in the <div> element:

```
<script language = "javascript">

  function callback(xmlDocument)
  {
      var obj = document.getElementById('targetDiv');

      colors = xmlDocument.getElementsByTagName("color");
      obj.innerHTML = "Here are the fetched colors:<ul>";
          .
          .
          .
  }

</script>
```

And we can loop over each individual color, displaying each one:

```
<script language = "javascript">

  function callback(xmlDocument)
  {
      var obj = document.getElementById('targetDiv');

      colors = xmlDocument.getElementsByTagName("color");
      obj.innerHTML = "Here are the fetched colors:<ul>";
      for (loopIndex = 0; loopIndex < colors.length; loopIndex++ )
      {
          .
          .
          .
      }
  }

</script>
```

To fetch an individual color, you access the <color> element as colors[loopIndex] in the loop. Then you can reach the text node that actually contains the text of the color:

```xml
<?xml version = "1.0" ?>
<colors>
  <color>red</color>
  <color>green</color>
  <color>blue</color>
</colors>
```

Those text nodes can be accessed as colors[loopIndex].firstChild, and the actual data in the text nodes (that is, the text of the color itself) can be accessed as colors[loopIndex].firstChild .data. So here's how to extract the colors and display them, one by one:

```javascript
<script language = "javascript">

    function callback(xmlDocument)
    {
        var obj = document.getElementById('targetDiv');

        colors = xmlDocument.getElementsByTagName("color");
        obj.innerHTML = "Here are the fetched colors:<ul>";
        for (loopIndex = 0; loopIndex < colors.length; loopIndex++ )
        {
            obj.innerHTML += "<li>" +
            colors[loopIndex].firstChild.data + "</li>";
        }
        obj.innerHTML += "</ul>";
    }

</script>
```

Here's all of downloadXml.html:

```html
<html>
  <head>

    <title>Downloading XML With the Ajax Framework Library Pack</title>

    <script type = "text/javascript" src = "ajaxframework.js"></script>

    <script language = "javascript">

      function callback(xmlDocument)
      {
          var obj = document.getElementById('targetDiv');

          colors = xmlDocument.getElementsByTagName("color");
          obj.innerHTML = "Here are the fetched colors:<ul>";
          for (loopIndex = 0; loopIndex < colors.length; loopIndex++ )
```

```
                  {
                      obj.innerHTML += "<li>" +
                      colors[loopIndex].firstChild.data + "</li>";
                  }
                  obj.innerHTML += "</ul>";
              }

          </script>
      </head>

      <body>

          <h1>Downloading XML With the Ajax Framework Library Pack</h1>

          <form>
              <input type = "button" value = "Get the colors"
                  onclick = "downloadXml('colors.xml', callback)">
          </form>

          <div id="targetDiv">The colors will appear here.</div>

      </body>

  </html>
```

You can see this page at work in Figure 5-2.

When you click the button, colors.xml is downloaded and displayed. Cool.

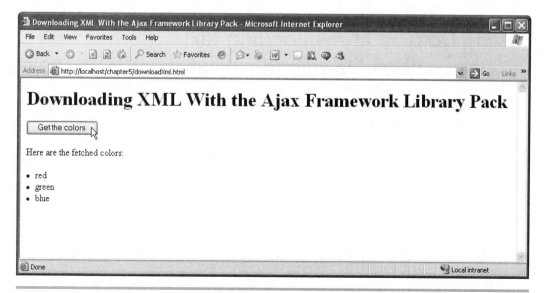

Figure 5-2   downloadXml.html at work

Get downloadXml.html to Work

Try adding URL encoding to downloadXml.html so that you can assign an argument named data a value of 1 or a value of 2, and have a different list of colors come back from the server.

You'll need a new PHP script to do this—here it is, colors.php:

```php
<?php
header("Content-type: text/xml");
if ($_GET["data"] == "1")
  $colors = array('red', 'green', 'blue');
if ($_GET["data"] == "2")
  $colors = array('orange', 'navy', 'viridian');
echo '<?xml version="1.0" ?>';
echo '<colors>';
foreach ($colors as $value)
{
  echo '<color>';
  echo $value;
  echo '</color>';
}
echo '</colors>';
?>
```

When you send URL-encoded data to this script, it will respond with the set of colors that you asked for, and the rest of the code in downloadXml.html will display it properly.

Posting Data and Downloading Text with the postDataDownloadText Function

You can also post data to the server (using POST) and download text using our Ajax framework's postDataDownloadText function. You pass the URL, the data you want sent, and the callback function to this function:

```
function postDataDownloadText(url, dataToSend, callbackFunction)
{
        .
        .
        .
    }
}
```

In the postDataDownloadText function, we start by creating an XMLHttpRequest object:

```
function postDataDownloadText(url, dataToSend, callbackFunction)
{
    var XMLHttpRequestObject = false;
```

```
  if (window.XMLHttpRequest) {
    XMLHttpRequestObject = new XMLHttpRequest();
  } else if (window.ActiveXObject) {
    XMLHttpRequestObject = new
     ActiveXObject("Microsoft.XMLHTTP");
  }
     .
     .
     .

}
```

And then we check if we were successful in creating that object:

```
function postDataDownloadText(url, dataToSend, callbackFunction)
{
  var XMLHttpRequestObject = false;

  if (window.XMLHttpRequest) {
    XMLHttpRequestObject = new XMLHttpRequest();
  } else if (window.ActiveXObject) {
    XMLHttpRequestObject = new
     ActiveXObject("Microsoft.XMLHTTP");
  }

  if(XMLHttpRequestObject) {
     .
     .
     .

  }
}
```

And if the XMLHttpRequest object exists, we open it, configuring it with the URL to access, and telling it to use the POST method:

```
function postDataDownloadText(url, dataToSend, callbackFunction)
{
  var XMLHttpRequestObject = false;

  if (window.XMLHttpRequest) {
    XMLHttpRequestObject = new XMLHttpRequest();
  } else if (window.ActiveXObject) {
    XMLHttpRequestObject = new
     ActiveXObject("Microsoft.XMLHTTP");
  }

  if(XMLHttpRequestObject) {
    XMLHttpRequestObject.open("POST", url);
     .
     .
     .


  }
}
```

We also set the Content-Type HTTP header to "application/x-www-form-urlencoded", as discussed in Chapter 3, when you use POST:

```
function postDataDownloadText(url, dataToSend, callbackFunction)
{
  var XMLHttpRequestObject = false;

  if (window.XMLHttpRequest) {
    XMLHttpRequestObject = new XMLHttpRequest();
  } else if (window.ActiveXObject) {
    XMLHttpRequestObject = new
     ActiveXObject("Microsoft.XMLHTTP");
  }

  if(XMLHttpRequestObject) {
    XMLHttpRequestObject.open("POST", url);
    XMLHttpRequestObject.setRequestHeader('Content-Type',
      'application/x-www-form-urlencoded');
        .
        .
        .

  }
}
```

Next, we connect an anonymous function to the XMLHttpRequest object's onreadystatechange property:

```
function postDataDownloadText(url, dataToSend, callbackFunction)
{
  var XMLHttpRequestObject = false;

  if (window.XMLHttpRequest) {
    XMLHttpRequestObject = new XMLHttpRequest();
  } else if (window.ActiveXObject) {
    XMLHttpRequestObject = new
     ActiveXObject("Microsoft.XMLHTTP");
  }

  if(XMLHttpRequestObject) {
    XMLHttpRequestObject.open("POST", url);
    XMLHttpRequestObject.setRequestHeader('Content-Type',
      'application/x-www-form-urlencoded');

    XMLHttpRequestObject.onreadystatechange = function()
    {
      if (XMLHttpRequestObject.readyState == 4 &&
        XMLHttpRequestObject.status == 200) {
        .
        .
        .

      }
    }

  }
}
```

When we receive the text back from the server, we can pass it on to the callback function that the user wants us to use:

```
function postDataDownloadText(url, dataToSend, callbackFunction)
{
  var XMLHttpRequestObject = false;

  if (window.XMLHttpRequest) {
    XMLHttpRequestObject = new XMLHttpRequest();
  } else if (window.ActiveXObject) {
    XMLHttpRequestObject = new
     ActiveXObject("Microsoft.XMLHTTP");
  }

  if(XMLHttpRequestObject) {
    XMLHttpRequestObject.open("POST", url);
    XMLHttpRequestObject.setRequestHeader('Content-Type',
      'application/x-www-form-urlencoded');

    XMLHttpRequestObject.onreadystatechange = function()
    {
      if (XMLHttpRequestObject.readyState == 4 &&
        XMLHttpRequestObject.status == 200) {
          callbackFunction(XMLHttpRequestObject.responseText);
          delete XMLHttpRequestObject;
          XMLHttpRequestObject = null;
      }
    }
  }
}
```

And that's almost it—all that remains is to use the XMLHttpRequest object's send method to post the data to the server:

```
function postDataDownloadText(url, dataToSend, callbackFunction)
{
  var XMLHttpRequestObject = false;

  if (window.XMLHttpRequest) {
    XMLHttpRequestObject = new XMLHttpRequest();
  } else if (window.ActiveXObject) {
    XMLHttpRequestObject = new
     ActiveXObject("Microsoft.XMLHTTP");
  }

  if(XMLHttpRequestObject) {
    XMLHttpRequestObject.open("POST", url);
    XMLHttpRequestObject.setRequestHeader('Content-Type',
      'application/x-www-form-urlencoded');
```

```
XMLHttpRequestObject.onreadystatechange = function()
{
  if (XMLHttpRequestObject.readyState == 4 &&
    XMLHttpRequestObject.status == 200) {
      callbackFunction(XMLHttpRequestObject.responseText);
      delete XMLHttpRequestObject;
      XMLHttpRequestObject = null;
  }
}

XMLHttpRequestObject.send(dataToSend);
}
}
```

Okay, that completes the postDataDownloadText function; let's give it a try with a new page, postDataDownloadText.html. In that page, we start by including ajaxframework.js, the library that includes the postDataDownloadText function:

```
<head>

  <title>Posting Data and Downloading
  Text With the Ajax Framework Library Pack</title>

  <script type = "text/javascript" src = "ajaxframework.js"></script>
    .
    .
    .
```

We'll display a button that calls the postDataDownloadText function:

```
<form>
  <input type = "button" value = "Get the text"
  onclick =
  "postDataDownloadText('repeater.php', 'message=Hello there.', display)">
</form>
```

Note what's happening here: we're calling the postDataDownloadText function with the URL repeater.php, a data string, and the name of a callback function, display. What does all this mean?

Let's start with repeater.php. This PHP script just sends back any text you post to it; here is the PHP code:

```
<?php
  echo ($_POST["message"]);
?>
```

How about the data string we're passing to the postDataDownloadText function? Here it is: 'message=Hello there.' We're passing that string because that's the kind of data you have to use with the POST method (see Chapter 3 for more information). This data string connects the text "Hello there." with the argument message, which means that repeater.php will be able to read that text and return it.

The display function is our callback function—that's the function that will be called back when the text has been downloaded from the server. In the display function, we can display the received text in a <div> element, targetDiv:

```
<script language = "javascript">

function display(text)
{
  document.getElementById('targetDiv').innerHTML = text;
}

</script>
```

Here's what the whole page, postDataDownloadText.html, looks like:

```
<html>
  <head>

    <title>Posting Data and Downloading Text With the Ajax
    Framework Library Pack</title>

    <script type = "text/javascript" src = "ajaxframework.js"></script>

    <script language = "javascript">

      function display(text)
      {
        document.getElementById('targetDiv').innerHTML = text;
      }

    </script>
  </head>

  <body>

    <h1>Posting Data and Downloading Text With the Ajax
    Framework Library Pack</h1>

    <form>
      <input type = "button" value = "Get the text"
      onclick =
      "postDataDownloadText('repeater.php', 'message=Hello there.', display)">
    </form>

    <div id="targetDiv">The fetched text will go here.</div>

  </body>

</html>
```

You can see this page at work in Figure 5-3, where the user has clicked the button and downloaded the text using the POST method. Not bad.

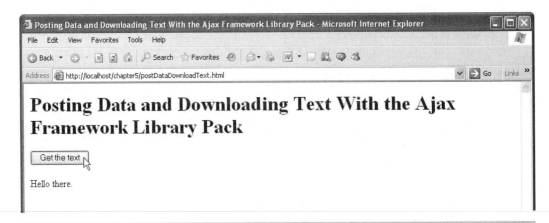

Figure 5-3 postDataDownloadText.html at work

Posting Data and Downloading XML with the postDataDownloadXml Function

We've used GET to download both text and XML, and POST to download text, so there's one topic left for ajaxframework.js—downloading XML with POST. That's handled by a function named postDataDownloadXml in ajaxframework.js, and we'll take a look at how to create this function now.

With POST, we can send data to the server, and we'll use a PHP script named colors.xml to return one of two color schemes in XML: one if we post a value of 1 as an argument named data, and one if we post a value of 2 to this script. Posting data to the server and getting back XML will let us test the postDataDownloadXml function. Here's what colors.php looks like—we start by telling the browser that we're sending it XML:

```php
<?php
header("Content-type: text/xml");
        .
        .
        .
?>
```

Then we can read the value of the argument named data—if it's 1, we'll use red, green, and blue as the colors we return to the browser by storing them in a PHP array named $colors (variables start with a $ in PHP):

```php
<?php
header("Content-type: text/xml");
if ($_POST["data"] == "1")
```

```php
$colors = array('red', 'green', 'blue');
      .
      .
      .
?>
```

And color scheme 2 will be orange, navy, and viridian:

```php
<?php
header("Content-type: text/xml");
if ($_POST["data"] == "1")
  $colors = array('red', 'green', 'blue');
if ($_POST["data"] == "2")
  $colors = array('orange', 'navy', 'viridian');
      .
      .
      .
?>
```

Having stored the colors to use in the array named $colors, we can put together the XML to send back to the user, which looks like this for color scheme 1:

```xml
<?xml version = "1.0" ?>
<colors>
  <color>red</color>
  <color>green</color>
  <color>blue</color>
</colors>
```

and this for color scheme 2:

```xml
<?xml version = "1.0" ?>
<colors>
  <color>orange</color>
  <color>navy</color>
  <color>viridian</color>
</colors>
```

To send that XML back to the browser, we start with the XML declaration that starts the XML document (<?xml version="1.0" ?>):

```php
<?php
header("Content-type: text/xml");
if ($_POST["data"] == "1")
  $colors = array('red', 'green', 'blue');
if ($_POST["data"] == "2")
  $colors = array('orange', 'navy', 'viridian');
echo '<?xml version="1.0" ?>';
      .
      .
      .
?>
```

Then we can echo the document element, <colors>:

```php
<?php
header("Content-type: text/xml");
if ($_POST["data"] == "1")
  $colors = array('red', 'green', 'blue');
if ($_POST["data"] == "2")
  $colors = array('orange', 'navy', 'viridian');
echo '<?xml version="1.0" ?>';
echo '<colors>';
        .
        .
        .
echo '</colors>';
?>
```

Then we can use a PHP foreach loop (see Chapter 9) to loop over the $colors array and put each color into a <color> element:

```php
<?php
header("Content-type: text/xml");
if ($_POST["data"] == "1")
  $colors = array('red', 'green', 'blue');
if ($_POST["data"] == "2")
  $colors = array('orange', 'navy', 'viridian');
echo '<?xml version="1.0" ?>';
echo '<colors>';
foreach ($colors as $value)
{
  echo '<color>';
  echo $value;
  echo '</color>';
}
echo '</colors>';
?>
```

Great, that completes colors.php. We just post an argument named data, set to 1 or 2, to this script, and it'll return color scheme 1 or 2.

Now that we know what the kind of script that the postDataDownloadXml function will be interacting with looks like, let's put that function together. We pass the URL to download the XML from to this function, as well as the data we want to post, and the callback function:

```
function postDataDownloadXml(url, dataToSend, callbackFunction)
{
        .
        .
        .
}
```

As usual, we start by creating an XMLHttpRequest object, and checking if we were successful in creating it:

```
function postDataDownloadXml(url, dataToSend, callbackFunction)
{
  var XMLHttpRequestObject = false;

  if (window.XMLHttpRequest) {
    XMLHttpRequestObject = new XMLHttpRequest();
    XMLHttpRequestObject.overrideMimeType("text/xml");
  } else if (window.ActiveXObject) {
    XMLHttpRequestObject = new
     ActiveXObject("Microsoft.XMLHTTP");
  }

  if(XMLHttpRequestObject) {
      .
      .
      .
  }
}
```

Then we can open the XMLHttpRequest object, configuring it with the URL the user wants to access, and specifying the POST method:

```
function postDataDownloadXml(url, dataToSend, callbackFunction)
{
  var XMLHttpRequestObject = false;

  if (window.XMLHttpRequest) {
    XMLHttpRequestObject = new XMLHttpRequest();
    XMLHttpRequestObject.overrideMimeType("text/xml");
  } else if (window.ActiveXObject) {
    XMLHttpRequestObject = new
     ActiveXObject("Microsoft.XMLHTTP");
  }

  if(XMLHttpRequestObject) {
    XMLHttpRequestObject.open("POST", url);
    XMLHttpRequestObject.setRequestHeader('Content-Type',
      'application/x-www-form-urlencoded');
      .
      .
      .
  }
}
```

Then we can set up the anonymous function that will be called with the XML returned from the server, which we pass to the user-specified callback function, and finish by sending the data string the user wants us to send to the server:

```
function postDataDownloadXml(url, dataToSend, callbackFunction)
{
  var XMLHttpRequestObject = false;

  if (window.XMLHttpRequest) {
    XMLHttpRequestObject = new XMLHttpRequest();
    XMLHttpRequestObject.overrideMimeType("text/xml");
  } else if (window.ActiveXObject) {
    XMLHttpRequestObject = new
      ActiveXObject("Microsoft.XMLHTTP");
  }

  if(XMLHttpRequestObject) {
    XMLHttpRequestObject.open("POST", url);
    XMLHttpRequestObject.setRequestHeader('Content-Type',
      'application/x-www-form-urlencoded');

    XMLHttpRequestObject.onreadystatechange = function()
    {
      if (XMLHttpRequestObject.readyState == 4 &&
        XMLHttpRequestObject.status == 200) {
          callbackFunction(XMLHttpRequestObject.responseXML);
          delete XMLHttpRequestObject;
          XMLHttpRequestObject = null;
      }
    }

    XMLHttpRequestObject.send(dataToSend);
  }
}
```

And that completes the postDataDownloadXml function in ajaxframework.js. All that remains now is to test it out, and we'll do that with a document named postDataDownloadXml .html. This HTML document will let the user click one of two buttons to download the two color schemes:

```
<form>
  <input type = "button" value = "Get color scheme 1"
    onclick = "postDataDownloadXml('colors.php', 'data=1', callback)">
  <input type = "button" value = "Get color scheme 2"
    onclick = "postDataDownloadXml('colors.php', 'data=2', callback)">
</form>
```

Note that we're calling the postDataDownloadXml function to download the color schemes in XML—both schemes come from the colors.php script, but for scheme 1, we post a value of 1, and for scheme 2, we post a value of 2. Here's what the whole postDataDownloadXml.html looks like:

```html
<html>
  <head>

    <title>Posting Data and Downloading Text With the Ajax
    Framework Library Pack</title>

    <script type = "text/javascript" src = "ajaxframework.js"></script>

    <script language = "javascript">

      function callback(xmlDocument)
      {
          var obj = document.getElementById('targetDiv');

          colors = xmlDocument.getElementsByTagName("color");
          obj.innerHTML = "Here are the fetched colors:<ul>";
          for (loopIndex = 0; loopIndex < colors.length; loopIndex++ )
          {
             obj.innerHTML +=
             "<li>" + colors[loopIndex].firstChild.data + "</li>";
          }
          obj.innerHTML += "</ul>";
      }

    </script>
  </head>

  <body>

    <h1>Posting Data and Downloading Text With the Ajax
    Framework Library Pack</h1>

    <form>
      <input type = "button" value = "Get color scheme 1"
        onclick = "postDataDownloadXml('colors.php', 'data=1', callback)">
      <input type = "button" value = "Get color scheme 2"
        onclick = "postDataDownloadXml('colors.php', 'data=2', callback)">
    </form>

    <div id="targetDiv">Your color scheme will appear here.</div>

  </body>

</html>
```

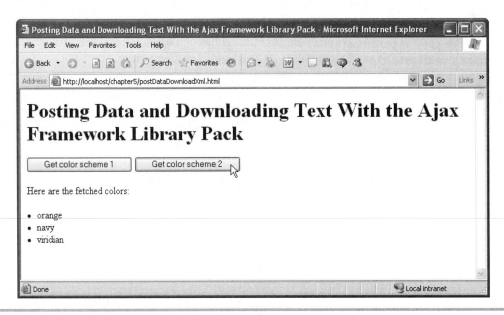

Figure 5-4 postDataDownloadXml.html at work

You can see this HTML document, postDataDownloadXml.html, at work in Figure 5-4—just click a button and the application will use the postDataDownloadXml function to download the matching color scheme. Nice.

And that completes the ajaxframework.js library, a convenient JavaScript library that includes these functions:

- downloadText(url, callbackFunction)

- downloadXml(url, callbackFunction)

- postDataDownloadText(url, dataToSend, callbackFunction)

- postDataDownloadXml(url, dataToSend, callbackFunction)

Using ajaxframework.js means that you don't have to write your own Ajax code if you don't want to—just include ajaxframework.js in your page and then call the appropriate function.

There are dozens of Ajax frameworks already out there, and we'll take a look at a couple of them next.

Using the libXmlRequest JavaScript Ajax Framework

Among the many Ajax frameworks available is the libXmlRequest JavaScript Ajax framework, which you can pick up for free at www.whitefrost.com/reference/2008/04/27/libXmlRequest .html. The JavaScript library itself is libXmlRequest.js, and when you include that file in a <script> element, you make the functions available in libXmlRequest accessible to your code.

The libXmlRequest framework centers on two Ajax functions—getXml and postXml. Note that this library is XML based, and contains a number of functions that let you handle XML. Here's an overview of the Ajax functions in the libXmlRequest library:

- **getXml(url)**   A synchronous GET request that returns null or an XML document object

- **getXml(url, callback, 1)**   An asynchronous GET request that returns 1 if the request was made successfully, and calls the callback function handler when the XML is downloaded

- **postXml(url, data)**   A synchronous POST request that returns null or an XML document object

- **postXml(url, data, callback, 1)**   An asynchronous POST request that returns 1 if the request was made successfully, and calls the callback function handler when the XML is downloaded

The callback functions are called with two arguments, and the second argument is the one we're interested in, because it contains the downloaded XML—in particular, the xdom property of that parameter is the XML object that contains the XML data we've requested.

Let's use libXmlRequest to download and read the data in an XML document named hellp .xml, which just holds the text "Hello from libXmlRequest.":

```
<?xml version = "1.0" ?>
<text>
Hello from libXmlRequest.
</text>
```

We'll test libXmlRequest in an HTML document named libxmlrequest.html. First, we include libXmlRequest.js:

```
<html>
  <head>
    <title>Using the libXmlRequest Ajax framework</title>

    <script src = "libXmlRequest.js"></script>
        .
        .
        .
</html>
```

Then we add a button that calls the libXmlRequest function to get XML, org.cote.js.xml .getXml:

```
<html>
  <head>
    <title>Using the libXmlRequest Ajax framework</title>
```

```
    <script src = "libXmlRequest.js"></script>
            .
            .
            .
  <body>

    <H1>Using the libXmlRequest Ajax framework</H1>

    <form>
      <input type = "button" value = "Get the message"
        onclick = "org.cote.js.xml.getXml('hello.xml', callback, 1)">
    </form>
  </body>
</html>
```

This call to org.cote.js.xml.getXml gives the name of our callback function simply as "callback," so we'll add that function now. We just want to extract the text from the <text> element in the downloaded XML, and we can do that by extracting the <text> element with the getElementsByTagName method, using the firstChild property to extract the text node from the <text> element, and then using the data property of the text node to finally reach the text itself:

```
<html>
  <head>
    <title>Using the libXmlRequest Ajax framework</title>

    <script src = "libXmlRequest.js"></script>

    <script language = "javascript">

      function callback(a, b)
      {
        var textElement = b.xdom.getElementsByTagName("text");

        var div = document.getElementById('targetDiv');

        div.innerHTML = textElement[0].firstChild.data;

      }
    </script>
  </head>

  <body>

    <H1>Using the libXmlRequest Ajax framework</H1>
```

Figure 5-5   libXmlRequest.html at work

```
<form>
  <input type = "button" value = "Get the message"
    onclick = "org.cote.js.xml.getXml('hello.xml', callback, 1)">
</form>

<div id="targetDiv">
  <p>The fetched data will go here.</p>
</div>

  </body>
</html>
```

And that's it—that completes our example that uses the libXmlRequest library. You can see this web page at work in Figure 5-5, where it is correctly downloading the hello.xml document.

Let's take a look at another Ajax framework now—AJAXLib.

Using the AJAXLib JavaScript Ajax Framework

AJAXLib is a free Ajax framework that you can get at http://karaszewski.com/tools/ajaxlib/. The actual framework's JavaScript library is named ajaxlib.js.

This framework is simple to use. You just pass this library's loadXMLDoc function the URL to your XML source, the callback function (to call with the downloaded XML), and a true/false parameter that lets you remove whitespace in the downloaded XML (if you pass a value of true, AJAXLib will remove indentation whitespace in your XML). After the XML is downloaded, it will be accessible to your JavaScript code in a JavaScript variable named resultXML.

Let's put this framework to work in an example named ajaxlib.html, using AJAXLib to download and extract the text "Hello from AJAXLib." from a document named hello2.xml:

```
<?xml version = "1.0" ?>
<text>
Hello from AJAXLib.
</text>
```

The ajaxlib.html web page begins with a button to download hello2.xml, and indicates that the callback function is just named callback:

```
<form>
  <input type = "button" value = "Get the message"
    onclick = "loadXMLDoc('hello2.xml', callback, false)">
</form>
```

In the callback function, we can make use of the JavaScript XML document object that will be stored in the resultXML variable to extract the text in hello2.xml. Here's what it looks like in ajaxlib.html:

```
<html>
  <head>
    <title>Using the AJAXLib Ajax framework</title>

    <script src = "ajaxlib.js"></script>

    <script language = "javascript">

      function callback()
      {
        var xmlData = resultXML.getElementsByTagName("text");

        var div = document.getElementById('targetDiv');

        div.innerHTML = xmlData[0].firstChild.data;

      }
    </script>
  </head>

  <body>

    <H1>Using the AJAXLib Ajax framework</H1>

    <form>
      <input type = "button" value = "Get the message"
        onclick = "loadXMLDoc('hello2.xml', callback, false)">
    </form>
```

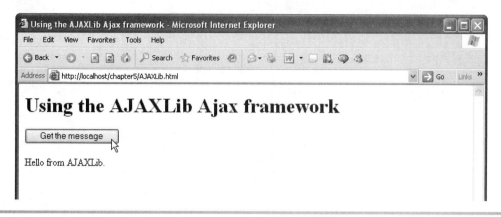

Figure 5-6 AJAXLib.html at work

```
<div id="targetDiv">
  <p>The fetched data will go here.</p>
</div>

</body>
</html>
```

And you can see the results in Figure 5-6—when the user clicks the button, the new message is indeed downloaded and displayed by AJAXLib. Cool.

Chapter 6

Handling XML in Ajax

Key Skills & Concepts

● Working with XML in JavaScript

● Navigating through XML documents

● Retrieving XML element data

● Retrieving XML element attribute data

The *x* in Ajax stands for XML, and this chapter is all about working with XML in Ajax applications. The bulk of the material in this chapter has to do with using XML in JavaScript, because, as you've already seen, doing so is not straightforward by any means. But you're going to gain valuable experience in XML handling in JavaScript in this chapter.

We'll start with a discussion of how XML works (this book assumes you know HTML, but doesn't make the same assumption about XML).

Building Some XML

Writing your own XML is a lot like writing your own HTML—you use tags, elements, and attributes, just as you do in HTML. The crucial difference is that in XML, you make up your own element names. For example, here's what an HTML document might look like, using the predefined element names in HTML 4.01:

```
<html>
  <head>
    <title>The Report</title>
  </head>

  <body>
    <h1>The Report</h1>
    All Quiet on the Western Front.
  </body>
<html>
```

This is fine as far as it goes, but what if you want to store your own private data? For example, say that you want to create a document that lets you keep track of your friends? There is no <friend> element in HTML, and no <first_name> or <last_name> element. But you can make up and use those elements in XML—no problem.

Here's what such a document might look like in XML—note that you're storing information about three friends here:

```
<?xml version="1.0"?>
<friends>
  <friend>
    <first_name>Cary</first_name>
    <last_name>Grant</last_name>
  </friend>
  <friend>
    <first_name>Myrna</first_name>
    <last_name>Loy</last_name>
  </friend>
  <friend>
    <first_name>James</first_name>
    <last_name>Stewart</last_name>
  </friend>
</friends>
```

You're free to use your own element names in XML, as long as they are legal element names syntactically. There are two sides to that coin: while browsers can be programmed to understand HTML elements and display your HTML document accordingly, you have to take extra steps with XML. That is, XML documents are all about storing data, not presenting that data visually (like HTML), and that means you have to provide a way of extracting that data and working with it yourself. That's where JavaScript is going to come into play in this chapter—you're going to see how to use JavaScript to read and navigate through XML documents in this chapter. Using your own programming (a step not necessary with HTML), you can extract the data in an XML document and make use of that data.

There are some XML rules here that you should know about, and we'll take a look at them now. We'll start by constructing an XML document from scratch that will document the people present at a party—in this case, a party given on the occasion of a snow day, when school has been cancelled.

First, you must start all XML documents with an *XML declaration*, which looks like this:

```
<?xml version="1.0" ?>
    .
    .
    .
```

This is an XML declaration, not an XML element, and it must be the first line in your XML document. The version attribute is required, and you can set it to "1.0" (the most common version, and the version we'll use) or "1.1". Besides the version attribute, you can also include the standalone attribute (set to "no" if this document includes other XML documents in it, "yes" otherwise) and the encoding attribute (set to the character encoding you're using—you can, for example, specify that you're using Japanese characters, or Russian characters). The default for the encoding is the UTF-8 character set, which is what WordPad and other standard editors use (actually, they use a subset of UTF-8):

```
<?xml version="1.0" standalone="yes" encoding="UTF-8" ?>
        .
        .
        .
```

Next up in an XML document are the elements that contain the data in the document. You make up your own tag names in XML, but there are some rules about what tag names are legal. Tag names can't start with a number, can't contain spaces, and can't contain a few other illegal characters, such as quotation marks or spaces. Here are some illegal tag names:

```
<12steps>
<big dog>
<"ok">
```

The first element in a document is the *document element*. In XML documents, one element encloses all the other elements, and that element is called the document element. In the case of our snow-day party example, we might call the document element <parties> so that we can keep track of a number of parties:

```
<?xml version="1.0"?>
<parties>
        .
        .
        .
</parties>
```

Every other element in the XML document must be contained within this document element, so, for example, if you want to keep track of the attendees at three different parties, you can have three <party> elements enclosed inside the <parties> element:

```
<?xml version="1.0"?>
<parties>
    <party>
        .
        .
        .
    </party>
    <party>
        .
        .
        .
    </party>
    <party>
        .
        .
        .
    </party>
</parties>
```

So you see that, just like HTML, XML elements can contain other XML elements. In fact, you can also have *empty elements*, just as you can in HTML (the <img> element is an example of an empty element in HTML). Empty elements have no content: no nested elements, no nested text. In XML, you end an empty element with the markup />, so, for example, if you have empty elements named <afternoon /> and <evening />, you can indicate when a party took place by using these elements:

```
<?xml version="1.0"?>
<parties>
    <party>
      <afternoon />
         .
         .
         .
    </party>
    <party>
      <evening />
         .
         .
         .
    </party>
    <party>
      <afternoon />
         .
         .
         .
    </party>
</parties>
```

XML elements can also include *attributes*, just as HTML elements can. Attributes can appear in the opening tags of elements, or inside empty elements, and they're name/value pairs. For example, say that you want to give the <party> element a type attribute, indicating that the party is a winter party; you can do that like this:

```
<?xml version="1.0"?>
<parties>
    <party type="winter">
         .
         .
         .
    </party>
</parties>
```

In XML (unlike HTML), you always have to assign attributes a value—in this example, type is the attribute name, and "winter" is the attribute value. The attribute value must *always* be inside quotation marks.

Besides other elements, you can enclose text inside XML elements. Here's what that might look like in our full party example (this is party.xml):

```xml
<?xml version="1.0"?>
<parties>
    <party type="winter">
        <party_title>Snow Day</party_title>
        <party_number>63</party_number>
        <subject>No school today!</subject>
        <date>2/2/2009</date>
        <people>
            <person attendance="present">
                <first_name>Ralph</first_name>
                <last_name>Kramden</last_name>
            </person>
            <person attendance="absent">
                <first_name>Alice</first_name>
                <last_name>Kramden</last_name>
            </person>
            <person attendance="present">
                <first_name>Ed</first_name>
                <last_name>Norton</last_name>
            </person>
        </people>
    </party>
</parties>
```

Now you're getting the idea. XML is actually pretty simple to construct, but there are pitfalls. The XML document that we've constructed is an example of a so-called *well-formed* XML document. However, it's easy to slip up, making your XML document not well formed—and XML-aware software, like browsers, are going to give you errors if your XML is not well formed. Not nesting the XML elements properly is the primary well-formedness error. For example, this version of our example XML document, where one <person> element hasn't ended before another one starts, would not be read by a browser because of the nesting error:

```xml
<?xml version="1.0"?>
<parties>
    <party type="winter">
        <party_title>Snow Day</party_title>
        <party_number>63</party_number>
        <subject>No school today!</subject>
        <date>2/2/2009</date>
        <people>
            <person attendance="present">
                <first_name>Ralph</first_name>
                <last_name>Kramden</last_name>
            <person attendance="absent">
            </person>
```

```
                <first_name>Alice</first_name>
                <last_name>Kramden</last_name>
            </person>
            <person attendance="present">
                <first_name>Ed</first_name>
                <last_name>Norton</last_name>
            </person>
        </people>
    </party>
</parties>
```

That kind of error is obvious, but what about the more subtle ones? Can you spot the error in the following version of our document?

```
<?xml version="1.0"?>
<parties>
    <party type="winter">
        <party_title>Snow Day</party_title>
        <party_number>63</party_number>
        <subject>No school today!</subject>
        <date>2/2/2009</date>
        <people>
            <person attendance="present">
                <first_name>Ralph</first_name>
                <last_name>Kramden</last_name>
            <person attendance="absent">
            </person>
                <first_name>Alice</first_name>
                <last_name>Kramden</last_name>
            </person>
            <person attendance="present">
                <first_name>Ed</first_name>
                <last_name>Norton</last_name>
            </person>
        </people>
    </party>
</parties>
```

The error is that the attendance attribute is spelled "attendence" in the first <person> element. The document is well formed, but it's not correct. So in addition to well-formedness, XML documents can also be checked for *validity*. To check if an XML document is valid, you have to specify the legal syntax of your document. For example, can a <friend> element contain a <people> element? What attributes does a <party> element have? And so on.

There are two methods to check the validity of XML documents: XML Document Type Definitions (DTD) and XML Schema. Each lets you specify the syntax rules of your XML document, and of the two, XML Schema is the newest and the most powerful.

Unfortunately, the browser you work with may not support XML Schema (the support in Internet Explorer is problematic), so you might want to stick to the older way of specifying the syntax of XML documents, DTDs, if you want to ensure that your document is checked for validity (we'll see an example near the end of this chapter—note that you do not have to check for validity to use XML in Ajax). Here's what a DTD for our example XML document looks like:

```
<?xml version="1.0"?>
<!DOCTYPE parties [
<!ELEMENT parties (party*)>
<!ELEMENT party (party_title, party_number, subject, date, people*)>
<!ELEMENT party_title (#PCDATA)>
<!ELEMENT party_number (#PCDATA)>
<!ELEMENT subject (#PCDATA)>
<!ELEMENT date (#PCDATA)>
<!ELEMENT first_name (#PCDATA)>
<!ELEMENT last_name (#PCDATA)>
<!ELEMENT people (person*)>
<!ELEMENT person (first_name,last_name)>
<!ATTLIST party
    type CDATA #IMPLIED>
<!ATTLIST person
    attendance CDATA #IMPLIED>
]>
<parties>
    <party type="winter">
        <party_title>Snow Day</party_title>
        <party_number>63</party_number>
        <subject>No school today!</subject>
        <date>2/2/2009</date>
        <people>
            <person attendance="present">
                <first_name>Ralph</first_name>
                <last_name>Kramden</last_name>
            </person>
            <person attendance="absent">
                <first_name>Alice</first_name>
                <last_name>Kramden</last_name>
            </person>
            <person attendance="present">
                <first_name>Ed</first_name>
                <last_name>Norton</last_name>
            </person>
        </people>
    </party>
</parties>
```

If you're interested in ensuring the validity of your XML documents, check out an XML book that covers DTDs and XML Schema.

Okay, that gives you a good XML foundation. Let's get started handling XML in JavaScript, as you're likely to do in Ajax applications.

Working with XML in JavaScript

To see how to work with XML in JavaScript, you have to understand how JavaScript sees XML. JavaScript sees XML in terms of *nodes*. Take this XML document as an example:

```
<?xml version="1.0" ?>
<document>
    <greeting>
        Welcome to XML
    </greeting>
    <text>
        Hello there!
    </text>
</document>
```

In this case, the <document> node has two child nodes, the <greeting> and <text> nodes. These nodes are sibling nodes of each other. Both the <greeting> and <text> elements themselves have one child node—a text node that holds character data. Looked at as a tree of nodes, this is what this document looks like:

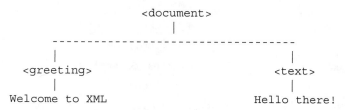

To JavaScript, an XML document is constructed of nodes—and not just element nodes, either. There are text nodes, attribute nodes, and so on. Table 6-1 diplays the node types (the numbers are the numbers that JavaScript has assigned to each type of node).

JavaScript has built-in properties you can use to work with the nodes in XML documents (like the document object that's returned in the XMLHttpRequest object's responseXML property), shown in Table 6-2.

Note in particular that the nodeType property holds the type of a node. You'll see how to use these properties in JavaScript in this chapter.

It's time to sling some code, and we'll start by extracting the document element from our example XML document, party.xml.

Number	Node type
1	Element node
2	Attribute node
3	Text node
4	CDATA (XML character data) section node
5	XML entity reference node
6	XML entity node
7	XML processing instruction node
8	XML comment node
9	XML document node
10	XML DTD node
11	XML document fragment node
12	XML notation node

Table 6-1   Node Types

Property	Means
attributes	Attributes by this node
childNodes	Array of child nodes
documentElement	The document element
firstChild	First child node
lastChild	Last child node
localName	Local name of the node
name	Name of the node
nextSibling	Next sibling node
nodeName	Name of the node
nodeType	Node type
nodeValue	Value of the node
previousSibling	Previous sibling node

Table 6-2   JavaScript Properties You Can Use to Work with Nodes

Getting the Document Element

Getting the document element—the element that contains all the other elements in an XML document—is usually the first step in working with XML documents. We'll now see how to extract the document element in an example named documentElement.html.

The documentElement.html example will read in our party.xml document and display the document element, which is <parties>. We start this application with a button:

```
<body>

  <h1>Getting the Document Element</h1>

  <form>
    <input type = "button" value = "Get the document element"
      onclick = "getDocumentElement()">
  </form>

</body>
```

When the user clicks this button, the browser calls a JavaScript function named getDocumentElement:

```
<script language = "javascript">

  function getDocumentElement()
  {
        .
        .
        .
  }
</script>
```

Okay, we want to read in the party.xml document here, using Ajax techniques. We start by creating a new XMLHttpRequest object:

```
<script language = "javascript">

  function getDocumentElement()
  {
    var XMLHttpRequestObject = false;

    if (window.XMLHttpRequest) {
      XMLHttpRequestObject = new XMLHttpRequest();
    } else if (window.ActiveXObject) {
      XMLHttpRequestObject = new
        ActiveXObject("Microsoft.XMLHTTP");
    }
```

```
            .
            .
            .
        }
    </script>
```

And if we were successful in creating that object, we configure XMLHttpRequestObject to access the party.xml document using the HTTP GET method:

```
<script language = "javascript">

    function getDocumentElement()
    {
      var XMLHttpRequestObject = false;

        if (window.XMLHttpRequest) {
          XMLHttpRequestObject = new XMLHttpRequest();
        } else if (window.ActiveXObject) {
          XMLHttpRequestObject = new
            ActiveXObject("Microsoft.XMLHTTP");
        }

        if(XMLHttpRequestObject) {
          XMLHttpRequestObject.open("GET", "party.xml", true);
          .
          .
          .
        }
    }
    </script>
```

Then we add the anonymous function to download party.xml:

```
<script language = "javascript">

    function getDocumentElement()
    {
      var XMLHttpRequestObject = false;

        if (window.XMLHttpRequest) {
          XMLHttpRequestObject = new XMLHttpRequest();
        } else if (window.ActiveXObject) {
          XMLHttpRequestObject = new
            ActiveXObject("Microsoft.XMLHTTP");
        }

        if(XMLHttpRequestObject) {
          XMLHttpRequestObject.open("GET", "party.xml", true);

          XMLHttpRequestObject.onreadystatechange = function()
```

```
        {
          if (XMLHttpRequestObject.readyState == 4 &&
            XMLHttpRequestObject.status == 200) {
              .
              .
              .
            }
          }
        }

      }
    }
</script>
```

After the download, we can get the XML as a JavaScript XML object from the XMLHttpRequest object's responseXML property. Then we can use that object's documentElement property to get the document element:

```
<script language = "javascript">

  function getDocumentElement()
  {
    var XMLHttpRequestObject = false;

    if (window.XMLHttpRequest) {
      XMLHttpRequestObject = new XMLHttpRequest();
    } else if (window.ActiveXObject) {
      XMLHttpRequestObject = new
        ActiveXObject("Microsoft.XMLHTTP");
    }

    if(XMLHttpRequestObject) {
      XMLHttpRequestObject.open("GET", "party.xml", true);

      XMLHttpRequestObject.onreadystatechange = function()
      {
        if (XMLHttpRequestObject.readyState == 4 &&
          XMLHttpRequestObject.status == 200) {
          var xmlDocument = XMLHttpRequestObject.responseXML;
          var documentElement = xmlDocument.documentElement;
            .
            .
            .
          }
        }
      }

    }
  }
</script>
```

Now we have the document element, and it's stored as a JavaScript element object. That one object contains all the other elements in the document. How do we confirm that we've gotten the document element, <parties>? We can print it out like this, using the nodeName property of the documentElement object (note that we write < as <, which is how you write markup that you want browsers simply to display, not react to as HTML):

```
<script language = "javascript">

  function getDocumentElement()
  {
    var XMLHttpRequestObject = false;

    if (window.XMLHttpRequest) {
      XMLHttpRequestObject = new XMLHttpRequest();
    } else if (window.ActiveXObject) {
      XMLHttpRequestObject = new
        ActiveXObject("Microsoft.XMLHTTP");
    }

    if(XMLHttpRequestObject) {
      XMLHttpRequestObject.open("GET", "party.xml", true);

      XMLHttpRequestObject.onreadystatechange = function()
      {
        if (XMLHttpRequestObject.readyState == 4 &&
          XMLHttpRequestObject.status == 200) {
          var xmlDocument = XMLHttpRequestObject.responseXML;
          var documentElement = xmlDocument.documentElement;
          if(documentElement){
            document.getElementById("targetDiv").innerHTML =
              "The document element is &lt;" +
              documentElement.nodeName + ">.";
          }
        }
      }

      XMLHttpRequestObject.send(null);
    }
  }
</script>
```

And that's it—here's the whole web page, documentElement.html:

```
<html>
  <head>

    <title>Getting the Document Element</title>

    <script language = "javascript">

      function getDocumentElement()
```

```
    {
      var XMLHttpRequestObject = false;

      if (window.XMLHttpRequest) {
        XMLHttpRequestObject = new XMLHttpRequest();
      } else if (window.ActiveXObject) {
        XMLHttpRequestObject = new
          ActiveXObject("Microsoft.XMLHTTP");
      }

      if(XMLHttpRequestObject) {
        XMLHttpRequestObject.open("GET", "party.xml", true);

        XMLHttpRequestObject.onreadystatechange = function()
        {
          if (XMLHttpRequestObject.readyState == 4 &&
            XMLHttpRequestObject.status == 200) {
            var xmlDocument = XMLHttpRequestObject.responseXML;
            var documentElement = xmlDocument.documentElement;
            if(documentElement){
              document.getElementById("targetDiv").innerHTML =
                "The document element is &lt;" +
                documentElement.nodeName + ">.";
            }
          }
        }

        XMLHttpRequestObject.send(null);
      }
    }
  </script>

</head>

<body>

  <h1>Getting the Document Element</h1>

  <form>
    <input type = "button" value = "Get the document element"
      onclick = "getDocumentElement()">
  </form>

  <div id="targetDiv" width =100 height=100>
    The result will appear here.
  </div>

</body>

</html>
```

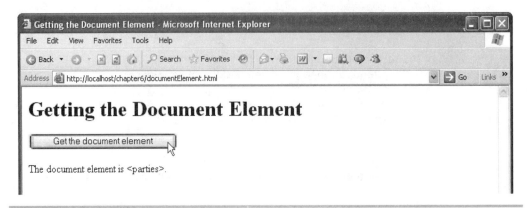

Figure 6-1 documentElement.html at work

You can see the results in Figure 6-1, where the application has correctly retrieved the document element of party.xml.

We're making progress—we've extracted and read the document element of an XML document. Now how about accessing any element in the XML document?

Try This Get the Number of Children of the Document Element

Want to find out how many child elements the document element has? Modify documentElement.html now to do that. You can use the childNodes property of the documentElement object to do this. That property holds an array that contains all the child nodes of the document element, and you can determine the length of that array—and hence the number of children of the document node—with the array's length property:

```
"The document element has " + documentElement.childNodes.length + "
children.";
```

Note that the document element, <parties>, has only one direct child node, <party>, in our party.xml example, which you should see when you run the modified form of documentElement.html.

Accessing Any XML Element

We've been able to access the document element in party.xml in JavaScript, after downloading party.xml using Ajax. But what if we want to access other elements in party.xml? For example, what if we want to access the third guest at the party and retrieve their first (Ed) and last (Norton) names?

```
<?xml version="1.0"?>
<parties>
    <party type="winter">
        <party_title>Snow Day</party_title>
        <party_number>63</party_number>
        <subject>No school today!</subject>
        <date>2/2/2009</date>
        <people>
            <person attendance="present">
                <first_name>Ralph</first_name>
                <last_name>Kramden</last_name>
            <person attendance="absent">
            </person>
                <first_name>Alice</first_name>
                <last_name>Kramden</last_name>
            </person>
            <person attendance="present">
                <first_name>Ed</first_name>
                <last_name>Norton</last_name>
            </person>
        </people>
    </party>
</parties>
```

Can you access the third guest using JavaScript? You sure can, and we'll take a look at how that works in a new example, party.html, now. This application starts with a button that, when clicked, calls a function named getData:

```
<body>

  <h1>Retrieving the Third Guest From party.xml</h1>

  <form>
    <input type = "button" value = "Get the third guest"
      onclick = "getData()">
  </form>

  <div id="targetDiv" width =100 height=100>
    Who was the third guest?
  </div>

</body>
```

In the getData function, we can create an XMLHttpRequest object:

```
<script language = "javascript">

  function getData()
  {
    var XMLHttpRequestObject = false;

    if (window.XMLHttpRequest) {
      XMLHttpRequestObject = new XMLHttpRequest();
      XMLHttpRequestObject.overrideMimeType("text/xml");
    } else if (window.ActiveXObject) {
      XMLHttpRequestObject = new
        ActiveXObject("Microsoft.XMLHTTP");
    }
      .
      .
      .

  }
</script>
```

Then we can use that XMLHttpRequest object to download party.xml using Ajax, get party.xml in JavaScript XML object form from the XMLHttpRequest object's responseXML property, and pass that XML object on to another function named displayGuest:

```
<script language = "javascript">

  function getData()
  {
    var XMLHttpRequestObject = false;

    if (window.XMLHttpRequest) {
      XMLHttpRequestObject = new XMLHttpRequest();
      XMLHttpRequestObject.overrideMimeType("text/xml");
    } else if (window.ActiveXObject) {
      XMLHttpRequestObject = new
        ActiveXObject("Microsoft.XMLHTTP");
    }

    if(XMLHttpRequestObject) {
      XMLHttpRequestObject.open("GET", "party.xml", true);

      XMLHttpRequestObject.onreadystatechange = function()
      {
        if (XMLHttpRequestObject.readyState == 4 &&
          XMLHttpRequestObject.status == 200) {
        var xmlDocument = XMLHttpRequestObject.responseXML;
```

```
      displayGuest(xmlDocument);
      }
    }

    XMLHttpRequestObject.send(null);
   }
  }
</script>
```

OK, now we've passed the XML object containing the XML data we want to work with to a function named displayGuest:

```
<script language = "javascript">
  function displayGuest (xmldoc)
  {
     .
     .
     .
  }

</script>
```

We start navigating through the XML document to the third guest by getting the document element for party.xml:

```
<script language = "javascript">
  function displayGuest (xmldoc)
  {
    var partiesNode;

    partiesNode = xmldoc.documentElement;
     .
     .
     .
  }

</script>
```

Okay, now that we've got the document element, how do we navigate to the third guest? We use navigation properties like these, which are supported by all element node objects (including the document element node):

childNodes	Array of child nodes
firstChild	First child node
lastChild	Last child node
nextSibling	Next sibling node
previousSibling	Previous sibling node

For example, the <party> element node is the first (and only) child of the <parties> node:

```
<?xml version="1.0"?>
<parties>
    <party type="winter">
        <party_title>Snow Day</party_title>
        <party_number>63</party_number>
        <subject>No school today!</subject>
        <date>2/2/2009</date>
        <people>
            <person attendance="present">
                <first_name>Ralph</first_name>
                <last_name>Kramden</last_name>
            <person attendance="absent">
            </person>
                <first_name>Alice</first_name>
                <last_name>Kramden</last_name>
            </person>
            <person attendance="present">
                <first_name>Ed</first_name>
                <last_name>Norton</last_name>
            </person>
        </people>
    </party>
</parties>
```

Since we have an object corresponding to the <parties> document element node already (partiesNode), we can access the <party> child node like this in the displayGuest function:

```
<script language = "javascript">
  function displayGuest (xmldoc)
  {
    var partiesNode, partyNode;

    partiesNode = xmldoc.documentElement;
    partyNode = partiesNode.firstChild;
    .
    .
    .
  }

</script>
```

The third guest is stored inside the <people> element, and the <people> element is the last child element of the <party> element, so we can access it with the <party> element's lastChild property:

```
<script language = "javascript">
  function displayGuest (xmldoc)
  {
    var partiesNode, partyNode, peopleNode;
    var firstNameNode, lastNameNode, displayText;
```

```
        partiesNode = xmldoc.documentElement;
        partyNode = partiesNode.firstChild;
        peopleNode = partyNode.lastChild;
            .
            .
            .

    }

    </script>
```

Now we've reached the <people> element. The <person> element we're interested in is the last child of the <people> element, so we can access that third <person> node like this:

```
    <script language = "javascript">
      function displayGuest (xmldoc)
      {
        var partiesNode, partyNode, peopleNode;
        var firstNameNode, lastNameNode, displayText;

        partiesNode = xmldoc.documentElement;
        partyNode = partiesNode.firstChild;
        peopleNode = partyNode.lastChild;
        personNode = peopleNode.lastChild;
            .
            .
            .

    }

    </script>
```

Almost there. Now we have to access the <first_name> and <last_name> elements inside the <person> element. The <first_name> element is the first child of the <person> element, so we grab it like this:

```
    <script language = "javascript">
      function displayGuest (xmldoc)
      {
        var partiesNode, partyNode, peopleNode;
        var firstNameNode, lastNameNode, displayText;

        partiesNode = xmldoc.documentElement;
        partyNode = partiesNode.firstChild;
        peopleNode = partyNode.lastChild;
        personNode = peopleNode.lastChild;
        firstNameNode = personNode.firstChild;
            .
            .
            .

    }

    </script>
```

The <last_name> element is the last child of the <person> element, so we could use the lastChild property of the personNode object to access it, but for variety, noting that the <last_name> element is a sibling of (that is, an element on the same level as) the <first_name> node, we can also access the <last_name> element as using the <first_name> element's nextSibling property:

```
<script language = "javascript">
  function displayGuest (xmldoc)
  {
    var partiesNode, partyNode, peopleNode;
    var firstNameNode, lastNameNode, displayText;

    partiesNode = xmldoc.documentElement;
    partyNode = partiesNode.firstChild;
    peopleNode = partyNode.lastChild;
    personNode = peopleNode.lastChild;
    firstNameNode = personNode.firstChild;
    lastNameNode = firstNameNode.nextSibling;
       .
       .
       .
  }

</script>
```

Whew. Now we've got two objects corresponding to the <first_name> and <last_name> elements—firstNameNode and lastNameNode. It took some effort to get here, but we got those objects.

So how do you extract the actual guest's name from the <first_name> and <last_name> elements? The first and last names are stored as text nodes inside these elements:

```
<person attendance="present">
    <first_name>Ed</first_name>
    <last_name>Norton</last_name>
</person>
```

And you can reach the text nodes, because they're the first child nodes of the <first_name> and <last_name> elements. So the text nodes containing the first and last names are firstNameNode.firstChild and lastNameNode.firstChild.

Are we done? Nope. The text nodes are themselves simply objects—you can't display them in a web page. To actually access the text in a text node, you have to use the text node's nodeValue property. So, finally, you can access the third guest's first name as firstNameNode .firstChild.nodeValue and their last name as lastNameNode.firstChild.nodeValue. Here's what it looks like in code:

```
<script language = "javascript">

  function displayGuest (xmldoc)
  {
    var partiesNode, partyNode, peopleNode;
    var firstNameNode, lastNameNode, displayText;
```

```
      partiesNode = xmldoc.documentElement;
      partyNode = partiesNode.firstChild;
      peopleNode = partyNode.lastChild;
      personNode = peopleNode.lastChild;
      firstNameNode = personNode.firstChild;
      lastNameNode = firstNameNode.nextSibling;

      displayText = "The third guest was " +
        firstNameNode.firstChild.nodeValue + ' '
        + lastNameNode.firstChild.nodeValue;

      var target = document.getElementById("targetDiv");
      target.innerHTML=displayText;
    }

  </script>
```

Here's the whole application, party.html:

```
<html>
  <head>

    <title>Retrieving the Third Guest From party.xml</title>

    <script language = "javascript">

      function getData()
      {
        var XMLHttpRequestObject = false;

        if (window.XMLHttpRequest) {
          XMLHttpRequestObject = new XMLHttpRequest();
          XMLHttpRequestObject.overrideMimeType("text/xml");
        } else if (window.ActiveXObject) {
          XMLHttpRequestObject = new
            ActiveXObject("Microsoft.XMLHTTP");
        }

        if(XMLHttpRequestObject) {
          XMLHttpRequestObject.open("GET", "party.xml", true);

          XMLHttpRequestObject.onreadystatechange = function()
          {
            if (XMLHttpRequestObject.readyState == 4 &&
              XMLHttpRequestObject.status == 200) {
            var xmlDocument = XMLHttpRequestObject.responseXML;
            displayGuest(xmlDocument);
            }
          }
```

```
        XMLHttpRequestObject.send(null);
      }
    }

  function displayGuest (xmldoc)
  {
    var partiesNode, partyNode, peopleNode;
    var firstNameNode, lastNameNode, displayText;

    partiesNode = xmldoc.documentElement;
    partyNode = partiesNode.firstChild;
    peopleNode = partyNode.lastChild;
    personNode = peopleNode.lastChild;
    firstNameNode = personNode.firstChild;
    lastNameNode = firstNameNode.nextSibling;

    displayText = "The third guest was " +
      firstNameNode.firstChild.nodeValue + ' '
      + lastNameNode.firstChild.nodeValue;

    var target = document.getElementById("targetDiv");
    target.innerHTML=displayText;
  }

</script>

</head>

<body>

  <h1>Retrieving the Third Guest From party.xml</h1>

  <form>
    <input type = "button" value = "Get the third guest"
      onclick = "getData()">
  </form>

  <div id="targetDiv" width =100 height=100>
    Who was the third guest?
  </div>

</body>

</html>
```

You can see this application at work in Figure 6-2, where it is correctly identifying Ed Norton as the third guest. Voilà.

So far so good—except that there's a problem. This example as written will work in Internet Explorer, but not in Firefox. What's wrong?

Figure 6-2   party.html at work

Try This   Find the Second Guest

Want to find the second guest's name? All you need to do is navigate to that person's <person> element. You can do that by navigating backward one sibling from the last <person> element, like this:

```
function displayGuest (xmldoc)
{
  var partiesNode, partyNode, peopleNode;
  var firstNameNode, lastNameNode, displayText;

  partiesNode = xmldoc.documentElement;
  partyNode = partiesNode.firstChild;
  peopleNode = partyNode.lastChild;
  personNode = peopleNode.lastChild;
  personNode = personNode.previousSibling;
  firstNameNode = personNode.firstChild;
  lastNameNode = firstNameNode.nextSibling;

  displayText = "The second guest was " +
    firstNameNode.firstChild.nodeValue + ' '
    + lastNameNode.firstChild.nodeValue;

  var target = document.getElementById("targetDiv");
  target.innerHTML=displayText;
}
```

Give this a try and confirm that you do get the second guest's name. And then try to get the first person's name.

Handling Whitespace in Firefox

When it comes to whitespace, Firefox by default acts differently than Internet Explorer. In Firefox, whitespace that you use to indent the elements in your XML counts as text nodes. So when navigating, we have to take all the whitespace nodes into account in Firefox, by default. For example, suppose we have an object corresponding to the <parties> element, say partiesNode:

```xml
<?xml version="1.0"?>
<parties>
    <party type="winter">
        <party_title>Snow Day</party_title>
        <party_number>63</party_number>
        <subject>No school today!</subject>
        <date>2/2/2009</date>
        <people>
            <person attendance="present">
                <first_name>Ralph</first_name>
                <last_name>Kramden</last_name>
            <person attendance="absent">
            </person>
                <first_name>Alice</first_name>
                <last_name>Kramden</last_name>
            </person>
            <person attendance="present">
                <first_name>Ed</first_name>
                <last_name>Norton</last_name>
            </person>
        </people>
    </party>
</parties>
```

What if we want to navigate to the <party> element? You might think that partiesNode .firstChild would do the trick, but not here. The expression partiesNode.firstChild would take you to the first child of the <parties> element node, and in Firefox, that's the text node used to indent the <party> element:

```xml
<?xml version="1.0"?>
<parties>
xxxx<party type="winter">
        <party_title>Snow Day</party_title>
        <party_number>63</party_number>
            .
            .
            .
```

So to get to the <party> element, you actually have to get to the text node's next sibling. That means that the correct JavaScript is partyNode = partiesNode.firstChild.nextSibling:

```
<?xml version="1.0"?>
<parties>
xxxx<party type="winter">
        <party_title>Snow Day</party_title>
        <party_number>63</party_number>
    .

    .

    .
```

Similarly, to get to the <party_title> element node, you'd use partyNode.firstChild .nextSibling to skip over the indentation whitespace text node:

```
<?xml version="1.0"?>
<parties>
    <party type="winter">
        <party_title>Snow Day</party_title>
        <party_number>63</party_number>
    .

    .

    .
```

So you can use the nextSibling and previousSibling properties to navigate over whitespace text nodes, but it's a pain. Here's what the displayGuest function turns into when you take into account the default whitespace handling in Firefox:

```
function displayGuest(xmldoc)
{
  var partiesNode, partyNode, peopleNode;
  var personNode, firstNameNode, lastNameNode, displayText;

  partiesNode = xmldoc.documentElement;
  partyNode = partiesNode.firstChild.nextSibling;
  peopleNode = partyNode.lastChild.previousSibling;
  personNode = peopleNode.firstChild.nextSibling
     .nextSibling.nextSibling.nextSibling.nextSibling;
  firstNameNode = personNode.firstChild.nextSibling;
  lastNameNode = firstNameNode.nextSibling.nextSibling;

  displayText = "The third guest is: " +
     firstNameNode.firstChild.nodeValue + ' '
     + lastNameNode.firstChild.nodeValue;

  var target = document.getElementById("targetDiv");
     target.innerHTML=displayText;
}
```

This looks like a mess—it's bad enough having to navigate from element to element, but now we have to navigate over text nodes as well? Isn't there a better way?

Handling Cross-Browser Whitespace

There is a better way—for example, you can strip out indentation whitespace before Firefox gets its hands on it. To do that, we might write a JavaScript function named removeWhitespace, which is passed a JavaScript XML document object:

```
function removeWhitespace(xml)
{
    .
    .
    .
}
```

We can set up a loop over all nodes in the XML document object by looping over all child nodes:

```
function removeWhitespace(xml)
{
  var loopIndex;

  for (loopIndex = 0; loopIndex < xml.childNodes.length;
    loopIndex++) {
      .
      .
      .
    }
  }
}
```

And we get the current node in the loop from the childNodes property, which holds an array of child nodes:

```
function removeWhitespace(xml)
{
  var loopIndex;

  for (loopIndex = 0; loopIndex < xml.childNodes.length;
    loopIndex++) {

    var currentNode = xml.childNodes[loopIndex];
      .
      .
      .
    }
}
```

If the current node is an element node, which we can check by seeing if its nodeType property equals 1 (see Table 6-1), it might have child nodes—and we've got to remove the whitespace from those child nodes as well, so we pass the current node to the removeWhitespace function again:

```
function removeWhitespace(xml)
{
  var loopIndex;

  for (loopIndex = 0; loopIndex < xml.childNodes.length;
    loopIndex++) {

  var currentNode = xml.childNodes[loopIndex];

  if (currentNode.nodeType == 1) {
    removeWhitespace(currentNode);
  }
    .
    .
    .
  }
}
```

Ask the Expert

Q: **Is calling removeWhitespace from inside that function an unusual practice?**

A: Calling a function from inside that function is called *recursion*, and JavaScript supports recursion. It's a legal technique, and, as you can see, it's a powerful one.

In this case, we use recursion to be able to loop over all the nodes in an XML document, no matter what the structure of that document. Fifteen nested levels of elements? No problem—removeWhitespace will handle it by operating at each level, and calling itself to handle the child nodes on the current node.

Now that we've eliminated element nodes, we have a candidate indentation whitespace node of the kind we want to remove. How do we check if it's removable whitespace? We can remove any text node that is pure whitespace—that is, only spaces. So how do we check if the current node is a text node that consists of only spaces?

Text nodes have the nodeType property value set to 3, so we want to check that for sure. We can also use a *regular expression* to check if the text node contains all spaces. Regular expressions let you test the contents of text strings, and JavaScript supports regular expressions with the string test method. The regular expression we'll test against is ^\s+$, which, translated, says that to match, the text node must contain one or more spaces (that's the \s+ part)—and nothing else from start (that's the ^ character) to finish (that's the $ character). Here's how we test for pure whitespace nodes:

```
function removeWhitespace(xml)
{
  var loopIndex;

  for (loopIndex = 0; loopIndex < xml.childNodes.length;
    loopIndex++) {

    var currentNode = xml.childNodes[loopIndex];

    if (currentNode.nodeType == 1) {
      removeWhitespace(currentNode);
    }

    if (((/^\s+$/.test(currentNode.nodeValue))) &&
      (currentNode.nodeType == 3)) {
        .
        .
        .
    }
  }
}
```

If the if statement's condition is satisfied, you know you have a text node that's pure whitespace, and should be removed. So how the heck do you remove a node from a JavaScript XML document? You do that with the XML document object's removeChild method. All you need to do is pass that method the node object you want to have removed. That means you can remove a whitespace node like this:

```
function removeWhitespace(xml)
{
  var loopIndex;
```

Regular Expressions

Are regular expressions leaving you reeling? You won't need to learn them to work with this book, or JavaScript, or XML, but they are useful. They have a syntax all their own, and it's not particularly easy to master. You can find out all about regular expressions and how to test strings with them (you can test if text is in the form of phone numbers or social security numbers, in all uppercase letters, or in any of a thousand other formats) at http://perldoc. perl.org/perlre.html.

```
    for (loopIndex = 0; loopIndex < xml.childNodes.length;
      loopIndex++) {

    var currentNode = xml.childNodes[loopIndex];

    if (currentNode.nodeType == 1) {
      removeWhitespace(currentNode);
    }

    if (((/^\s+$/.test(currentNode.nodeValue))) &&
      (currentNode.nodeType == 3)) {
        xml.removeChild(xml.childNodes[loopIndex--]);
    }
  }
}
```

Presto, we're done. All that remains is to make sure to call removeWhitspace if we're operating in Firefox, which we can check through a variable named firefoxFlag. If firefoxFlag is set to true, we're operating in Firefox, in which case we call removeWhitespace. Here's the final version of party.html that does just this:

```
<html>
  <head>

    <title>Retrieving the Third Guest From party.xml</title>

    <script language = "javascript">

    function getData()
    {
      var firefoxFlag = false;
      var XMLHttpRequestObject = false;

      if (window.XMLHttpRequest) {
        XMLHttpRequestObject = new XMLHttpRequest();
        XMLHttpRequestObject.overrideMimeType("text/xml");
        firefoxFlag = true;
      } else if (window.ActiveXObject) {
        XMLHttpRequestObject = new
          ActiveXObject("Microsoft.XMLHTTP");
      }

      if(XMLHttpRequestObject) {
        XMLHttpRequestObject.open("GET", "party.xml", true);

        XMLHttpRequestObject.onreadystatechange = function()
        {
          if (XMLHttpRequestObject.readyState == 4 &&
```

```
              XMLHttpRequestObject.status == 200) {
         var xmlDocument = XMLHttpRequestObject.responseXML;
         if(firefoxFlag){
           removeWhitespace(xmlDocument);
         }
         displayGuest(xmlDocument);
         }
      }

    XMLHttpRequestObject.send(null);
  }
}

function displayGuest (xmldoc)
{
  var partiesNode, partyNode, peopleNode;
  var firstNameNode, lastNameNode, displayText;

  partiesNode = xmldoc.documentElement;
  partyNode = partiesNode.firstChild;
  peopleNode = partyNode.lastChild;
  personNode = peopleNode.lastChild;
  firstNameNode = personNode.firstChild;
  lastNameNode = firstNameNode.nextSibling;

  displayText = "The third guest was " +
    firstNameNode.firstChild.nodeValue + ' '
    + lastNameNode.firstChild.nodeValue;

  var target = document.getElementById("targetDiv");
  target.innerHTML=displayText;
}

function removeWhitespace(xml)
{
  var loopIndex;

  for (loopIndex = 0; loopIndex < xml.childNodes.length;
    loopIndex++) {

    var currentNode = xml.childNodes[loopIndex];

    if (currentNode.nodeType == 1) {
      removeWhitespace(currentNode);
    }

    if ((((/^\s+$/.test(currentNode.nodeValue))) &&
      (currentNode.nodeType == 3)) {
```

```
                xml.removeChild(xml.childNodes[loopIndex--]);
            }
        }
    }
</script>

</head>

<body>

    <h1>Retrieving the Third Guest From party.xml</h1>

    <form>
      <input type = "button" value = "Get the third guest"
        onclick = "getData()">
    </form>

    <div id="targetDiv" width =100 height=100>
      Who was the third guest?
    </div>

</body>

</html>
```

The results are displayed in Figure 6-3 in Firefox—now party.html works in Firefox as well as in Internet Explorer. Cool.

As you can see, navigating from element to element using methods like firstChild and lastChild works, but it's awkward, and you have to know the exact structure of the XML document. One variation from the normal XML structure of your XML document and the whole application will fail.

Figure 6-3   party.html at work in Firefox

So is there a better way of locating and extracting your data from an XML document downloaded with Ajax? There is.

Accessing XML Data Directly

You can actually search XML documents for just the data you're looking for by using the XML document object's getElementsByTagName method, which returns an array of XML element nodes.

For example, to find the third guest's first and last names, you only need to search for all <first_name> and <last_name> elements, and extract the necessary text from the third of each of these:

```
<?xml version="1.0"?>
<parties>
    <party type="winter">
        <party_title>Snow Day</party_title>
        <party_number>63</party_number>
        <subject>No school today!</subject>
        <date>2/2/2009</date>
        <people>
            <person attendance="present">
                <first_name>Ralph</first_name>
                <last_name>Kramden</last_name>
            <person attendance="absent">
            </person>
                <first_name>Alice</first_name>
                <last_name>Kramden</last_name>
            </person>
            <person attendance="present">
                <first_name>Ed</first_name>
                <last_name>Norton</last_name>
            </person>
        </people>
    </party>
</parties>
```

We can perform this search in a new Ajax application, party2.html, based on our previous example, party.html. Here, however, we can simply modify the displayGuest function to search for <first_name> and <last_name> elements:

```
function displayGuest (xmldoc)
{
  firstnamenodes = xmldoc.getElementsByTagName("first_name");
  lastnamenodes = xmldoc.getElementsByTagName("last_name");
  .
  .
  .
}
```

After we have an array of <first_name> and <last_name> elements, we can use the third element in each array (which has array index 2, since array indexes start at 0) to locate the name we're looking for. It looks like this (in party2.html):

```html
<html>
  <head>

    <title>Accessing XML Data Directly</title>

    <script language = "javascript">

      function getData()
      {
        var XMLHttpRequestObject = false;

        if (window.XMLHttpRequest) {
          XMLHttpRequestObject = new XMLHttpRequest();
          XMLHttpRequestObject.overrideMimeType("text/xml");
        } else if (window.ActiveXObject) {
          XMLHttpRequestObject = new
            ActiveXObject("Microsoft.XMLHTTP");
        }

        if(XMLHttpRequestObject) {
          XMLHttpRequestObject.open("GET", "party.xml", true);

          XMLHttpRequestObject.onreadystatechange = function()
          {
            if (XMLHttpRequestObject.readyState == 4 &&
              XMLHttpRequestObject.status == 200) {
            var xmlDocument = XMLHttpRequestObject.responseXML;
            displayGuest(xmlDocument);
            }
          }

          XMLHttpRequestObject.send(null);
        }
      }

      function displayGuest (xmldoc)
      {
        firstnamenodes = xmldoc.getElementsByTagName("first_name");
        lastnamenodes = xmldoc.getElementsByTagName("last_name");

        var displayText = "The third guest was: " +
          firstnamenodes[2].firstChild.nodeValue + ' '
          + lastnamenodes[2].firstChild.nodeValue;
```

```
          var target = document.getElementById("targetDiv");
          target.innerHTML=displayText;
        }

    </script>

  </head>

  <body>

    <h1>Accessing XML Data Directly</h1>

    <form>
      <input type = "button" value = "Get the third guest"
        onclick = "getData()">
    </form>

    <div id="targetDiv" width =100 height=100>
      Who was the third guest?
    </div>

  </body>

</html>
```

You can see the results in Figure 6-4, where party2.html has correctly identified the third guest. That was easy—no fuss, no muss.

Okay, we've been able to extract data from XML elements, but what about XML attributes? For example, what if you want to read the value of the attendance attribute of the third guest at the party, to see whether they were present or absent?

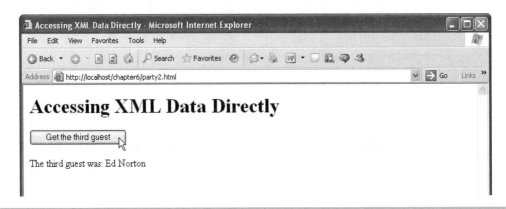

Figure 6-4   party2.html at work

```
<?xml version="1.0"?>
<parties>
    <party type="winter">
        <party_title>Snow Day</party_title>
        <party_number>63</party_number>
        <subject>No school today!</subject>
        <date>2/2/2009</date>
        <people>
            <person attendance="present">
                <first_name>Ralph</first_name>
                <last_name>Kramden</last_name>
            <person attendance="absent">
            </person>
                <first_name>Alice</first_name>
                <last_name>Kramden</last_name>
            </person>
            <person attendance="present">
                <first_name>Ed</first_name>
                <last_name>Norton</last_name>
            </person>
        </people>
    </party>
</parties>
```

You can get an array of an element's attributes with an element node's attributes property, which looks like this in a new example, attributes.html:

```
function displayGuest  (xmldoc)
{
  var partiesNode, partyNode, peopleNode;
  var firstNameNode, lastNameNode, displayText;

  partiesNode = xmldoc.documentElement;
  partyNode = partiesNode.firstChild;
  peopleNode = partyNode.lastChild;
  personNode = peopleNode.lastChild;
  firstNameNode = personNode.firstChild;
  lastNameNode = firstNameNode.nextSibling;
  attributes = personNode.attributes
     .
     .
     .

}
```

Actually, the attributes variable doesn't hold an array—technically, it's a *named node map*. And that's helpful, because named node map objects support a method called getNamedItem, to which you can pass the name of the attribute you want to get. The getNamedItem method will return an object corresponding to that attribute, and you can recover the value of the attribute with the object's nodeValue property.

In other words, it's easy to read attributes; here's how we read the third guest's attendance attribute (in attributes.html):

```html
<html>
  <head>

    <title>Accessing Data in XML Attributes</title>

    <script language = "javascript">

      function getData()
      {
        var mozillaFlag = false;
        var XMLHttpRequestObject = false;

        if (window.XMLHttpRequest) {
          XMLHttpRequestObject = new XMLHttpRequest();
          XMLHttpRequestObject.overrideMimeType("text/xml");
          mozillaFlag = true;
        } else if (window.ActiveXObject) {
          XMLHttpRequestObject = new
            ActiveXObject("Microsoft.XMLHTTP");
        }

        if(XMLHttpRequestObject) {
          XMLHttpRequestObject.open("GET", "party.xml", true);

          XMLHttpRequestObject.onreadystatechange = function()
          {
            if (XMLHttpRequestObject.readyState == 4 &&
              XMLHttpRequestObject.status == 200) {
            var xmlDocument = XMLHttpRequestObject.responseXML;
            if(mozillaFlag){
              removeWhitespace(xmlDocument);
            }
            displayGuest (xmlDocument);
            }
          }

          XMLHttpRequestObject.send(null);
        }
      }

      function displayGuest  (xmldoc)
      {
        var partiesNode, partyNode, peopleNode;
        var firstNameNode, lastNameNode, displayText;

        partiesNode = xmldoc.documentElement;
        partyNode = partiesNode.firstChild;
        peopleNode = partyNode.lastChild;
        personNode = peopleNode.lastChild;
```

```
        firstNameNode = personNode.firstChild;
        lastNameNode = firstNameNode.nextSibling;
        attributes = personNode.attributes
        attendancePerson = attributes.getNamedItem("attendance");

        var displayText = firstNameNode.firstChild.nodeValue
          + ' ' + lastNameNode.firstChild.nodeValue
          + " was " + attendancePerson.nodeValue;


      var target = document.getElementById("targetDiv");
      target.innerHTML=displayText;
    }

    function removeWhitespace(xml)
    {
      var loopIndex;

      for (loopIndex = 0; loopIndex < xml.childNodes.length;
        loopIndex++) {

        var currentNode = xml.childNodes[loopIndex];

        if (currentNode.nodeType == 1) {
          removeWhitespace(currentNode);
        }

        if (((/^\s+$/.test(currentNode.nodeValue))) &&
          (currentNode.nodeType == 3)) {
            xml.removeChild(xml.childNodes[loopIndex--]);
        }
      }
    }
  </script>

</head>

<body>

  <h1>Accessing Data in XML Attributes</h1>

  <form>
    <input type = "button" value = "Get the third guest's attendance"
      onclick = "getData()">
  </form>

  <div id="targetDiv" width =100 height=100>
    Was the third guest present?
  </div>

</body>

</html>
```

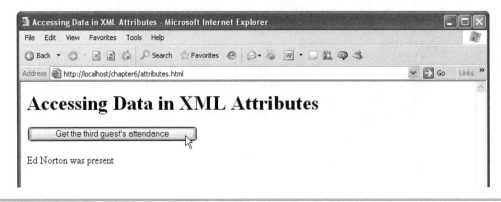

Figure 6-5 Reading XML attribute values

You can see attributes.html at work in Figure 6-5, where it's reporting that the third guest, Ed Norton, was present. Excellent.

Validating Your XML

The final XML topic for this chapter is how to validate your XML. As discussed earlier in this chapter, you can specify the syntax of your XML documents and test to see whether or not it adheres to your rules. There are two methods of specifying an XML document's syntax: with XML Schema, and with a DTD. Unfortunately, support for schema is shaky to nonexistent in browsers—even Internet Explorer's support for schema is very shaky. So in this example, we'll stick with the older form of specifying XML syntax, DTDs.

We saw what the DTD for party.xml looked like earlier in this chapter, and we'll call the document that includes the DTD for party.xml, partydtd.xml:

```
<?xml version="1.0"?>
<!DOCTYPE parties [
<!ELEMENT parties (party*)>
<!ELEMENT party (party_title, party_number, subject, date, people*)>
<!ELEMENT party_title (#PCDATA)>
<!ELEMENT party_number (#PCDATA)>
<!ELEMENT subject (#PCDATA)>
<!ELEMENT date (#PCDATA)>
<!ELEMENT first_name (#PCDATA)>
<!ELEMENT last_name (#PCDATA)>
<!ELEMENT people (person*)>
<!ELEMENT person (first_name,last_name)>
<!ATTLIST party
    type CDATA #IMPLIED>
<!ATTLIST person
    attendance CDATA #IMPLIED>
]>
```

```
<parties>
    <party type="winter">
        <party_title>Snow Day</party_title>
        <party_number>63</party_number>
        <subject>No school today!</subject>
        <data>2/2/2009</data>
        <people>
            <person attendance="present">
                <first_name>Ralph</first_name>
                <last_name>Kramden</last_name>
            </person>
            <person attendance="absent">
                <first_name>Alice</first_name>
                <last_name>Kramden</last_name>
            </person>
            <person attendance="present">
                <first_name>Ed</first_name>
                <last_name>Norton</last_name>
            </person>
        </people>
    </party>
</parties>
```

Note that there's an error here—this document uses a <data> element, not a <date> element, and you can catch that error in browsers like Internet Explorer. To check the document's validity, you can create an XML parser object of the MSXML2.DOMDocument type in Internet Explorer, which we do in our getData function:

```
function getData()
{
  var XMLHttpRequestObject = false;

  XMLHttpRequestObject = new
    ActiveXObject("Microsoft.XMLHTTP");

  if(XMLHttpRequestObject) {
    XMLHttpRequestObject.open("GET", "partydtd.xml?b=5", true);

    XMLHttpRequestObject.onreadystatechange = function()
    {
      if (XMLHttpRequestObject.readyState == 4 &&
        XMLHttpRequestObject.status == 200) {
        var xmlDocument = XMLHttpRequestObject.responseXML;

        var parser = new ActiveXObject("MSXML2.DOMDocument");
        parser.validateOnParse = true;
          .
          .
          .
  }
```

Note that you also must set the parser object's validateOnParse property to true to make it actually parse XML. Now you can pass the XML you've downloaded to the parser using its load method like this:

```
function getData()
{
  var XMLHttpRequestObject = false;

  XMLHttpRequestObject = new
    ActiveXObject("Microsoft.XMLHTTP");

  if(XMLHttpRequestObject) {
    XMLHttpRequestObject.open("GET", "partydtd.xml?b=5", true);

    XMLHttpRequestObject.onreadystatechange = function()
    {
      if (XMLHttpRequestObject.readyState == 4 &&
        XMLHttpRequestObject.status == 200) {
        var xmlDocument = XMLHttpRequestObject.responseXML;

        var parser = new ActiveXObject("MSXML2.DOMDocument");
        parser.validateOnParse = true;
        parser.load(XMLHttpRequestObject.responseXML);
          .
          .
          .

}
```

If the parser found an error, the parser.parseError.errorCode property will be non-zero, and you can report the error like this in a new example (validation.html):

```
<html>
  <head>

    <title>Validating an XML Document</title>

    <script language = "javascript">

      function getData()
      {
        var XMLHttpRequestObject = false;

        XMLHttpRequestObject = new
          ActiveXObject("Microsoft.XMLHTTP");

        if(XMLHttpRequestObject) {
          XMLHttpRequestObject.open("GET", "partydtd.xml?b=5", true);

          XMLHttpRequestObject.onreadystatechange = function()
          {
            if (XMLHttpRequestObject.readyState == 4 &&
              XMLHttpRequestObject.status == 200) {
              var xmlDocument = XMLHttpRequestObject.responseXML;
```

```
              var parser = new ActiveXObject("MSXML2.DOMDocument");
              parser.validateOnParse = true;
              parser.load(XMLHttpRequestObject.responseXML);
              var target = document.getElementById("targetDiv");

              if (parser.parseError.errorCode != 0) {
                target.innerText = "Error in " +
                  parser.parseError.url +
                  " line " + parser.parseError.line +
                  " position " + parser.parseError.linepos +
                  ".\nError source: " + parser.parseError.srcText +
                  "\n" + parser.parseError.reason +
                  "\n" +  "Error: " +
                  parser.parseError.errorCode;
              }
              else {

                displayGuest(xmlDocument);
              }
            }
          }

        XMLHttpRequestObject.send(null);
      }
    }

    function displayGuest(xmldoc)
    {
      var partiesNode, partyNode, peopleNode;
      var firstNameNode, lastNameNode, displayText;

      partiesNode = xmldoc.documentElement;
      partyNode = partiesNode.firstChild;
      peopleNode = partyNode.lastChild;
      personNode = peopleNode.lastChild;
      firstNameNode = personNode.firstChild;
      lastNameNode = firstNameNode.nextSibling;

      displayText = "The third guest was " +
        firstNameNode.firstChild.nodeValue + ' '
        + lastNameNode.firstChild.nodeValue;

      var target = document.getElementById("targetDiv");
      target.innerHTML=displayText;
    }

  </script>

</head>

<body>
```

```
<h1>Validating an XML Document</h1>

<form>
  <input type = "button" value = "Get the third guest"
    onclick = "getData()">
</form>

<div id="targetDiv" width =100 height=100>
  Your data will appear here.
</div>

</body>

</html>
```

You can see that partydtd.xml fails the validation process because the parser found a <data> element when it was expecting a <date> element, as shown in Figure 6-6.

You now have a good foundation in working with XML in Ajax.

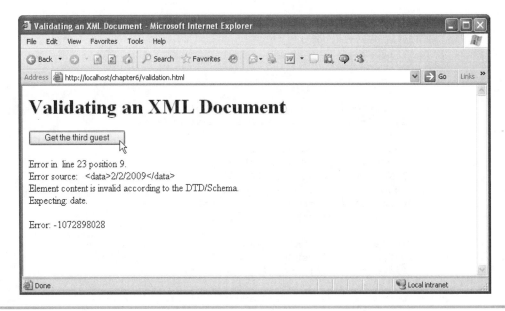

Figure 6-6 Validating an XML document

Chapter 7

Working with Cascading Style Sheets with Ajax

Key Skills & Concepts

- Getting text noticed with CSS

- Styling fonts with CSS

- Styling colors with CSS

- Setting absolute positions using CSS

- Creating a full Ajax-enabled CSS-driven menu system

As you've already seen in the previous chapters, the primary reason to use Ajax is that it enables web pages to be updated without requiring a page refresh, which makes the page update rather seamless to the viewer. An important consideration when using this technique is how you present the data downloaded from the server. So far, you've been presenting the downloaded data simply by overwriting a <div> element. As this chapter explains, you have many more options available in how you present that new data, enabling you to draw the reader's attention to the changes.

Because the way you present your downloaded data is such a big part of Ajax applications, that's the subject of this chapter. For example, a frequent question among professional Ajax developers is, will the user notice the download when it appears in the page? In pages that present tables of data, where you're updating only one or two items, that can be an issue. As you'll see, one way of handling this issue is to display downloaded text with a flash of color.

You'll also see that you don't have to display downloaded text in simple <div> elements. You can display such data anywhere in a page, as you're going to see while creating a pop-up menu system with text that's downloaded interactively with Ajax, allowing the menu items to be updated in real time.

In this chapter, updating the page with Ajax-downloaded data is going to take place using Cascading Style Sheets, CSS. Familiarity with CSS is essential for the Ajax developer, and you're going to get a good introduction to the topic in this chapter. CSS is one of the most important Ajax topics because updating web pages is so important in Ajax.

CSS is a formal specification for arranging and styling items in web pages. You can set data's font, color, appearance, visibility, and placement using CSS. You're going to get a good CSS foundation in this chapter, but for full, complete details on CSS, see the CSS specification at www.w3.org/TR/CSS21/.

Drawing the User's Attention to Downloaded Text

One of the main issues of Ajax applications is also its main advantage—there's no page refresh when you download data. That's great, but it can also mean the user misses data updates, especially in pages with lots of content.

There are various ways to address this issue, but the easiest solution is simply to make newly displayed data stand out in some way. For example, you can enlarge that text, or color it momentarily, when it's newly displayed. This section presents an example, attentionGetter .html, which displays text in red for half a second after it is downloaded. After that time, the newly downloaded text goes back to black. Making newly downloaded data flash in this way is a great way to get that data noticed in Ajax applications.

We can create this example with a combination of CSS and JavaScript. We start attentionGetter.html with a button that, when clicked, calls a function named getData, asking that function to download a file named message.txt and display its contents in a <div> element with the ID targetDiv:

```
<body>

  <H1>Getting the user's attention</H1>

  <form>
    <input type = "button" value = "Get the text"
      onclick = "getData('message.txt', 'targetDiv')">
  </form>

  <div id="targetDiv">
    <p>The fetched data will go here.</p>
  </div>

</body>
```

In the getData function, we create an XMLHttpRequest object:

```
<script language = "javascript">
  function getData(dataSource, divID)
  {
    var XMLHttpRequestObject = false;

    if (window.XMLHttpRequest) {
      XMLHttpRequestObject = new XMLHttpRequest();
    } else if (window.ActiveXObject) {
      XMLHttpRequestObject = new
        ActiveXObject("Microsoft.XMLHTTP");
    }
    .
    .
    .
  }
```

If we were successful in creating an XMLHttpRequest object, we open it, configuring it to use the GET method:

```
<script language = "javascript">
  function getData(dataSource, divID)
  {
    var XMLHttpRequestObject = false;

    if (window.XMLHttpRequest) {
      XMLHttpRequestObject = new XMLHttpRequest();
    } else if (window.ActiveXObject) {
      XMLHttpRequestObject = new
        ActiveXObject("Microsoft.XMLHTTP");
    }

    if(XMLHttpRequestObject) {
      XMLHttpRequestObject.open("GET", dataSource);
        .
        .
        .
    }
  }
```

And we set up an anonymous JavaScript function to handle the download, like this:

```
<script language = "javascript">
  function getData(dataSource, divID)
  {
    var XMLHttpRequestObject = false;

    if (window.XMLHttpRequest) {
      XMLHttpRequestObject = new XMLHttpRequest();
    } else if (window.ActiveXObject) {
      XMLHttpRequestObject = new
        ActiveXObject("Microsoft.XMLHTTP");
    }

    if(XMLHttpRequestObject) {
      XMLHttpRequestObject.open("GET", dataSource);

      XMLHttpRequestObject.onreadystatechange = function()
      {
        if (XMLHttpRequestObject.readyState == 4 &&
          XMLHttpRequestObject.status == 200) {
            .
            .
            .
        }

      }
  }
```

When the text is downloaded, we want to display it in red initially. You can style the <div> element to display its text in red by using the color property of the <div> element's built-in style object. The style object gives you access to a visible element's CSS styles via JavaScript.

You style items in CSS by setting CSS *properties*. The following are the color-related properties:

- **color**   Sets the foreground color. You set it to an HTML color (like #FFFFFF).

- **background-color**   Sets the background color. Again, you set it to an HTML color.

You set colors using HTML color values—just as in web pages—like this: rrggbb, where rr is the hexadecimal value (00 up to FF) of the red component, gg is the green component, and bb is the blue component. (This is essential HTML to know. If you're not familiar with setting colors in HTML, do an online search for "HTML color values.")

So, for example, to set the text color of a <div> element with the ID targetDiv to red (which, in HTML terms, is "#FF0000"), you could do this in our example, attentionGetter .html, as follows:

```
<script language = "javascript">
  function getData(dataSource, divID)
  {
    var XMLHttpRequestObject = false;

    if (window.XMLHttpRequest) {
      XMLHttpRequestObject = new XMLHttpRequest();
    } else if (window.ActiveXObject) {
      XMLHttpRequestObject = new
        ActiveXObject("Microsoft.XMLHTTP");
    }

    if(XMLHttpRequestObject) {
      var obj = document.getElementById("targetDiv");
      XMLHttpRequestObject.open("GET", dataSource);

      XMLHttpRequestObject.onreadystatechange = function()
      {
        if (XMLHttpRequestObject.readyState == 4 &&
          XMLHttpRequestObject.status == 200) {
          obj.style.color = "#FF0000";
            .
            .
            .

      }

    }
  }
```

That's the way you can access CSS style properties of visible elements in web pages—as, for example, obj.style.color. What if the CSS style property name has a hyphen in it, such as background-color? Hyphens aren't allowed in JavaScript variable names, so the convention is that you capitalize the letter following the hyphen, and then remove the hyphen. So, for example, if you wanted to set the <div> element's background color to red, how would you do it? You'd do it like this: obj.style.backgroundColor = "#FF0000".

Great, that allows you to set the foreground and background colors of HTML elements using CSS from JavaScript. Here's how we complete the getData function, displaying the downloaded text in red:

```
<script language = "javascript">
  function getData(dataSource, divID)
  {
      var XMLHttpRequestObject = false;

      if (window.XMLHttpRequest) {
        XMLHttpRequestObject = new XMLHttpRequest();
      } else if (window.ActiveXObject) {
        XMLHttpRequestObject = new
          ActiveXObject("Microsoft.XMLHTTP");
      }

      if(XMLHttpRequestObject) {
        var obj = document.getElementById("targetDiv");
        XMLHttpRequestObject.open("GET", dataSource);

        XMLHttpRequestObject.onreadystatechange = function()
        {
          if (XMLHttpRequestObject.readyState == 4 &&
            XMLHttpRequestObject.status == 200) {
              obj.style.color = "#FF0000";
              obj.innerHTML = XMLHttpRequestObject.responseText;
          }
        }

        XMLHttpRequestObject.send(null);
      }
  }
```

That displays the downloaded text in red, but we only want the downloaded text to flash red for a half second and then go back to black. So how the heck do we do that?

This is where JavaScript comes in. We can use the JavaScript setTimeout function to pass to JavaScript the name of another function and the amount of time (in milliseconds—that is, thousandths of a second) that we want to elapse before JavaScript calls that other function. So we can set up JavaScript to call another function named, say, attentionGetter, that would change the color of the text back to black after a half second (that is, 500 ms) like this:

```
<script language = "javascript">
  function getData(dataSource, divID)
  {
    var XMLHttpRequestObject = false;

    if (window.XMLHttpRequest) {
      XMLHttpRequestObject = new XMLHttpRequest();
    } else if (window.ActiveXObject) {
      XMLHttpRequestObject = new
        ActiveXObject("Microsoft.XMLHTTP");
    }

    if(XMLHttpRequestObject) {
      var obj = document.getElementById("targetDiv");
      XMLHttpRequestObject.open("GET", dataSource);

      XMLHttpRequestObject.onreadystatechange = function()
      {
        if (XMLHttpRequestObject.readyState == 4 &&
          XMLHttpRequestObject.status == 200) {
            obj.style.color = "#FF0000";
            obj.innerHTML = XMLHttpRequestObject.responseText;
            setTimeout(attentionGetter, 500);
        }
      }

      XMLHttpRequestObject.send(null);
    }
  }
</script>
```

And in the attentionGetter function, we just set the color of the text back to black (HTML color value "#000000"):

```
<script language = "javascript">
  function getData(dataSource, divID)
  {
    .
      .
        .
  }

  function attentionGetter()
  {
      var target = document.getElementById("targetDiv");
      target.style.color = "#000000";
  }
</script>
```

And that's it—the downloaded text originally appears in red, and then changes back to black after half a second. Here's the whole of attentionGetter.html:

```html
<html>
  <head>
    <title>Getting the user's attention</title>

    <script language = "javascript">
      function getData(dataSource, divID)
      {
        var XMLHttpRequestObject = false;

        if (window.XMLHttpRequest) {
          XMLHttpRequestObject = new XMLHttpRequest();
        } else if (window.ActiveXObject) {
          XMLHttpRequestObject = new
            ActiveXObject("Microsoft.XMLHTTP");
        }

        if(XMLHttpRequestObject) {
          var obj = document.getElementById("targetDiv");
          XMLHttpRequestObject.open("GET", dataSource);

          XMLHttpRequestObject.onreadystatechange = function()
          {
            if (XMLHttpRequestObject.readyState == 4 &&
              XMLHttpRequestObject.status == 200) {
                obj.style.color = "#FF0000";
                obj.innerHTML = XMLHttpRequestObject.responseText;
                setTimeout(attentionGetter, 500);
            }
          }

          XMLHttpRequestObject.send(null);
        }
      }

      function attentionGetter()
      {
        var target = document.getElementById("targetDiv");
        target.style.color = "#000000";
      }
    </script>
  </head>

  <body>
```

Figure 7-1   attentionGetter.html at work

```
<H1>Getting the user's attention</H1>

<form>
  <input type = "button" value = "Get the text"
    onclick = "getData('message.txt', 'targetDiv')">
</form>

<div id="targetDiv">
  <p>The fetched data will go here.</p>
</div>

  </body>
</html>
```

You can see this example at work in Figure 7-1, although the text appears in glorious black and white here because this book is not in color; to see the message displayed in red, you can download and try this example for yourself.

Cool. That's one way to make sure the user's attention is drawn to newly downloaded text. And there are other ways to style text using CSS, as you're about to see.

Styling Text Using CSS

Besides making newly downloaded text flash in color in a web page, you have your choice of other CSS effects to draw the user's attention to that text. For example, you could enlarge it temporarily, display it in bold, underline it, or use some other text style.

Property	Description
font-family	Specifies the actual font, like Arial or Helvetica. If you want to list alternative fonts in case the target computer is missing your first choice, specify them as a comma-separated list, such as {font-family: Arial, Helvetica}.
font-style	Specifies how the text is to be rendered. Set to normal, italic, or oblique.
font-weight	Refers to the boldness or lightness of the glyphs used to render the text, relative to other fonts in the same font family. Set to normal, bold, bolder, lighter, 100, 200, 300, 400, 500, 600, 700, 800, or 900.
line-height	Indicates the height given to each line.
font-size	Refers to the size of the font.
text-decoration	Underlines text. Set to none, underline, overline, line-through, or blink.
text-align	Centers text. Set to left, right, or center.

Table 7-1 CSS Style Properties

CSS has many different text styles that you can use to make newly downloaded text stand out. Table 7-1 lists and describes the most popular style properties.

Here's an example, textStyles.html, that puts these text properties to work. This example sets the styles for the <body> element of a web page (you've already seen how to set the styles for an individual element by ID, such as a <div> element, in JavaScript). In addition to JavaScript, you can set styles in a <style> element, which usually goes in the <head> element of a web page:

```
<html>
    <head>
        <title>
            Styling text with CSS
        </title>

        <style type="text/css">
            .
            .
            .
        </style>
    </head>
        .
        .
        .
    </html>
```

You set styles here for web page elements by using *style rules*, collections of style property and style value pairs separated by semicolons. For example, here's how you could set up a style rule for this <body> element, setting various style properties:

```
<html>
    <head>
        <title>
            Styling text with CSS
        </title>
        <style type="text/css">
            body {font-style: italic; font-weight: bold;
            font-size: 16pt; line-height: 12pt; font-family: arial,
            helvetica; text-align: center}
        </style>
    </head>
        .
        .
        .
</html>
```

This sets the font-style property of the <body> element to italic, the font-weight style property to bold, and so on. Now we can add some text to the <body> element:

```
<html>
    <head>
        <title>
            Styling text with CSS
        </title>
        <style type="text/css">
            body {font-style: italic; font-weight:
            bold; font-size: 16pt; line-height: 12pt; font-family:
            arial, helvetica; text-align: center}
        </style>
    </head>

    <body>
        <br>
        <h1>Styling text with CSS</h1>
        <br>
        This page displays text styled with CSS.
        .
        .
        .
    </body>
</html>
```

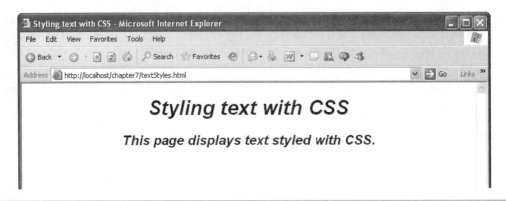

Figure 7-2 Styling a <body> element

You can see the results in Figure 7-2.

Now let's add a button that, when clicked, will underline the text. To underline text, you use the text-decoration style property, setting it to "underline". In JavaScript, that property becomes the textDecoration property, so we can have the button do its work like this (in textStyles.html):

```html
<html>
    <head>
        <title>
            Styling text with CSS
        </title>
        <style type="text/css">
            body {font-style: italic; font-weight: bold; font-size:
            16pt; line-height: 12pt; font-family: arial, helvetica;
            text-align: center}
        </style>
    </head>

    <body>
        <br>
        <h1>Styling text with CSS</h1>
        <br>
        This page displays text styled with CSS.

      <form>
        <input type = "button" value = "Underline the text"
          onclick = "body.style.textDecoration = 'underline'">
      </form>

    </body>
</html>
```

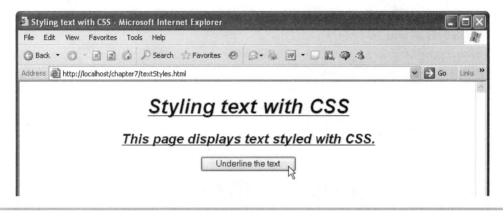

Figure 7-3 Underlining text in a <body> element

You can see this new button at work in Figure 7-3.
Here are the CSS style properties and their values in this example:

- font-style: italic

- font-weight: bold

- font-size: 16pt

- line-height: 12pt

- text-decoration: underline

- font-family: arial, helvetica

- text-align: center

What if you had several HTML elements of the same type (such as <div> or <p> elements) and wanted to style them all differently? In that case, you could give them different ID values, and create a style rule for each one using the ID value preceded by a sharp sign (#). For example, if you had a <div> element with the ID targetDiv, here's how you could style it to use 36-point font in the textStyles.html <style> element:

```
<html>
    <head>
        <title>
            Styling text with CSS
        </title>
        <style type="text/css">
            body {font-style: italic; font-weight: bold; font-size: 16pt;
line-height: 12pt; font-family: arial, helvetica; text-align: center}
            #targetDiv {font-size: 36pt}
```

Figure 7-4   Styling a <div> element

```
        </style>
    </head>

    <body>
        <br>
        <h1>Styling text with CSS</h1>
        <br>
        This page displays text styled with CSS.

      <form>
        <input type = "button" value = "Underline the text"
          onclick = "body.style.textDecoration = 'underline'">
      </form>

      <div id="targetDiv">Here is more text</div>
    </body>
</html>
```

You can see this new version of the page at work in Figure 7-4.

Try This   Change the Size of Text

Try changing the size of the text in the textStyles.html page to 48-point font when the user clicks the button. Here's how to do that:

```
<html>
    <head>
        <title>
            Styling text with CSS
```

```
    </title>
    <style type="text/css">
        body {font-style: italic; font-weight: bold; font-size:
        16pt; line-height: 12pt; font-family: arial, helvetica;
        text-align: center}
        #targetDiv {font-size: 36pt}
    </style>
</head>

<body>
    <br>
    <h1>Styling text with CSS</h1>
    <br>
    This page displays text styled with CSS.

  <form>
    <input type = "button" value = "Change the text size"
      onclick = "body.style.fontSize = '48pt'">
  </form>

    <div id="targetDiv">Here is more text</div>
</body>
</html>
```

Besides styling text, you can also style colors and backgrounds in Ajax-enabled pages.

Styling Colors and Backgrounds Using CSS

There are a number of CSS properties to set colors and backgrounds. Table 7-2 lists and describes the most popular color and background properties.

Property	Description
color	Sets the foreground color. Set to an HTML color (like #FFFFFF).
background-color	Sets the background color. Set to an HTML color.
background-image	Sets the background image. Set to an URL.
background-repeat	Specifies whether the background image should be tiled. Set to repeat, repeat-x, repeat-y, or no-repeat.
background-attachment	Specifies whether the background scrolls with the rest of the document. Set to scroll or fixed.
background-position	Sets the initial position of the background. Set to top, center, bottom, left, or right.

Table 7-2   CSS Color and Background Properties

Here's an example, letter.html, that styles a business letter's colors and background colors:

```
<html>
    <head>
        <title>
            Styling Foregrounds and Backgrounds
        </title>
    </head>

    <body style="background-color: #EEDDDD">

        <div align="left">
            Chief Web Designer
            <br>
            Pretty Pleasing Web Designs, Inc.
            <br>
            Los Angeles
        </div>

        <p>
            Dear you:
            <br>
            <br>
            <div align="center"
              style="color: #FF0000; background-color: #55FF55;
              font-weight: bold; font-size: 16pt">
            <br>
                What do you think of this style?
            <br>
            <br>
            </div>

            <div align="right">
                <br>
                <p>
                Chief Stylist
                <br>
                Dynamo CSS Stylers, Inc.
                <br>
                London
            </div>

    </body>
</html>
```

You can also add a button that, when clicked, can change the background of the <div> in the middle of the letter. You've seen that you can refer to elements such as the <body> element like body.style.backgroundColor—but how do you refer to a specific <div> element? You can use the getElementById method to get an object corresponding to that <div> element, as we did in the beginning of this chapter, but there's another way as well.

You can give the <div> element an ID value, and refer to that element in JavaScript simply using that ID value—no need to call the getElementById method. For example, if you give the <div> element the ID div1, you could refer to its background color like this: div1.style .backgroundColor.

Here's how we change the <div> element's background color to white when the user clicks a button:

```
<html>
    <head>
        <title>
            Styling Foregrounds and Backgrounds
        </title>
    </head>

    <body style="background-color: #EEDDDD">

        <div align="left">
            Chief Web Designer
            <br>
            Pretty Pleasing Web Designs, Inc.
            <br>
            Los Angeles
        </div>

        <p>
            Dear you:
            <br>
            <br>
            <div align="center" id="div1"
              style="color: #FF0000; background-color: #55FF55;
              font-weight: bold; font-size: 16pt">
            <br>
                What do you think of this style?
            <br>
            <br>
            </div>

            <div align="right">
                <br>
                <p>
                Chief Stylist
```

```
        <br>
        Dynamo CSS Stylers, Inc.
        <br>
        London
    </div>
    <center>
      <form>
        <input type = "button" value = "Change background color"
          onclick = "div1.style.backgroundColor = '#FFFFFF'">
      </form>
    </center>

    </body>
</html>
```

That's useful in Ajax applications when just making the text flash isn't enough—you want to make the change you've made in the web page really stand out by making the background of the element change color (particularly useful when you're dealing with cells in an HTML table).

You can see this example at work in Figure 7-5, where clicking the button has changed the color of the central <div> element to white. Nice.

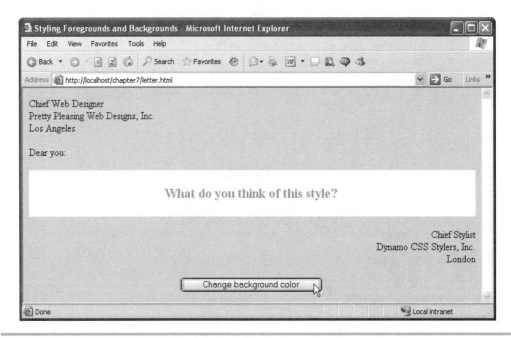

Figure 7-5 Setting a <div> element's background

Use Preassigned Colors

Besides letting you use color values to set colors (like '#FFCCEE'), modern browsers also support dozens of predefined color names like "green," "red," "ivory," "sand," "viridian," and more.

Try changing the background of the central <div> element in letter.html to coral instead of white. Here's the code:

```
<center>
  <form>
    <input type = "button" value = "Change background color"
      onclick = "div1.style.backgroundColor = 'coral'">
  </form>
</center>
```

Setting Element Location in Web Pages

A major use in Ajax for CSS is setting absolute positions of the elements in a web page, such as when you create pop-up menus, dialog boxes, drop-down auto-complete list boxes, and so on. Table 7-3 lists and describes the CSS properties you use when setting absolute positions.

NOTE

By default, the top, bottom, left, and right measurements are taken to be in pixels. You can append px to the end of these values to make sure the browser interprets the measurement as pixels, as in 50px.

Property	Description
position	Set to absolute for absolute positioning.
top	Offset of the top of the element on the screen.
bottom	Offset of the bottom of the element in the browser's client area.
left	Offset of the left edge of the element in the browser's client area.
right	Offset of the right edge of the element in the browser's client area.
z-order	Sets the stacking order of the item with respect to other elements.

Table 7-3   CSS Absolute Position Properties

Here's an example, location.html, that positions images in a web page. Each image will be stored in a <div> element, and we'll set the position of the <div> element. We'll start off by positioning image 1 (image01.jpg) with an HTML style attribute:

```html
<html>

    <head>
        <title>
            Using Absolute Positioning
        </title>
    </head>

    <body>

        <h1 align="center">
            Using Absolute Positioning
        </h1>

        <div style="position:absolute; left:40; top:60;" id="image01">
            <img src="image01.jpg" width="200" height="100">
            <br>
            Image 1
        </div>
            .
            .
            .

    </body>

</html>
```

Note that we're displaying both the image and a caption ("Image 1") in the <div> element, to which we've given the ID "image01". Note also that in order to position the image, we set the position style property to "absolute," and then set the location of the top-left point of the image with the top and left style properties—by default, these positions are measured in pixels.

And we can add the other two images as well:

```html
<html>

    <head>
        <title>
            Using Absolute Positioning
        </title>
    </head>

    <body>

        <h1 align="center">
            Using Absolute Positioning
        </h1>
```

```
<div style="position:absolute; left:40; top:60;" id="image01">
    <img src="image01.jpg" width="200" height="100">
    <br>
    Image 1
</div>

<div style="position:absolute; left:195; top:90;" id="image02">
    <img src="image02.jpg" width="200" height="100">
    <br>
    Image 2
</div>

<div style="position:absolute; left:350; top:120;" id="image03">
    <img src="image03.jpg" width="200" height="100">
    <br>
    Image 3
</div>
    .
    .
    .

</body>

</html>
```

And, just for fun, let's add a button that lets the user move one of the <div> elements containing an image—say image01—this way:

```
<html>

<head>
    <title>
        Using Absolute Positioning
    </title>
</head>

<body>

    <h1 align="center">
        Using Absolute Positioning
    </h1>

    <div style="position:absolute; left:40; top:60;" id="image01">
        <img src="image01.jpg" width="200" height="100">
        <br>
        Image 1
    </div>

    <div style="position:absolute; left:195; top:90;" id="image02">
        <img src="image02.jpg" width="200" height="100">
        <br>
        Image 2
    </div>
```

```
<div style="position:absolute; left:350; top:120;" id="image03">
    <img src="image03.jpg" width="200" height="100">
    <br>
    Image 3
</div>

<center>
  <form>
    <input type = "button" value = "Change location"
      style="position:absolute; left:220; top:260;"
      onclick = "image02.style.top = '150'">
  </form>
</center>

</body>
```

```
</html>
```

Note that we access the top position of the second div using its ID: image02.style.top. And note also that we position the button in the same way as we position the images, with absolute positioning.

You can see the results in Figure 7-6, where, as you can see, the images have positioned properly.

When you click the button, the second image moves, as you'd expect and as shown in Figure 7-7.

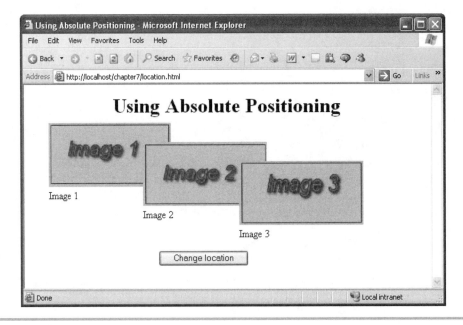

Figure 7-6   Positioning images

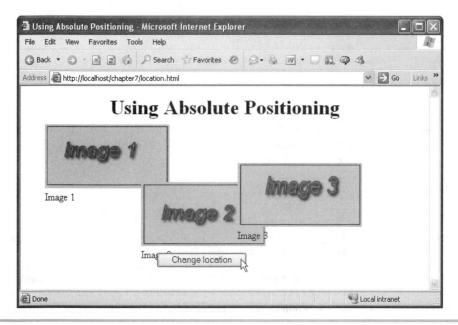

Figure 7-7   Positioning an image dynamically

Absolute positioning is exceptionally useful in Ajax applications, because you can place your new data anywhere you want in a page; no refresh needed.

Try This   Adding an Additional Button

Try adding an additional button that moves the third image. Here's one way of doing that:

```html
<html>

    <head>
        <title>
            Using Absolute Positioning
        </title>
    </head>

    <body>

        <h1 align="center">
            Using Absolute Positioning
        </h1>

        <div style="position:absolute; left:40; top:60;" id="image01">
            <img src="image01.jpg" width="200" height="100">
            <br>
            Image 1
```

(continued)

```
        </div>

        <div style="position:absolute; left:195; top:90;" id="image02">
            <img src="image02.jpg" width="200" height="100">
            <br>
            Image 2
        </div>

        <div style="position:absolute; left:350; top:120;" id="image03">
            <img src="image03.jpg" width="200" height="100">
            <br>
            Image 3
        </div>

        <center>
          <form>
            <input type = "button" value = "Change location of image 2"
              style="position:absolute; left:220; top:260;"
              onclick = "image02.style.top = '150'">
            <input type = "button" value = "Change location of image 3"
              style="position:absolute; left:220; top:290;"
              onclick = "image03.style.left = '400'">
          </form>
        </center>

    </body>

</html>
```

Setting the Stacking Order of Web Page Elements

You can also use the *stacking order* of web page elements to position them with respect to one another, and that's especially important when you're doing drag-and-drop in Ajax applications, to make sure the element being dragged slides over other elements in the page. An element with a high stacking order—as set by the style property z-index—will appear on top of elements lower in the stacking order.

Here's a quick example, stacker.html, that displays the three stacked images from the previous example:

```
<html>

    <head>
        <title>
            Using Stacking Order
        </title>
    </head>

    <body>
```

```
    <h1 align="center">
        Using Stacking Order
    </h1>

    <div style="position:absolute; left:40; top:60;" id="image01">
        <img src="image01.jpg" width="200" height="100">
        <br>
        Image 1
    </div>

    <div style="position:absolute; left:195; top:90;" id="image02">
        <img src="image02.jpg" width="200" height="100">
        <br>
        Image 2
    </div>

    <div style="position:absolute; left:350; top:120;" id="image03">
        <img src="image03.jpg" width="200" height="100">
        <br>
        Image 3
    </div>
        .
        .
        .

    </body>

</html>
```

Now let's add a button that reverses the stacking order by assigning a z-index of 300 to image01, 200 to image02, and 100 to image03:

```
<html>

    <head>
        <title>
            Using Stacking Order
        </title>
    </head>

    <body>

        <h1 align="center">
            Using Stacking Order
        </h1>

        <div style="position:absolute; left:40; top:60;" id="image01">
            <img src="image01.jpg" width="200" height="100">
            <br>
            Image 1
        </div>
```

```
<div style="position:absolute; left:195; top:90;" id="image02">
    <img src="image02.jpg" width="200" height="100">
    <br>
    Image 2
</div>

<div style="position:absolute; left:350; top:120;" id="image03">
    <img src="image03.jpg" width="200" height="100">
    <br>
    Image 3
</div>

<center>
  <form>
    <input type = "button" value = "Flip stacking order"
        style="position:absolute; left:200; top:260;"
        onclick = "image01.style.zIndex = '300';
        image02.style.zIndex = '200'; image03.style.zIndex =
        '100'">
  </form>
</center>

</body>

</html>
```

You can see the original stacking order in Figure 7-8.

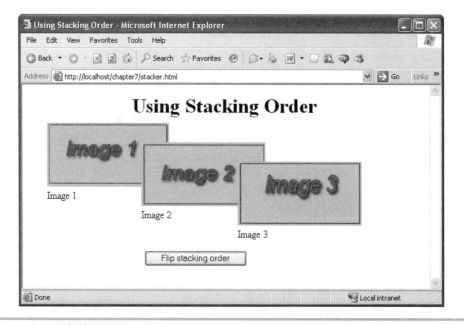

Figure 7-8   Stacked images

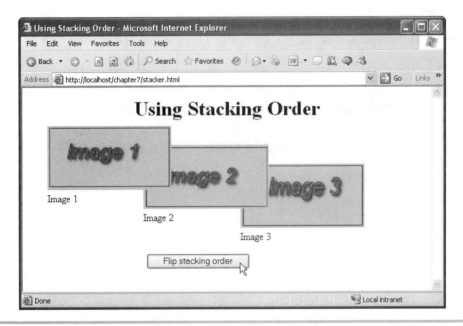

Figure 7-9   Setting stacking order

When you click the button, the stacking order reverses, as you can see in Figure 7-9.
Not bad.

A Complete Ajax CSS Example: menus.html

As the final CSS-intensive example in this chapter, we'll take a look at an Ajax-enabled CSS-driven menu system. This real-world example, menus.html, downloads menu items from a server and displays its menus using CSS. Because the menu items are downloaded in real time, you can update and change the menu items that the application displays. For example, if your menus are for a restaurant that serves ice cream and sandwiches, and the restaurant runs out of licorice ice cream, you can remove that item from the menu before the menu items are downloaded.

You can see menus.html at work in Figure 7-10, where the user is selecting chocolate ice cream from a pop-up menu whose items were just downloaded behind the scenes using Ajax.

When the user makes their selection, the application reports on that selection, as you see in Figure 7-11.

This is a full-scale Ajax application, and it's a long one, so don't feel that you have to catch all the details. The idea is to show an example of how you can use CSS to display Ajax-downloaded data in a unique way—in drop-down menus that respond to mouse clicks. You'll pick up some CSS and JavaScript skills in the process.

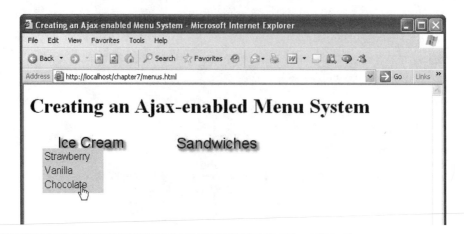

Figure 7-10 Selecting an item in a menu

Responding to the mouse makes up a significant amount of this example. When the user moves the mouse over an image ("Ice Cream" or "Sandwiches"), the corresponding menu needs to pop open. If the user moves the mouse away from the menu, the menu needs to close. If the user clicks an item in the menu to make a selection, the application must respond accordingly. On top of all that, the application has to respond to the mouse in both Internet Explorer and Firefox-type browsers, which handle the mouse in completely different ways.

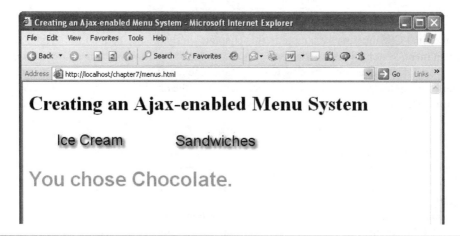

Figure 7-11 Reporting a menu item selection

First, in the <body> of the application, we'll set up the images ("Ice Cream" and "Sandwiches") that the user can move the mouse over to open the menus, and create the <div> elements that will hold the menus as well:

```
<body onclick = "hideMenu()" onmousemove = "checkMenu(event)">

  <H1>Creating an Ajax-enabled Menu System</H1>

    <img id = "image1" src="image1.jpg"
      style="left:30; top:50; width:200; height:40;">
    <div id = "menu1Div" style="position: absolute; left:30; top:100;
      width:100; height: 70; visibility:hidden;"><div></div></div>
    <img id = "image2" style="left:270; top:50; width:200;
      height:40;" src="image2.jpg">
    <div id = "menu2Div" style="position: absolute; left:270; top:100;
      width:100; height: 70; visibility:hidden;"><div></div></div>
    <br>
    <br>
    <div id = "targetDiv"></div>
</body>
```

Note that we connect the <body> element's onmousemove event to the JavaScript function checkMenu here (see the <body> tag above). This is the function that will respond to mouse movements, opening and closing menus as needed.

In the checkMenu function, we start by creating a new mouse event object with another function, mouseEventCreator:

```
function checkMenu(evt)
{
  var e = new mouseEventCreator(evt);
    .
    .
    .
}
```

The reason that we create our own mouse event object is that Internet Explorer and Firefox handle the mouse in totally different ways, and we need to merge those ways into one object to make our code easier. The mouse event we'll create will have these properties:

- **e** Holds the actual browser's event object (which contains information about the event, such as whether the mouse was being clicked, dragged, or just moved).

- **x** and **y** Hold the (x, y) location at which the event happened, in pixels.

- **target** Contains an object corresponding to the HTML element that was the target of the mouse event. For example, if the event was a mouse click, this property would hold an object corresponding to the HTML element that was clicked.

Here is mouseEventCreator, which we just used to create our unified mouse event object, taking into account the different ways that Internet Explorer and Firefox work with the mouse:

```
function mouseEventCreator(e)
{
  if(e) {
    this.e = e;
  } else {
    this.e = window.event;
  }

  if(e.pageX) {
    this.x = e.pageX;
  } else {
    this.x = e.clientX;
  }

  if(e.pageY) {
    this.y = e.pageY;
  } else {
    this.y = e.clientY;
  }

  if(e.target) {
    this.target = e.target;
  } else {
    this.target = e.srcElement;
  }
}
```

So now, back in checkMenu, we have a unified mouse event object that has the e, x, y, and target properties. In checkMenu, we'll check if the mouse moved over either image, in which case we'll have to download menu items and display the corresponding menu. We check that by examining the target property of the mouse event. If target holds an object matching either image, we download the menu items for the corresponding menu (that is, menu 1 or 2). We'll use a function named getData to download the menu items—calling getData(1) will download the items for the first menu (the Ice Cream menu) and calling getData(2) will download the items for the second menu (the Sandwiches menu). Here's what it looks like in checkMenu:

```
function checkMenu(evt)
{
  var e = new mouseEventCreator(evt);
  var imgObject;

  imgObject = document.getElementById("image1");

  if(e.target == imgObject){
    getData(1);
  }
```

```
    imgObject = document.getElementById("image2");

    if(e.target == imgObject){
      getData(2);
    }
        .
        .
        .

}
```

The whole job of the getData function is to download the menu items and to call a function, showMenu, that will display the requested menu. The menu items for the first menu are stored in the document items1.text:

```
Strawberry, Vanilla, Chocolate
```

The menu items for the second menu are stored in the document items2.text:

```
Turkey, Beef, Sardine
```

Here's what the getData function looks like—note that it just downloads the text stored in items1.txt or items2.txt using Ajax and passes that text to the showMenu function:

```
function getData(menuNumber)
{

  var XMLHttpRequestObject = false;

  if (window.XMLHttpRequest) {
    XMLHttpRequestObject = new XMLHttpRequest();
  } else if (window.ActiveXObject) {
    XMLHttpRequestObject = new
      ActiveXObject("Microsoft.XMLHTTP");
  }

  var itemsSource;

  if(menuNumber== 1){
    itemsSource = "items1.txt";
  } else {
    itemsSource = "items2.txt";
  }

  if(XMLHttpRequestObject) {
    XMLHttpRequestObject.open("GET", itemsSource);

    XMLHttpRequestObject.onreadystatechange = function()
    {
      if (XMLHttpRequestObject.readyState == 4 &&
```

```
            XMLHttpRequestObject.status == 200) {
                showMenu(menuNumber, XMLHttpRequestObject.responseText);
            }
        }

        XMLHttpRequestObject.send(null);
    }
}
```

The getData function calls the showMenu function, passing it the number of the menu to display (1 or 2), and the text downloaded from the server that holds the menu items ("Strawberry, Vanilla, Chocolate" or "Turkey, Beef, Sardine"). The showMenu function displays the correct menu with those menu items. This function begins by splitting the downloaded text into a global array of items named menuItems, using the handy JavaScript split function. The split function will split a text string into an array of strings, if we pass that function the character or characters to split the string on (which is a comma here). Here's how we create menuItems, the array of menu items we want to display:

```
<html>
  <head>
    <script language = "javascript">
      var menuItems;
        .
        .
        .

      function showMenu(menuNumber, itemsString)
      {
        menuItems = itemsString.split(", ");
        .
        .
        .
      }
```

Each menu will actually be an HTML table of menu items, and we'll construct that array with a loop over the menu items in the menuItems array, which looks like this in code:

```
      function showMenu(menuNumber, itemsString)
      {
        var loopIndex;

        menuItems = itemsString.split(", ");

        var menuText = "<table width = '100%'>";

        if (menuItems.length != 0) {
          for (var loopIndex = 0; loopIndex < menuItems.length;
            loopIndex++) {
            var text = "displaySelection(" + loopIndex + ")";
```

```
          menuText += "<tr><td "
            + "onclick='" + text + "'>" +
            menuItems[loopIndex] +
            "</td></tr>";
        }
      }

      menuText += "</table>";
          .
          .
          .

    }
```

You might note that the onclick event in each cell in the menu's HTML table is connected to a function named displaySelection. When the user clicks a table cell in the HTML table (that is, an item in our displayed menu), the browser will call the displaySelection function, which is how we'll handle menu item clicks.

Now that we've assembled the HTML for the menu, we can display that menu. We can control the visibility of an HTML element with the CSS property visibility, which we can set to "visible" or "hidden". Here's how we load the HTML for the menu into the correct <div> element and then make that menu visible:

```
function showMenu(menuNumber, itemsString)
{
  var loopIndex;
  var menuObject;

  menuItems = itemsString.split(", ");

  var menuText = "<table width = '100%'>";

  if (menuItems.length != 0) {
    for (var loopIndex = 0; loopIndex < menuItems.length;
      loopIndex++) {
      var text = "displaySelection(" + loopIndex + ")";
      menuText += "<tr><td "
        + "onclick='" + text + "'>" +
        menuItems[loopIndex] +
        "</td></tr>";
    }
  }

  menuText += "</table>";

  if(menuNumber == "1"){
    menuObject = document.getElementById("menu1Div");
  }
```

```
      if (menuNumber == "2") {
        menuObject = document.getElementById("menu2Div");
      }

      if (menuObject.style.visibility == "hidden") {
        menuObject.innerHTML = menuText;
        menuObject.style.visibility = "visible";
      }
    }
```

Whew. That displays a menu if the mouse moved over the matching image (that is, if the target of the mouse move event was an image).

But what if the user is moving the mouse away from an image? In that case, we should hide any menu that's visible. We've already checked if the mouse is moving over an image and displayed the corresponding menu in the checkMenu function; now we have to add code to checkMenu to hide the menus when the user moves the mouse away from an image. Here's what that looks like in checkMenu—we'll call a function named hideMenu to hide the menus:

```
function checkMenu(evt)
{
  var e = new mouseEventCreator(evt);
  var menuObject = null;
  var imgObject;

  imgObject = document.getElementById("image1");

  if(e.target == imgObject){
    getData(1);
  }

  imgObject = document.getElementById("image2");

  if(e.target == imgObject){
    getData(2);
  }

  menuObject = document.getElementById("menu1Div");

  imgObject = document.getElementById("image1");

  if (menuObject.style.visibility == "visible"){
    if(e.x < parseInt(menuObject.style.left) || e.y <
      parseInt(imgObject.style.top) ||
      e.x > (parseInt(imgObject.style.left) +
      parseInt(imgObject.style.width))
      || e.y > (parseInt(menuObject.style.top) +
      parseInt(menuObject.style.height))){
      hideMenu();
    }
  }
```

```
menuObject = document.getElementById("menu2Div");

imgObject = document.getElementById("image2");

if (menuObject.style.visibility == "visible"){
  if(e.x < parseInt(menuObject.style.left) || e.y <
  parseInt(imgObject.style.top) ||
  e.x > (parseInt(imgObject.style.left) +
  parseInt(imgObject.style.width))
  || e.y > (parseInt(menuObject.style.top) +
  parseInt(menuObject.style.height))){
    hideMenu();
  }
}
}
```

Ask the Expert

Q: What's the JavaScript parseInt function in this code?

A: That code is checking whether the mouse is outside the boundaries of an image. It gets those boundaries using style properties like menuObject.style.top or menuObject.style .left—and those properties are stored as text. To convert them from text to a number you can compare the mouse position to, you use the JavaScript parseInt function. That function converts text into an integer.

To hide the menus if the user has moved the mouse outside an image, the preceding code calls the hideMenu function. That function just sets the visibility property of the menus to "hidden" to hide the menus. Here's what the code looks like:

```
function hideMenu()
{
  var menu1Div = document.getElementById("menu1Div");

  if(menu1Div.style.visibility == "visible"){
    menu1Div.innerHTML = "<div></div>";
    menu1Div.style.visibility = "hidden";
  }

  var menu2Div = document.getElementById("menu2Div");

  if(menu2Div.style.visibility == "visible"){
    menu2Div.innerHTML = "<div></div>";
    menu2Div.style.visibility = "hidden";
  }
}
```

Wow, that's a lot of JavaScript. But we're coming to the end of this example. The last function is the displaySelection function, which is called by the browser when a menu item is clicked. The displaySelection function is passed the number of the menu item that was clicked (for example, in the first menu, "Strawberry" is item 0, "Vanilla" is item 1, and "Chocolate" is item 2), and the job of this function is to display the user's selection in the web page. The displaySelection function translates the item number (0, 1, or 2) into the English-language item name ("Strawberry", "Vanilla", or "Chocolate") by using that item number as an index in the array of menu item names that we created earlier—menuItems. So here, finally, is the way that we display the user's menu selection:

```
function displaySelection(index)
{
  var targetDiv = document.getElementById("targetDiv");

  targetDiv.innerHTML = "You chose " + menuItems[index] + ".";
}
```

And that completes this example. Here's the whole code for this application—note that we also style the menu and display <div> elements in a <style> element here (menus.html):

```
<html>
  <head>

    <title>Creating an Ajax-enabled Menu System</title>

    <style>
    #targetDiv {
      color: #00BBBB;
      font-size: 24pt;
      font-weight: bold;
      font-family: arial;
    }

    #menu1Div {
      color: #222222;
      background-color: #FFCCFF;
      font-weight: bold;
      font-family: arial;
      visibility: hidden;
      cursor: hand;
    }

    #menu2Div {
      color: #222222;
      background-color: #FFCCFF;
      font-weight: bold;
      font-family: arial;
      visibility: hidden;
      cursor: hand;
    }
```

```
</style>

<script language = "javascript">
  var menuItems;

  function checkMenu(evt)
  {
    var e = new mouseEventCreator(evt);
    var menuObject = null;
    var imgObject;

    imgObject = document.getElementById("image1");

    if(e.target == imgObject){
      getData(1);
    }

    imgObject = document.getElementById("image2");

    if(e.target == imgObject){
      getData(2);
    }

    menuObject = document.getElementById("menu1Div");

    imgObject = document.getElementById("image1");

    if (menuObject.style.visibility == "visible"){
      if(e.x < parseInt(menuObject.style.left) || e.y <
        parseInt(imgObject.style.top) ||
        e.x > (parseInt(imgObject.style.left) +
        parseInt(imgObject.style.width))
        || e.y > (parseInt(menuObject.style.top) +
        parseInt(menuObject.style.height))){
        hideMenu();
      }
    }

    menuObject = document.getElementById("menu2Div");

    imgObject = document.getElementById("image2");

    if (menuObject.style.visibility == "visible"){
      if(e.x < parseInt(menuObject.style.left) || e.y <
      parseInt(imgObject.style.top) ||
      e.x > (parseInt(imgObject.style.left) +
      parseInt(imgObject.style.width))
      || e.y > (parseInt(menuObject.style.top) +
      parseInt(menuObject.style.height))){
        hideMenu();
      }
    }
  }
```

```
function mouseEventCreator(e)
{
  if(e) {
    this.e = e;
  } else {
    this.e = window.event;
  }

  if(e.pageX) {
    this.x = e.pageX;
  } else {
    this.x = e.clientX;
  }

  if(e.pageY) {
    this.y = e.pageY;
  } else {
    this.y = e.clientY;
  }

  if(e.target) {
    this.target = e.target;
  } else {
    this.target = e.srcElement;
  }
}

function getData(menuNumber)
{

  var XMLHttpRequestObject = false;

  if (window.XMLHttpRequest) {
    XMLHttpRequestObject = new XMLHttpRequest();
  } else if (window.ActiveXObject) {
    XMLHttpRequestObject = new
      ActiveXObject("Microsoft.XMLHTTP");
  }

  var itemsSource;

  if(menuNumber== 1){
    itemsSource = "items1.txt";
  } else {
    itemsSource = "items2.txt";
  }

  if(XMLHttpRequestObject) {
    XMLHttpRequestObject.open("GET", itemsSource);

    XMLHttpRequestObject.onreadystatechange = function()
```

```
      {
        if (XMLHttpRequestObject.readyState == 4 &&
          XMLHttpRequestObject.status == 200) {
            showMenu(menuNumber, XMLHttpRequestObject.responseText);
        }
      }

    XMLHttpRequestObject.send(null);
  }
}

function showMenu(menuNumber, itemsString)
{
  var loopIndex;
  var menuObject;

  menuItems = itemsString.split(", ");

  var menuText = "<table width = '100%'>";

  if (menuItems.length != 0) {
    for (var loopIndex = 0; loopIndex < menuItems.length;
      loopIndex++) {
      var text = "displaySelection(" + loopIndex + ")";
      menuText += "<tr><td "
        + "onclick='" + text + "'>" +
        menuItems[loopIndex] +
        "</td></tr>";
    }
  }

  menuText += "</table>";

  if(menuNumber == "1"){
    menuObject = document.getElementById("menu1Div");
  }

  if(menuNumber == "2"){
    menuObject = document.getElementById("menu2Div");
  }

  if(menuObject.style.visibility == "hidden"){
    menuObject.innerHTML = menuText;
    menuObject.style.visibility = "visible";
  }
}

function hideMenu()
{
  var menu1Div = document.getElementById("menu1Div");

  if(menu1Div.style.visibility == "visible"){
```

```
        menu1Div.innerHTML = "<div></div>";
        menu1Div.style.visibility = "hidden";
      }

      var menu2Div = document.getElementById("menu2Div");
      if(menu2Div.style.visibility == "visible"){
        menu2Div.innerHTML = "<div></div>";
        menu2Div.style.visibility = "hidden";
      }
    }

    function displaySelection(index)
    {
      var targetDiv = document.getElementById("targetDiv");

      targetDiv.innerHTML = "You chose " + menuItems[index] + ".";
    }

  </script>

</head>

<body onclick = "hideMenu()" onmousemove = "checkMenu(event)">

  <H1>Creating an Ajax-enabled Menu System</H1>

    <img id = "image1" src="image1.jpg"
      style="left:30; top:50; width:200; height:40;">
    <div id = "menu1Div" style="position: absolute; left:30; top:100;
      width:100; height: 70; visibility:hidden;"><div></div></div>
    <img id = "image2" style="left:270; top:50; width:200;
      height:40;" src="image2.jpg">
    <div id = "menu2Div" style="position: absolute; left:270; top:100;
      width:100; height: 70; visibility:hidden;"><div></div></div>
    <br>
    <br>
    <div id = "targetDiv"></div>
  </body>

</html>
```

That finishes menus.html, our first full-scale in-depth Ajax example. There's a lot of CSS and JavaScript going on here—and that's precisely the point. There is usually a lot of CSS and JavaScript going on in most Ajax applications.

You now have a working knowledge of how to handle CSS—not to mention the mouse—in Ajax applications, and you can make the data that you download using Ajax appear anywhere in a page you want it to appear, no page refresh needed. Cool.

Chapter 8

Handling Dynamic HTML with Ajax

Key Skills & Concepts

- Updating pages with dynamic HTML methods
- Updating pages with dynamic HTML properties
- Creating elements on-the-fly
- Updating tables with data
- Writing documents to the browser

As stated in Chapter 7, the primary reason to use Ajax is that it enables you to update web pages without requiring a page refresh in the browser. You have seen how to use CSS to accomplish that; in this chapter, you're going to see how to work with Ajax and dynamic HTML.

Like CSS, dynamic HTML offers ways to update and manage your web page. In many ways, dynamic HTML is more powerful than CSS, because by using dynamic HTML, you can alter the HTML in a page. We'll start off by examining just how that works.

Updating Pages with Dynamic HTML Methods

There are two main ways to modify the HTML in a web page using dynamic HTML: *methods* or *properties*. We've already used the innerHTML dynamic HTML property throughout this book to insert downloaded data into a web page:

```
if(XMLHttpRequestObject) {
  var obj = document.getElementById("targetDiv");
  XMLHttpRequestObject.open("GET", dataSource);

  XMLHttpRequestObject.onreadystatechange = function()
  {
    if (XMLHttpRequestObject.readyState == 4 &&
      XMLHttpRequestObject.status == 200) {
        obj.innerHTML = XMLHttpRequestObject.responseText;
    }
  }
}
```

There are other dynamic HTML properties available, too, as you're going to see in this chapter. But what's this about using dynamic HTML methods? The main methods that you can use to modify the HTML in a web page are the following:

- **insertAdjacentHTML**   Lets you insert HTML next to an element that already exists
- **insertAdjacentText**   Lets you insert text next to an element that already exists

You can specify where the new text or HTML will go with respect to the already existing element by passing the constants "BeforeBegin", "AfterBegin", "BeforeEnd", or "AfterEnd" to the insertAdjacentHTML and insertAdjacentText methods.

In the following example, insertAdjacent.html, we're going to use the insertAdjacent method to insert some text and a text field when the user clicks a button. We start with the button inside a <div> element named targetDiv:

```
<body>

  <center>
    <h1>
      Updating a Page With insertAdjacentHTML
    </h1>
  </center>

  <div id="targetDiv">
    <center>
      <form>
        <input type=button value="Click here"
          onclick="addHTML()">
      </form>
    </center>
  </div>

</body>
```

The button is connected to a JavaScript function named addHTML, which will add the HTML needed for the new text and text field:

```
<script language="JavaScript">

  function addHTML()
  {
      .
      .
      .
  }

</script>
```

In addHTML, we can use the insertAdjacentHTML method to add the HTML we want after the targetDiv <div> element. To add that HTML after the end of the targetDiv <div> element, we can pass the constant "AfterEnd" to the insertAdjacentHTML method like this:

```
<script language="JavaScript">

  function addHTML()
```

```
    {
      targetDiv.insertAdjacentHTML("AfterEnd",
        .
        .
        .
    }

</script>
```

And we have to specify what HTML we want to insert, which we can do like this to create a text field and some new text:

```
<script language="JavaScript">

    function addHTML()
    {
      targetDiv.insertAdjacentHTML("AfterEnd",
      "<p><input type=text value='Hello there.'> See? A new text
        field.</p>");
    }

</script>
```

Here's the whole thing, insertAdjacent.html:

```
<html>
  <head>
    <title>
      Updating a Page With insertAdjacentHTML
    </title>

    <script language="JavaScript">
      function addHTML()
      {
        targetDiv.insertAdjacentHTML("AfterEnd",
          "<p><input type=text value='Hello there.'> See? A new text
            field.</p>");
      }
    </script>
  </head>

  <body>

    <center>
      <h1>
        Updating a Page With insertAdjacentHTML
      </h1>
    </center>
```

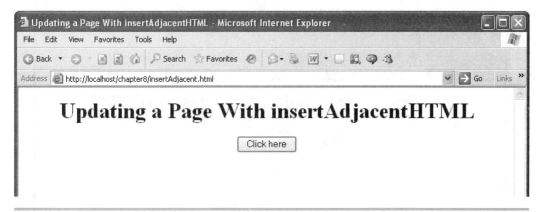

Figure 8-1   insertAdjacent.html at work

```
<div id="targetDiv">
  <center>
    <form>
      <input type=button value="Click here"
        onclick="addHTML()">
    </form>
  </center>
</div>

</body>
</html>
```

You can see this page at work in Figure 8-1.

When you click the button, a new text field (complete with text in it) and some additional text appears, as shown in Figure 8-2. Cool.

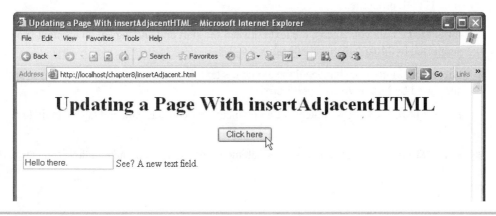

Figure 8-2   Adding HTML to insertAdjacent.html

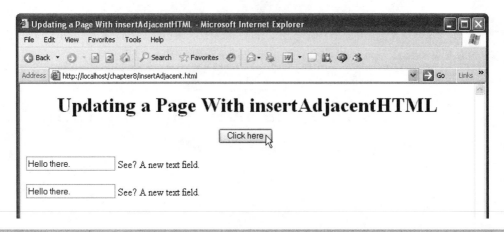

Figure 8-3 Adding more HTML to insertAdjacent.html

If you click the button again, the new HTML is added to the page again, as you see in Figure 8-3.

That's a great way to go if you want to use Ajax to reconfigure your web page, as when you want to add (or remove) tables from the page, depending on what data you've downloaded.

On the other hand, there's an issue here. The insertAdjacentHTML and insertAdjacentText methods won't work in Firefox-type browsers. If you want to maintain cross-browser compatibility, you can work with the dynamic HTML properties that are coming up next.

Updating Pages with Dynamic HTML Properties

No matter whether you're in Internet Explorer or Firefox, each item in a web page supports the dynamic HTML properties:

- **innerText**   Lets you change the text between the start and end tags of an element (not supported by Mozilla/Netscape/Firefox)

- **outerText**   Lets you change all the element's text, including the start and end tags (not supported by Mozilla/Netscape/Firefox)

- **innerHTML**   Changes contents of an element between start and end tags; can include HTML

- **outerHTML**   Changes contents of an element, including start and end tags; treats text as HTML

As mentioned earlier, you've already seen the innerHTML property throughout the book:

```
if(XMLHttpRequestObject) {
  var obj = document.getElementById("targetDiv");
  XMLHttpRequestObject.open("GET", dataSource);

  XMLHttpRequestObject.onreadystatechange = function()
  {
    if (XMLHttpRequestObject.readyState == 4 &&
      XMLHttpRequestObject.status == 200) {
        obj.innerHTML = XMLHttpRequestObject.responseText;
    }
  }
}
```

Here's an example, innerText.html, that uses the innerText property. This example lets you click an HTML <h1> header—and when you do, it changes the text in that header. We start with the header itself, and connect a function named changeHeader to the header's onclick event:

```
<body>

    <center>
        <h1 id = "header"
          onclick = "changeHeader()">
          Changing Text With the innerText Property
        </h1>

        Click the above header to make it change.
    </center>

</body>
```

Now when the user clicks the header, the changeHeader function will be called:

```
<head>
    <title>
        Changing Text With the innerText Property
    </title>

    <script language = "JavaScript">

    function changeHeader()
    {
      .
      .
      .
    }

    </script>

</head>
```

In the changeHeader function, you can place new text inside the <h1> header using the innerText property:

```
<head>
    <title>
        Changing Text With the innerText Property
    </title>

    <script language = "JavaScript">

     function changeHeader()
     {
       var header = document.getElementById("header");
       header.innerText = "Here is the new header.";
     }

    </script>

</head>
```

Here's what the whole example, innerText.html, looks like:

```
<html>

    <head>
        <title>
            Changing Text With the innerText Property
        </title>

        <script language = "JavaScript">

         function changeHeader()
         {
           var header = document.getElementById("header");
           header.innerText = "Here is the new header.";
         }

        </script>

    </head>

    <body>

        <center>
            <h1 id = "header"
              onclick = "changeHeader()">
              Changing Text With the innerText Property
            </h1>
```

Figure 8-4   innerText.html at work

```
        Click the above header to make it change.
    </center>

  </body>

</html>
```

You can see this page at work in Figure 8-4.

When you click the header, the text in that header is changed, as you see in Figure 8-5. Nice.

You use the innerText property to set the inner text of an element, rather than rewrite it entirely. Note that if you had wanted to insert HTML into the header, you could have used the innerHTML property instead. Here's an example that inserts a <marquee> element into

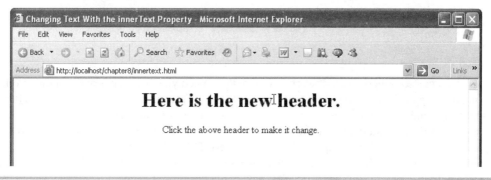

Figure 8-5   Changing the text in a header in innerText.html

the header that displays a scrolling marquee—note that this element only works in Internet Explorer (innerHTML.html):

```html
<html>

    <head>
        <title>
            Changing HTML With the innerHTML Property
        </title>

        <script language = "JavaScript">

         function changeHeader()
         {
           var header = document.getElementById("header");
           header.innerHTML = "<marquee>Here is the new
           header.</marquee>";
         }

        </script>

    </head>

    <body>

        <center>
            <h1 id = "header"
              onclick = "changeHeader()">
              Changing HTML With the innerHTML Property
            </h1>

            Click the above header to make it change.
        </center>

    </body>

</html>
```

You can see innerHTML at work in Figure 8-6. When you click the header, a new scrolling marquee appears (in Internet Explorer, anyway). The HTML inside the <h1> header has been replaced, and the new marquee is displayed as a scrolling <h1> header.

What if you want to change the <h1> header itself to, say, an <h3> header instead? You could use the outerHTML property instead of innerHTML. The outerHTML property lets you rewrite the HTML that contains the element you're working on. In other words, using the innerHTML property lets you edit the HTML inside the current element, while the outerHTML property lets you change all the HTML of the current element.

Figure 8-6 Changing the HTML in a header

Here's how that might work, in a new example, outerHTML.html. When you click the
<h1> header in this example, the changeHeader function will change it to an <h3> header
using the outerHTML property:

```
<script language = "JavaScript">

function changeHeader()
{
  var header = document.getElementById("header");
  header.outerHTML =
  "<h3>Here is the new, smaller header</h3>"
}

</script>
```

Here's what the whole example, outerHTML.html, looks like:

```
<html>

  <head>
    <title>
        Changing HTML With the outerHTML Property
    </title>

    <script language = "JavaScript">

     function changeHeader()
     {
       var header = document.getElementById("header");
       header.outerHTML =
       "<h3>Here is the new, smaller header</h3>"
     }

    </script>

  </head>
```

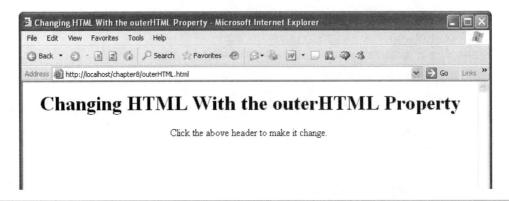

Figure 8-7 outerHTML.html in action

```
<body>

    <center>
        <h1 id = header
          onclick = "changeHeader()">
          Changing HTML With the outerHTML Property
        </h1>

        Click the above header to make it change.
    </center>

</body>

</html>
```

You can see outerHTML.html doing its thing in Figure 8-7.

When the user clicks the <h1> header in Figure 8-7, the changeHeader function changes it into the <h3> header that you see in Figure 8-8, using the outerHTML property. Nice.

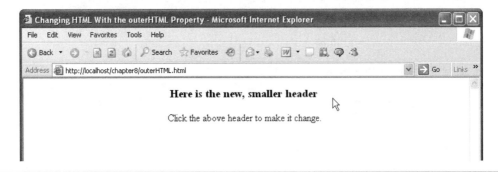

Figure 8-8 Changing an <h1> header to an <h3> header

When it comes to dynamic HTML, you're going to find that Internet Explorer has more functionality than any other browser—and that's true of the topics thus far in this chapter as well: of the dynamic HTML properties we've been discussing, only innerHTML is supported in Firefox; all the others (innerText, outerText, and outerHTML) are supported in Internet Explorer only.

In fact, there's even more dynamic HTML built into Internet Explorer that will let you alter the contents of a web page, as you might do in Ajax-enabled applications. Besides the methods and properties we've discussed in this chapter, you can also use *text ranges*.

Using Text Ranges in Internet Explorer

In Internet Explorer, you can address sections of text and handle them using text ranges. There are all kinds of methods built into text ranges, but we'll only take a look at a simple example in this chapter because text ranges are only available in Internet Explorer.

Here's an example, textRanges.html, that places text into a text range and then pastes HTML over that range to replace it. This example starts with a button that, when clicked, calls a function named changeText:

```
<body>
    <center>
        <h1>
            Replacing Text With Text Ranges
        </h1>
    </center>

    <input type="button" value="Click here"
      onclick="changeText()">

    <br>
    <br>

    <div id="div1">
        Click the button to change this text.
    </div>

</body>
```

In the changeText function, we create a new text range for the document:

```
<script language="JavaScript">

    function changeText()
    {
        var range = document.body.createTextRange();
        .
        .
        .
    }

</script>
```

We then create an object corresponding to the <div> element we want to overwrite:

```
<script language="JavaScript">

  function changeText()
  {
      var range = document.body.createTextRange();
      var div = document.getElementById("div1");
      .
      .
      .

  }

</script>
```

Next, we move the text range so that it encompasses the <div> element:

```
<script language="JavaScript">

  function changeText()
  {
      var range = document.body.createTextRange();
      var div = document.getElementById("div1");
      range.moveToElementText(div);
      .
      .
      .

  }

</script>
```

Finally, we can use the new text range's pasteHTML method to paste some text, replacing the text that's in the <div> now ("Click the button to change this text.") to the new text ("You have successfully clicked the button."):

```
<script language="JavaScript">

  function changeText()
  {
      var range = document.body.createTextRange();
      var div = document.getElementById("div1");
      range.moveToElementText(div);
      range.pasteHTML("You have successfully clicked the
        button.");
  }

</script>
```

Here's the whole example, textRanges.html:

```html
<html>
    <head>
        <title>
            Replacing Text With Text Ranges
        </title>

        <script language="JavaScript">

            function changeText()
            {
                var range = document.body.createTextRange();
                var div = document.getElementById("div1");
                range.moveToElementText(div);
                range.pasteHTML("You have successfully clicked the
                  button.");
            }

        </script>
    </head>

    <body>
        <center>
            <h1>
                Replacing Text With Text Ranges
            </h1>
        </center>

        <input type="button" value="Click here"
          onclick="changeText()">

        <br>
        <br>

        <div id="div1">
            Click the button to change this text.
        </div>

    </body>
</html>
```

You can see this example in Figure 8-9.

When you click the button in this example, the code pastes new text over the text range enclosing the <div> element, and you can see the result in Figure 8-10.

Text ranges are powerful tools, but you should probably stay away from them in Ajax applications unless you're sure that you're going to be dealing only with Internet Explorer; otherwise, you'll have to duplicate the same operation in code for other browsers.

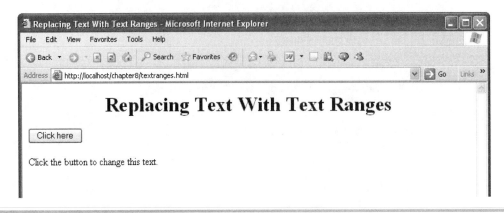

Figure 8-9 textRanges.html in action

As you know, you can configure your page with data downloaded using Ajax. And you can even write new HTML to the page to add controls as needed—for example, you might be downloading house listings from a real estate site, and need to create buttons so the user can e-mail the listing agent. Creating new HTML is a very common thing to do in Ajax, and as you've seen, you can create that new HTML just by writing it to the page. On the other hand, if you have a lot of HTML to write, it can get confusing.

There is a special dynamic HTML method, createElement, you can use to create new HTML elements, saving you time if you have to create a lot of new elements. createElement has the added benefit of working in both Internet Explorer and Firefox-type browsers.

Figure 8-10 Replacing the text in a text range

Creating New HTML Elements with createElement

Ajax applications frequently need to create new HTML elements. For example, if you download data for a Rolodex-like phone directory, you'll have to create the HTML for the controls used in the Rolodex. Or if you write an Ajax e-mail application that downloads e-mail text before the user asks for it, to avoid delays, you'll have to create buttons and text fields to enable the user to answer their e-mail. Or if you're interacting with an online database, you'll have to create an HTML table on-the-fly to display that data in.

All these tasks can be performed with the createElement method, and we'll take a look at that method in a new example, createElement.html, now. When you click a button in this example, the example creates a text field with text in it, a working button (clicking it will display a JavaScript alert dialog box), and some text. How can we create just text? It turns out that we can create text nodes with a method named createTextNode, and that's what we'll do, adding the text we want to display to that text node.

We start the createElement.html example with the button the user clicks to create the new elements:

```html
<body>
  <center>
    <h1>
      Creating New Elements
    </h1>
  </center>

  <form>
    <input type="button" value="Click here"
      onclick="createNewElements()">
  </form>

</body>
```

When the button is clicked, a function named createNewElements is called:

```html
<script language="JavaScript">
  function createNewElements()
  {
      .
      .
      .
  }
</script>
```

We'll add the new elements we create in this example (a text field, a button, and a text node) to a <div> element, and start by creating the <div> element now:

```html
<script language="JavaScript">
  function createNewElements()
```

```
  {
    var newDiv;

    newDiv = document.createElement("div");
        .
        .
        .

  }
</script>
```

Note the use of the createElement method here, which creates the new <div> element. We can access the attributes of newly created elements as properties of the element objects. For example, to set the ID property of the new <div> element, we only have to use the <div> object's id property:

```
<script language="JavaScript">
  function createNewElements()
  {
    var newDiv;

    newDiv = document.createElement("div");
    newDiv.id = "NewDIV";
        .
        .
        .

  }
</script>
```

Now we'll create the new HTML elements that we'll add to the <div> element, starting with the new text field. Text fields are <input> elements, so we create them like this:

```
<script language="JavaScript">
  function createNewElements()
  {
    var newDiv, newTextfield, newText, newButton;

    newDiv = document.createElement("div");
    newDiv.id = "NewDIV";

    newTextfield = document.createElement("input");
        .
        .
        .

  }
</script>
```

That creates a generic <input> element. How do we make it a text field? We have to set the type attribute to "text", and we can do that like this:

```
<script language="JavaScript">
  function createNewElements()
  {
    var newDiv, newTextfield, newText, newButton;

    newDiv = document.createElement("div");
    newDiv.id = "NewDIV";

    newTextfield = document.createElement("input");
    newTextfield.type = "text";
      .
      .
      .

  }
</script>
```

We can also add text to the new text field by setting its value attribute like this, where we're storing the text "Hello!" in the new text field:

```
<script language="JavaScript">
  function createNewElements()
  {
    var newDiv, newTextfield, newText, newButton;

    newDiv = document.createElement("div");
    newDiv.id = "NewDIV";

    newTextfield = document.createElement("input");
    newTextfield.type = "text";
    newTextfield.value = "Hello!";
      .
      .
      .

  }
</script>
```

Okay, that creates the new text field, which is now stored in the newTextfield object. Next, let's create the new button, which will also be an <input> control:

```
<script language="JavaScript">
  function createNewElements()
  {
    var newDiv, newTextfield, newText, newButton;

    newDiv = document.createElement("div");
    newDiv.id = "NewDIV";
```

```
newTextfield = document.createElement("input");
newTextfield.type = "text";
newTextfield.value = "Hello!";

newButton = document.createElement("input");
 .
 .
 .

}
</script>
```

We'll make it a button by setting its type attribute to "button" and set its caption to "New Button":

```
<script language="JavaScript">
  function createNewElements()
  {
    var newDiv, newTextfield, newText, newButton;

    newDiv = document.createElement("div");
    newDiv.id = "NewDIV";

    newTextfield = document.createElement("input");
    newTextfield.type = "text";
    newTextfield.value = "Hello!";

    newButton = document.createElement("input");
    newButton.type = "button";
    newButton.value = "New Button";
     .
     .
     .

  }
</script>
```

Now we can create some code—a function named sayHello—that will be called when the button is clicked. That new function will call the JavaScript alert function to display an alert dialog box that says "Hello!":

```
<script language="JavaScript">
  function createNewElements()
  {
    var newDiv, newTextfield, newText, newButton;

    newDiv = document.createElement("div");
    newDiv.id = "NewDIV";
```

```
newTextfield = document.createElement("input");
newTextfield.type = "text";
newTextfield.value = "Hello!";

newButton = document.createElement("input");
newButton.type = "button";
newButton.value = "New Button";
    .
    .
    .
}

function sayHello()
{
  alert("Hello!");
}
</script>
```

And we can connect the sayHello function to the new button by assigning the sayHello function to the button's onclick attribute this way:

```
<script language="JavaScript">
  function createNewElements()
  {
    var newDiv, newTextfield, newText, newButton;

    newDiv = document.createElement("div");
    newDiv.id = "NewDIV";

    newTextfield = document.createElement("input");
    newTextfield.type = "text";
    newTextfield.value = "Hello!";

    newButton = document.createElement("input");
    newButton.type = "button";
    newButton.value = "New Button";
    newButton.onclick = sayHello;
      .
      .
      .
  }

  function sayHello()
  {
    alert("Hello!");
  }
</script>
```

Now it's time to create the text node, which we can do with the createTextNode method:

```
<script language="JavaScript">
  function createNewElements()
  {
    var newDiv, newTextfield, newText, newButton;

    newDiv = document.createElement("div");
    newDiv.id = "NewDIV";

    newTextfield = document.createElement("input");
    newTextfield.type = "text";
    newTextfield.value = "Hello!";

    newButton = document.createElement("input");
    newButton.type = "button";
    newButton.value = "New Button";
    newButton.onclick = sayHello;

    newText = document.createTextNode("Here is the new text.");
        .
        .
        .
  }
</script>
```

Great, we've created a text field, a button, and a text node. The next step is to install all those items into the <div> element we've created, newDiv, and we'll use the dynamic HTML insertBefore method. You use this method to insert new elements into a web page, passing it the new element object to insert and the current element object you want to insert the new object before. In this case, we'll insert the new objects into the <div> element we created—and since there's no existing object in the <div> element to place our new objects before, we'll pass a value of null for that argument. Here's how we insert the new button, text field, and text node into the <div> element we created:

```
<script language="JavaScript">
  function createNewElements()
  {
    var newDiv, newTextfield, newText, newButton;

    newDiv = document.createElement("div");
    newDiv.id = "NewDIV";

    newTextfield = document.createElement("input");
    newTextfield.type = "text";
    newTextfield.value = "Hello!";
```

```
    newButton = document.createElement("input");
    newButton.type = "button";
    newButton.value = "New Button";
    newButton.onclick = sayHello;

    newText = document.createTextNode("Here is the new text.");

    newDiv.insertBefore(newButton, null);
    newDiv.insertBefore(newTextfield, null);
    newDiv.insertBefore(newText, null);
              .

              .

              .

    }
  </script>
```

Next, we insert the <div> element, which now contains the new text field, button, and text node, into the web page. We can insert that <div> element into the page's <body> element by referring to the <body> element as document.body this way:

```
  <script language="JavaScript">
    function createNewElements()
    {
      var newDiv, newTextfield, newText, newButton;

      newDiv = document.createElement("div");
      newDiv.id = "NewDIV";

      newTextfield = document.createElement("input");
      newTextfield.type = "text";
      newTextfield.value = "Hello!";

      newButton = document.createElement("input");
      newButton.type = "button";
      newButton.value = "New Button";
      newButton.onclick = sayHello;

      newText = document.createTextNode("Here is the new text.");

      newDiv.insertBefore(newButton, null);
      newDiv.insertBefore(newTextfield, null);
      newDiv.insertBefore(newText, null);

      document.body.insertBefore(newDiv, null);
    }
  </script>
```

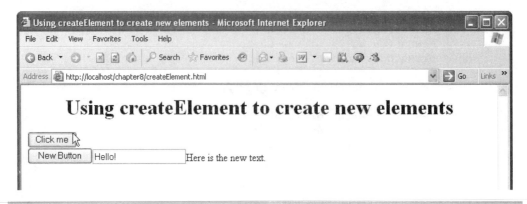

Figure 8-11   Creating new elements on-the-fly

Figure 8-12   Clicking the button displays an alert dialog box.

And that's it—we've created three new objects, inserted them into a <div> element, and inserted the <div> element into the web page. You can see the results in Figure 8-11; when the user clicks the button, a new button, text field, and text node are all added.

The button is functional, too—clicking it displays the alert dialog box you see in Figure 8-12. Very nice.

That gives you an overview of creating new HTML elements and adding them to a web page. One of the items Ajax developers find themselves creating from scratch often is the HTML table, such as when they download data from a database and need to display it. In fact, creating and editing tables is such a common thing to do that there is special support for it in dynamic HTML that is supported by both Internet Explorer and Firefox-type browsers.

Editing Tables On-the-Fly

In dynamic HTML, table objects (that is, objects corresponding to a <table> element) have these properties and methods that you can use to edit their contents:

- **tableObject.rows(index)**   Returns a collection (array) of the rows in the table.

- **tableObject.insertRow(index)**   Inserts a new row. Returns the inserted <tr> element (which will be empty), or null for failure. If index isn't supplied, then the <tr> element will be inserted at the end.

● **tableObject.deleteRow(index)**   Deletes a row. The index value indicates the row index of the row to delete.

And here are the properties and methods for objects corresponding to table row objects (that is, objects corresponding to <tr> elements):

● **tableObject.cells(index)**   Returns a collection (array) of the cells in the row.

● **tableObject.row(index)**   Returns the row index of the row. Useful for inserting and deleting rows.

● **tableObject.insertCell(index)**   Inserts a new cell and returns the inserted <td> element (which will be empty), or null for failure. If index isn't supplied, then the <td> element will be inserted at the end of the row.

● **tableObject.deleteCell(index)**   Deletes a cell. The index value indicates the position in the cell collection to delete.

Let's put editing tables on-the-fly to work in an example, editTable.html. This example will edit a table by adding new rows at the click of a button (and it'll work in Internet Explorer and Firefox). We start by displaying an HTML table:

```
<body>
    <center>
        <h1>
            Editing HTML Tables
        </h1>

        <table id="table1" border="2">
            <tr>
                <td>Fe</td>
                <td>Fi</td>
                <td>Fo</td>
                <td>Fum</td>
            </tr>
            <tr>
                <td>Fe</td>
                <td>Fi</td>
                <td>Fo</td>
                <td>Fum</td>
            </tr>
            <tr>
                <td>Fe</td>
                <td>Fi</td>
                <td>Fo</td>
                <td>Fum</td>
            </tr>
        </table>
            .
            .
            .
    </center>
</body>
```

Note that we've given an ID to the table, "table1", which will allow us to access that table in JavaScript. Let's add a button with the caption "Add a new row" that connects to a JavaScript function named createRow:

```
<body>
    <center>
        <h1>
            Editing HTML Tables
        </h1>

        <table id="table1" border="2">
            <tr>
                <td>Fe</td>
                <td>Fi</td>
                <td>Fo</td>
                <td>Fum</td>
            </tr>
            <tr>
                <td>Fe</td>
                <td>Fi</td>
                <td>Fo</td>
                <td>Fum</td>
            </tr>
            <tr>
                <td>Fe</td>
                <td>Fi</td>
                <td>Fo</td>
                <td>Fum</td>
            </tr>
        </table>

        <br>

        <input type="button" value="Add a new row"
          onclick="createRow()">

    </center>
</body>
```

In the createRow function, we can get an object corresponding to table1:

```
<script language="javascript">
    function createRow()
    {
        var table1 = document.getElementById("table1");
        .
        .
        .
    }
</script>
```

Then we call the table object's insertRow method to insert a new row into the table—this method returns the new row object so that we can work with it, adding cells to the row:

```
<script language="javascript">
    function createRow()
    {
        var table1 = document.getElementById("table1");
        var newRow = table1.insertRow(3);
            .
            .
            .


    }
</script>
```

Note that we're inserting row 3 here because the table already has three rows—that is, rows 0, 1, and 2. Now we've got a new row object to work with, and we'll do that by adding cells to it with the row object's insertCell method.

Each row in the table has four cells, cells 0, 1, 2, and 3. You can add cell 0 to the newly created row this way:

```
<script language="javascript">
    function createRow()
    {
        var table1 = document.getElementById("table1");
        var newRow = table1.insertRow(3);

        var newCell = newRow.insertCell(0);
            .
            .
            .


    }
</script>
```

The insertCell method returns the new cell object. How do we add data to this new cell? We can use its innerHTML property, as we've done so often before with <div> elements:

```
<script language="javascript">
    function createRow()
    {
        var table1 = document.getElementById("table1");
        var newRow = table1.insertRow(3);

        var newCell = newRow.insertCell(0);
        newCell.innerHTML = "Fe";
            .
            .
            .


    }
</script>
```

That's fine—we've been able to insert text data into the cell we just inserted into the new row. We can also create the other three cells in the row and add data to them as well:

```
<script language="javascript">
    function createRow()
    {
        var table1 = document.getElementById("table1");
        var newRow = table1.insertRow(3);

        var newCell = newRow.insertCell(0);
        newCell.innerHTML = "Fe";

        newCell = newRow.insertCell(1);
        newCell.innerHTML = "Fi";

        newCell = newRow.insertCell(2);
        newCell.innerHTML = "Fo";

        newCell = newRow.insertCell(3);
        newCell.innerHTML = "Fum";
    }
</script>
```

Great—here's the entire example, editTable.html:

```
<html>
    <head>
        <title>
            Editing HTML Tables
        </title>

        <script language="javascript">
            function createRow()
            {
                var table1 = document.getElementById("table1");
                var newRow = table1.insertRow(3);

                var newCell = newRow.insertCell(0);
                newCell.innerHTML = "Fe";

                newCell = newRow.insertCell(1);
                newCell.innerHTML = "Fi";

                newCell = newRow.insertCell(2);
                newCell.innerHTML = "Fo";
```

```
                newCell = newRow.insertCell(3);
                newCell.innerHTML = "Fum";
            }
        </script>
    </head>

    <body>
        <center>
            <h1>
                Editing HTML Tables
            </h1>

            <table id="table1" border="2">
                <tr>
                    <td>Fe</td>
                    <td>Fi</td>
                    <td>Fo</td>
                    <td>Fum</td>
                </tr>
                <tr>
                    <td>Fe</td>
                    <td>Fi</td>
                    <td>Fo</td>
                    <td>Fum</td>
                </tr>
                <tr>
                    <td>Fe</td>
                    <td>Fi</td>
                    <td>Fo</td>
                    <td>Fum</td>
                </tr>
            </table>

            <br>

            <input type="button" value="Add a new row"
              onclick="createRow()">

        </center>
    </body>
</html>
```

You can see this example at work in Figure 8-13, where the table appears in its original state.

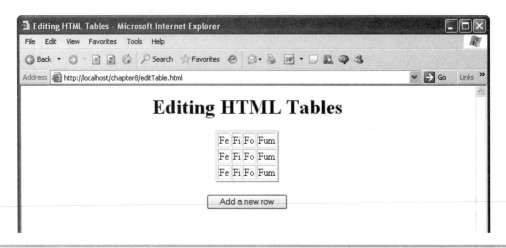

Figure 8-13 The original table in editTable.html

A new row appears at the bottom of the table when you click the button, as shown in Figure 8-14.

Cool, now you know how to edit a table on-the-fly. That's an exceptionally useful skill to have for Ajax applications, because you can update a table—and even rewrite it with new data—without refreshing the page.

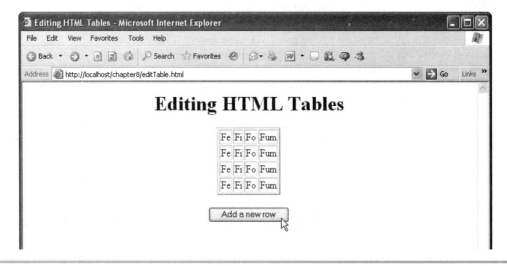

Figure 8-14 Adding a new row in editTable.html

Try This Remove Table Rows On-the-Fly

To truly be able to edit HTML tables on-the-fly, you need to know how to remove rows as well as add them. Try using the deleteRow method to let the user remove a row after the user adds a new row. Here's what the code looks like:

```html
<html>
    <head>
        <title>
            Editing HTML Tables
        </title>

        <script language="javascript">
            function createRow()
            {
                var table1 = document.getElementById("table1");
                var newRow = table1.insertRow(3);

                var newCell = newRow.insertCell(0);
                newCell.innerHTML = "Fe";

                newCell = newRow.insertCell(1);
                newCell.innerHTML = "Fi";

                newCell = newRow.insertCell(2);
                newCell.innerHTML = "Fo";

                newCell = newRow.insertCell(3);
                newCell.innerHTML = "Fum";
            }

            function removeRow()
            {
                var table1 = document.getElementById("table1");
                table1.deleteRow(3);
            }
        </script>
    </head>

    <body>
        <center>
            <h1>
                Editing HTML Tables
            </h1>

            <table id="table1" border="2">
                <tr>
                    <td>Fe</td>
```

(continued)

```
                    <td>Fi</td>
                    <td>Fo</td>
                    <td>Fum</td>
                </tr>
                <tr>
                    <td>Fe</td>
                    <td>Fi</td>
                    <td>Fo</td>
                    <td>Fum</td>
                </tr>
                <tr>
                    <td>Fe</td>
                    <td>Fi</td>
                    <td>Fo</td>
                    <td>Fum</td>
                </tr>
            </table>

            <br>

            <input type="button" value="Add a new row"
              onclick="createRow()">
            <input type="button" value="Remove the new row"
              onclick="removeRow()">

        </center>
    </body>
</html>
```

Using document.write to Write Documents to the Browser

Another dynamic HTML method you should know about is the document.write method, which allows you to write to a web page from JavaScript. Unlike the techniques you have seen earlier in this chapter, document.write is designed to write entire pages at once, not just update sections of a page. Using document.write in Ajax applications, you can download and examine data from the server before writing the web page and, depending on that data, write different web pages.

Here's an example, restaurant.html, that shows how document.write can respond to current conditions. In this case, we'll create for a restaurant a web page that displays a different menu—breakfast, lunch, or dinner—depending on the time of day. This web page will be entirely written from JavaScript, so it has an empty <body> element:

```
<body>
</body>
```

In the <script> element, we first determine what the current hour of the day is by creating a JavaScript Date object and using its getHours method:

```
<script language="JavaScript">
    var currentDate = new Date();
    var currentHour = currentDate.getHours();
        .
        .
        .
</script>
```

Next, we can write a header welcoming people to the restaurant ("Welcome to Our Restaurant") using document.write:

```
<script language="JavaScript">
    var currentDate = new Date();
    var currentHour = currentDate.getHours();
    document.write( "<center>");
    document.write( "<h1>");
    document.write("Welcome to Our Restaurant");
    document.write( "</h1>");
    document.write( "</center>");
        .
        .
        .
</script>
```

That's how it works—you use document.write to write to the web page. You can check what the hour of the day is, and write the web page to match. For example, if the restaurant is currently closed, you can write the web page to reflect that:

```
<script language="JavaScript">
    var currentDate = new Date();
    var currentHour = currentDate.getHours();
    document.write( "<center>");
    document.write( "<h1>");
    document.write("Welcome to Our Restaurant");
    document.write( "</h1>");
    document.write( "</center>");

    if (currentHour < 5 || currentHour > 23){
        document.write( "<center>");
        document.write( "<h1>");
        document.write( "Sorry, we are currently closed." );
        document.write( "</h1>");
        document.write( "</center>");
    }
        .
        .
        .
</script>
```

Or, if it's breakfast time, you can display the breakfast menu in, say, an HTML table:

```
<script language="JavaScript">
    var currentDate = new Date();
    var currentHour = currentDate.getHours();
    document.write( "<center>");
    document.write( "<h1>");
    document.write("Welcome to Our Restaurant");
    document.write( "</h1>");
    document.write( "</center>");

    if (currentHour < 5 || currentHour > 23){
        document.write( "<center>");
        document.write( "<h1>");
        document.write( "Sorry, we are currently closed." );
        document.write( "</h1>");
        document.write( "</center>");
    }

    if (currentHour > 6 && currentHour < 12 ) {
        document.write( "<center>");
        document.write(
          "<h2><i>We're now serving breakfast!</i></h2>");
        document.write( "<table border bgcolor='aqua'>");
        document.write(
          "<tr><th colspan = 2>Our Breakfast Menu</th></tr>");
        document.write(
           "<tr><td>Fried Eggs</td><td>$3.50</td></tr>");
        document.write(
           "<tr><td>Boiled eggs</td><td>$3.00</td></tr>");
        document.write(
           "<tr><td>Waffles</td><td>$2.00</td></tr>");
        document.write("<tr><td>Gruel</td><td>$2.50</td></tr>");
        document.write(
           "<tr><td>Spinach</td><td>$2.50</td></tr>");
        document.write( "</table>");
        document.write( "</center>");
        document.write( "</table>");
        document.write( "</center>");
    }
        .
        .
        .
</script>
```

Here's the whole document.write example, restaurant.html:

```
<html>
    <head>

        <script language="JavaScript">
            var currentDate = new Date();
            var currentHour = currentDate.getHours();
            document.write( "<center>");
            document.write( "<h1>");
            document.write("Welcome to Our Restaurant");
            document.write( "</h1>");
            document.write( "</center>");

            if (currentHour < 5 || currentHour > 23){
                document.write( "<center>");
                document.write( "<h1>");
                document.write( "Sorry, we are currently closed." );
                document.write( "</h1>");
                document.write( "</center>");
            }

            if (currentHour > 6 && currentHour < 12 ) {
                document.write( "<center>");
                document.write(
                  "<h2><i>We're now serving breakfast!</i></h2>");
                document.write( "<table border bgcolor='aqua'>");
                document.write(
                  "<tr><th colspan = 2>Our Breakfast Menu</th></tr>");
                document.write(
                   "<tr><td>Fried Eggs</td><td>$3.50</td></tr>");
                document.write(
                   "<tr><td>Boiled eggs</td><td>$3.00</td></tr>");
                document.write(
                  "<tr><td>Waffles</td><td>$2.00</td></tr>");
                document.write("<tr><td>Gruel</td><td>$2.50</td></tr>");
                document.write(
                  "<tr><td>Spinach</td><td>$2.50</td></tr>");
                document.write( "</table>");
                document.write( "</center>");
                document.write( "</table>");
                document.write( "</center>");
            }

            if ( currentHour >= 12 && currentHour < 17 ) {
                document.write( "<center>");
                document.write(
                  "<h2><i>We're now serving lunch!</i></h2>");
                document.write( "<table border bgcolor='aqua'>");
                document.write(
                  "<tr><th colspan = 2>Our Lunch Menu</th></tr>");
```

```
            document.write(
              "<tr><td>Ham Sandwich</td><td>$4.50</td></tr>");
            document.write(
              "<tr><td>Pickle Sandwich</td><td>$4.50</td></tr>");
            document.write(
              "<tr><td>Peacock Sandwich</td><td>$4.00</td></tr>");
            document.write(
              "<tr><td>Alligator Nuggets</td><td>$6.00</td></tr>");
            document.write(
               "<tr><td>Python Salad</td><td>$5.50</td></tr>");
            document.write(
               "<tr><td>Rattler Soup</td><td>$2.50</td></tr>");
            document.write( "</table>");
            document.write( "</center>");
        }

        if ( currentHour >= 17 && currentHour < 22 ) {
            document.write( "<center>");
            document.write(
              "<h2><i>We're now serving dinner!</i></h2>");
            document.write( "<table border bgcolor='aqua'>");
            document.write(
              "<tr><th colspan = 2>Our Dinner Menu</th></tr>");
            document.write(
              "<tr><td>Filet Mignon</td><td>$9.00</td></tr>");
            document.write(
              "<tr><td>Lobster Thermador</td><td>$8.50</td></tr>");
            document.write(
              "<tr><td>Strip Steak</td><td>$8.00</td></tr>");
            document.write(
              "<tr><td>Tube Steak</td><td>$4.50</td></tr>");
            document.write(
              "<tr><td>Baked Potato</td><td>$3.50</td></tr>");
            document.write(
              "<tr><td>Broiled Potato</td><td>$2.50</td></tr>");
            document.write(
              "<tr><td>Eggplant Drops</td><td>$2.50</td></tr>");
            document.write("</table>");
            document.write( "</center>");
        }

    </script>
  </head>

  <body>
  </body>

</html>
```

Figure 8-15   A restaurant menu that depends on the time of day

You can see in Figure 8-15 restaurant.html at work, where it's reporting the lunch menu.

Here's the key about document.write: it really is only for writing whole pages at once; there's no way to write just to a specific section of the page. When you use document.write, it "opens" a web page for writing, and when that web page is displayed, it's "closed" for writing. If you attempt to use document.write on a closed web page, that page is opened again—which means it's erased and blanked. That's fine if you want to rewrite the whole page, but it's not good if you just want to update data in a specific section of that page.

Chapter 9

Introducing PHP with Ajax

Key Skills & Concepts

- Mixing PHP with HTML

- Echoing text to the browser

- Working with variables

- Working with arrays

- Using if statements

- Using for loops

- Using while loops

- Using foreach loops

You can use Ajax to download static text and XML files from the server, of course, but there's not really much advantage to doing so. If your data doesn't change, why not just store it in your web page to start with? The true power of Ajax comes when your web page interacts with the server, and the server can send data that varies. That's why Ajax is usually used with some programming language that runs on the server—and the most common server-side language used with Ajax today is PHP.

For that reason, this and the following two chapters concentrate on introducing PHP as it relates to Ajax. You'll get a good working knowledge of PHP in these chapters, enough to provide a solid foundation for nearly any Ajax work you want to do.

Getting Started with PHP

To run PHP, you have to have a server that supports it. You can seek out an Internet service provider (ISP) that hosts PHP, or you can install it yourself from www.php.net/. To run PHP code, you have to give your file on the server the extension .php (and bear in mind that if you're using WordPad, you should enclose the filename in quotation marks when you save it, so that WordPad doesn't add the extension .txt to your file).

Inside the file, you can enclose PHP code between the markup <?php and ?>:

```
<?php
  .
  .
  .
[Put your PHP code here]
  .
  .
  .
?>
```

Then, when you access the file on the server via a web browser, the server sees that the file has the extension .php and checks to see if there's any PHP code in it. If the server finds PHP code, it runs that code, which can send results back to the browser.

Here's an example that runs the PHP built-in function phpinfo, which displays an HTML table of data about the version of PHP the server is running. This example will be named phpinfo.php.

We can also include HTML in PHP files, and in phpinfo.php, we want to send a web page back to the browser, so let's start with some HTML:

```html
<html>
    <head>
        <title>
            Running phpinfo
        </title>
    </head>

    <body>
        <h1>
            Running phpinfo
        </h1>
            .
            .
            .
    </body>
</html>
```

Now we can add the PHP markup that tells the server that there's PHP code to be run:

```html
<html>
    <head>
        <title>
            Running phpinfo
        </title>
    </head>

    <body>
        <h1>
            Running phpinfo
        </h1>
        <?php
            .
            .
            .
        ?>
    </body>
</html>
```

In this case, the only PHP we'll run is the phpinfo function, which will display an HTML table:

```
<html>
    <head>
        <title>
            Running phpinfo
        </title>
    </head>

    <body>
        <h1>
            Running phpinfo
        </h1>
        <?php
            phpinfo();
        ?>
    </body>
</html>
```

As you can see in Figure 9-1, the phpinfo function did indeed run, and the results appear in the figure. Not bad—our first PHP example in this chapter has run successfully.

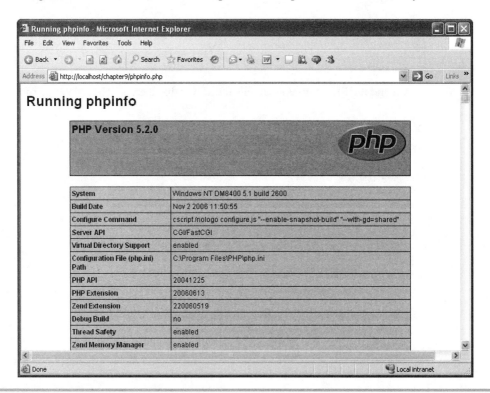

Figure 9-1   Running the phpinfo function

Returning Text to the Browser

Of course, running PHP scripts on the server wouldn't be much use unless you could send data back to the browser, where your Ajax application can make use of that data in JavaScript. In PHP, the primary function that sends data back to the browser is the echo function.

Here's an example, echo.php, that puts this function to work. We'll start echo.php with some HTML:

```html
<html>
    <head>
        <title>
            Echoing text
        </title>
    </head>

    <body>
        <h1>
            Echoing text
        </h1>
        .
        .
        .
    </body>
</html>
```

Next, we'll add a call to the echo function in a PHP block—we only have to pass the echo function the text we want to send back to the browser (echo.php):

```html
<html>
    <head>
        <title>
            Echoing text
        </title>
    </head>

    <body>
        <h1>
            Echoing text
        </h1>
        <?php
            echo("Hello from PHP.");
        ?>
    </body>
</html>
```

You can see the results in Figure 9-2, where the text we sent back to the browser does appear in the browser. Nice.

Figure 9-2 Using the echo function

Send HTML to the Browser

Besides simple text, you can also send HTML back to the browser using the echo function. Try this: make the message in echo.php appear in the browser in bold, italic font using the HTML tags <b> and <i>.

Here's what that would look like in code:

```
<html>
    <head>
        <title>
            Echoing text
        </title>
    </head>

    <body>
        <h1>
            Echoing text
        </h1>
        <?php
            echo("<b><i>Hello from PHP.</i></b>");
        ?>
    </body>
</html>
```

Now how about sending XML back to the browser?

Returning XML to the Browser

It's easier to send simple text back to the browser, but after all, the *x* in Ajax stands for XML. Let's take a look at how to send XML back to the browser from a PHP script with a new example, xml.php.

Let's say that we want to send this XML document to the browser:

```
<?xml version="1.0" ?>
<document>

  <item>Raspberry</item>

  <item>Strawberry</item>

  <item>Blueberry</item>

  <item>Tomato</item>

</document>
```

Because this is XML, we can't send any HTML back to the browser, so this example will be all PHP, no HTML:

```
<?php
    .
    .
    .
?>
```

We start by setting the header that the server sends to the browser to a Content-Type header set to "text/xml," which tells the browser that this document is XML (the default, if you don't set this header, is HTML):

```
<?php
  header('Content-Type: text/xml');
    .
    .
    .
?>
```

Every (legal) XML document starts with an XML declaration:

```
<?xml version="1.0" ?>
<document>

  <item>Raspberry</item>

  <item>Strawberry</item>
```

Ask the Expert

Q: Why did we set the Content-Type header to "text/xml"?

A: To send XML back to the browser, you tell the browser what that data's format is by setting the Content-Type header to the MIME (Multipurpose Internet Mail Extensions) type "text/xml."

Q: Who sets the MIME types of data formats, and what other types are available?

A: Data formats are named and given MIME types by the Internet Assigned Numbers Authority (IANA). You can find all the MIME types available at www.iana.org/assignments/media-types/. Examples include "text/rtf" for Rich Text Format text and text/html for HTML, the default for web servers.

```
<item>Blueberry</item>

<item>Tomato</item>

</document>
```

We can echo such a declaration to the browser like this:

```php
<?php
  header('Content-Type: text/xml');
  echo '<?xml version="1.0" ?>';
        .
        .
        .
?>
```

Next, we'll send the opening tag of the document element, just named <document>, back to the browser:

```xml
<?xml version="1.0" ?>
<document>

  <item>Raspberry</item>

  <item>Strawberry</item>

  <item>Blueberry</item>

  <item>Tomato</item>

</document>
```

Here's what that looks like in xml.php:

```php
<?php
  header('Content-Type: text/xml');
  echo '<?xml version="1.0" ?>';

  echo '<document>';
          .
          .
          .
?>
```

Next come the actual XML <item> elements:

```xml
<?xml version="1.0" ?>
<document>

  <item>Raspberry</item>

  <item>Strawberry</item>

  <item>Blueberry</item>

  <item>Tomato</item>

</document>
```

These XML <item> elements look like this in xml.php:

```php
<?php
  header('Content-Type: text/xml');
  echo '<?xml version="1.0" ?>';

  echo '<document>';

  echo '<item>';
  echo 'Raspberry';
  echo '</item>';

  echo '<item>';
  echo 'Strawberry';
  echo '</item>';

  echo '<item>';
  echo 'Blueberry';
  echo '</item>';

  echo '<item>';
  echo 'Tomato';
  echo '</item>';
          .
          .
          .
?>
```

We end by closing the <document> element:

```php
<?php
  header('Content-Type: text/xml');
  echo '<?xml version="1.0" ?>';

  echo '<document>';

  echo '<item>';
  echo 'Raspberry';
  echo '</item>';

  echo '<item>';
  echo 'Strawberry';
  echo '</item>';

  echo '<item>';
  echo 'Blueberry';
  echo '</item>';

  echo '<item>';
  echo 'Tomato';
  echo '</item>';

  echo '</document>';
?>
```

Excellent—now we've created and returned XML from a PHP script (see Figure 9-3).

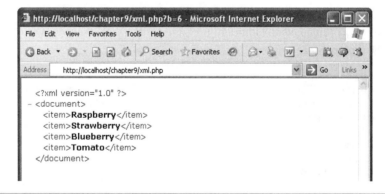

Figure 9-3   Viewing the XML sent from xml.php

Adding Comments to Your PHP Code

Comments are annotations that you can add to a program to make it more human-readable. Comments are ignored by the server, but they help you explain to other people (or yourself) what your program does.

There are three types of comments in PHP. The first type is a single-line comment, which begins with // and tells PHP not to read anything else for the remainder of the current line. Here's an example:

```php
<?php
  header('Content-Type: text/xml');
  echo '<?xml version="1.0" ?>';

  //Print the document element
  echo '<document>';

  //Print the elements
  echo '<item>';
  echo 'Raspberry';
  echo '</item>';

  echo '<item>';
  echo 'Strawberry';   //Strawberries are good!
  echo '</item>';

  echo '<item>';
  echo 'Blueberry';
  echo '</item>';

  echo '<item>';
  echo 'Tomato';
  echo '</item>';

  echo '</document>';
?>
```

Note that each comment doesn't have to have its own line; you can place a comment at the end of the line, as with the comment about strawberries above.

The second type of PHP comment is also a single-line comment, but it starts with the sharp symbol (#) instead of //:

```php
<?php
  header('Content-Type: text/xml');
  echo '<?xml version="1.0" ?>';

  #Print the document element
  echo '<document>';
```

```php
#Print the elements
echo '<item>';
echo 'Raspberry';
echo '</item>';

echo '<item>';
echo 'Strawberry';   #Strawberries are good!
echo '</item>';

echo '<item>';
echo 'Blueberry';
echo '</item>';

echo '<item>';
echo 'Tomato';
echo '</item>';

echo '</document>';
?>
```

Besides these two types of single-line comments, PHP also supports mutliline comments with the markup /* (which starts the comment) and */ (which ends the comment). All the text between /* and */ is ignored by PHP. Here's what our single-line comments look like when converted to multiline comments:

```php
<?php
header('Content-Type: text/xml');
echo '<?xml version="1.0" ?>';

/* Print the
document
element */
echo '<document>';

/* Print
the
elements */
echo '<item>';
echo 'Raspberry';
echo '</item>';

echo '<item>';
/* Strawberries are good! */
echo 'Strawberry';
echo '</item>';

echo '<item>';
echo 'Blueberry';
echo '</item>';
```

```
    echo '<item>';
    echo 'Tomato';
    echo '</item>';

    echo '</document>';
?>
```

Storing Data in Variables

As you know, variables are placeholders in memory for data, and using variables in PHP is as easy as using them in JavaScript. In PHP, variable names begin with a dollar sign, like this: $numberOfBooks or $moneyOwedToMe. As in JavaScript, you can use variables in PHP to store numbers or text strings.

Storing Numbers in Variables

Here's an example, variables.html, showing how to store numbers. This example will keep track of a number of apples, and starts by storing two apples in a variable named $apples, like this:

```
<html>
    <head>
        <title>
            Storing numbers in variables
        </title>
    </head>

    <body>
        <h1>
            Storing numbers in variables
        </h1>

        <?php
            echo "I'm setting the number of apples to 2...<br>";

            $apples = 2;
                .
                .
                .
        ?>

    </body>

</html>
```

Now $apples holds 2, as you can verify by displaying its contents in the browser using the echo statement:

```
<html>
    <head>
        <title>
            Storing numbers in variables
        </title>
    </head>

    <body>
        <h1>
            Storing numbers in variables
        </h1>

        <?php
            echo "I'm setting the number of apples to 2...<br>";

            $apples = 2;

            echo "The current number of apples is ", $apples, ".<br>";
                .
                .
                .
            .
        ?>

    </body>

</html>
```

Note how this works: you can echo a variety of items back to the browser if you separate those items with commas. Now you can add three more apples to the total, and echo the new total (variables.php):

```
<html>
    <head>
        <title>
            Storing numbers in variables
        </title>
    </head>

    <body>
        <h1>
            Storing numbers in variables
        </h1>
```

```php
<?php
    echo "I'm setting the number of apples to 2...<br>";

    $apples = 2;

    echo "The current number of apples is ", $apples, ".<br>";

    echo "Now I'm adding three more apples...<br>";

    $apples = $apples + 3;

    echo "The number of apples I have now is ", $apples, "<br>";
?>

    </body>

</html>
```

That's all you need to do—you can see the results in Figure 9-4.

Storing Text Strings in Variables

Besides numbers, you can also store strings in PHP variables, as in this example:

```php
$name = "Eythmoid Studge, Jr.";
```

In JavaScript, you can concatenate (that is, assemble) strings using the + operator, but in PHP, you use the dot (.) operator:

```php
$name = "Eythmoid" . " Studge," . " Jr.";
```

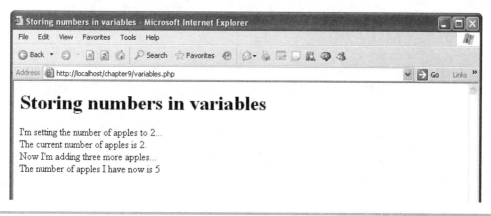

Figure 9-4 Using variables in variables.php

You can also use the many built-in string functions in PHP to work with strings. For example, the strtoupper function converts text to uppercase letters. The statement

```
$name = strtoupper("Eythmoid Studge, Jr.");
```

would leave "EYTHMOID STUDGE, JR." in $name.

The next example, string.php, uses the following popular string functions to get you started working with strings in PHP:

- **trim** Trims spaces from the beginning and end of a string
- **substr** Extracts substrings from a string
- **strlen** Returns the length of a string
- **substr_replace** Replaces text in a string
- **strtoupper** Converts a whole string to uppercase letters

We'll start off with the string " Good old PHP!", which has leading spaces, and use the trim function to trim off those spaces—this is a great function, because users often type leading or trailing spaces that you want to get rid of:

```html
<html>
    <head>
        <title>
            Working with PHP strings
        </title>
    </head>

    <body>
        <h1>
            Working With PHP strings
        </h1>

        <?php
          echo trim("    Good old PHP!"), "<br>";
            .
            .
            .
        ?>

    </body>

</html>
```

Next, we'll use the substr function to extract a substring from a string. You pass this function the string you start with, the (0-based) position in the string at which to start the substring, and the length of the substring. For example, to extract "PHP" from "Good old PHP!", we would do this:

```php
<?php
    echo trim("    Good old PHP!"), "<br>";

    echo substr("Good old PHP!", 9, 3), "<br>";
    .
    .
    .
?>
```

You can check the length of a string with the strlen function, which returns the length of the string you pass to it, in characters:

```php
<?php
    echo trim("    Good old PHP!"), "<br>";

    echo substr("Good old PHP!", 9, 3), "<br>";

    echo "'PHP' starts at position ", strpos("Good old PHP!",
      "PHP"), "<br>";

    echo "'Good old PHP!' is ", strlen("Good old PHP!"), "
      characters long.<br>";
    .
    .
    .
?>
```

You can also replace a substring in a string with another substring, using the substr_ replace function. You pass this function the string you want to edit, the new string to insert, the location at which you want to insert the new string in the old string, and the number of characters you want to replace. Here's how we might convert "Good old PHP!" to "Great old PHP!" using substr_replace:

```php
<?php
    echo trim("    Good old PHP!"), "<br>";

    echo substr("Good old PHP!", 9, 3), "<br>";

    echo "'PHP' starts at position ", strpos("Good old PHP!",
      "PHP"), "<br>";

    echo "'Good old PHP!' is ", strlen("Good old PHP!"), "
      characters long.<br>";
```

```php
    echo substr_replace("Good old PHP!", "Great", 0, 4), "<br>";
    .
    .
    .

?>
```

Finally, we use the strtoupper function to convert "Good old PHP!" to all uppercase letters:

```php
<?php
  echo trim("    Good old PHP!"), "<br>";

  echo substr("Good old PHP!", 9, 3), "<br>";

  echo "'PHP' starts at position ", strpos("Good old PHP!",
    "PHP"), "<br>";

  echo "'Good old PHP!' is ", strlen("Good old PHP!"), "
    characters long.<br>";

  echo substr_replace("Good old PHP!", "Great", 0, 4), "<br>";

  echo strtoupper("Good old PHP!"), "<br>";
?>
```

You can see this example, string.php, at work in Figure 9-5.

Many string functions are available in PHP, and you can find a sample in Table 9-1.

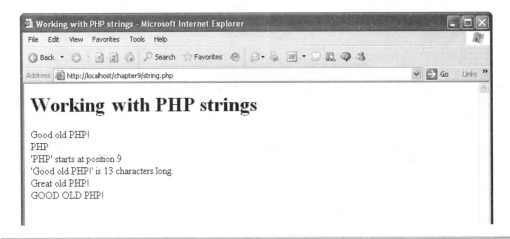

Figure 9-5 Using string functions in string.php

Function	Description
addcslashes	Quotes a string with slashes
addslashes	Quotes a string with slashes
bin2hex	Converts binary data into hexadecimal representation
chop	Alias of the rtrim function
chr	Returns a specific character given its ASCII code
chunk_split	Splits a string into smaller chunks
convert_cyr_string	Converts from one Cyrillic character set to another
count_chars	Returns information about characters in a string
crc32	Calculates the crc32 polynomial of a string
crypt	Supports one-way string encryption (hashing)
echo	Displays one or more strings
explode	Splits a string on a substring
fprintf	Writes a formatted string to a stream
get_html_translation_table	Returns the translation table
hebrev	Converts Hebrew text to visual text
hebrevc	Converts logical Hebrew text to visual text
html_entity_decode	Converts all HTML entities to their applicable characters
htmlentities	Converts all applicable characters to HTML entities
htmlspecialchars	Converts special characters to HTML entities
implode	Joins array elements with a string
join	Alias of the implode function
levenshtein	Calculates the Levenshtein distance between two strings
localeconv	Gets the numeric formatting information
ltrim	Strips whitespace from the beginning of a string
md5	Calculates the MD5 hash of a string
md5_file	Calculates the MD5 hash of a given filename
metaphone	Calculates the metaphone key of a string
money_format	Formats a number as a currency string
nl_langinfo	Queries language and locale information
nl2br	Inserts HTML line breaks before all newlines in a string
number_format	Formats a number with grouped thousands separators

Table 9-1 The String Functions

(continued)

Function	Description
ord	Returns the ASCII value of a character
parse_str	Parses a string into variables
print	Displays a string
printf	Displays a formatted string
quoted_printable_decode	Converts a quoted-printable string to an 8-bit string
quotemeta	Quotes metacharacters
rtrim	Strips whitespace from the end of a string
setlocale	Sets locale information
sha1	Calculates the SHA1 hash of a string
sha1_file	Calculates the SHA1 hash of a file
similar_text	Calculates the similarity between two strings
soundex	Calculates the soundex key of a string
sprintf	Returns a formatted string
sscanf	Parses input from a string according to a format
str_ireplace	Case-insensitive version of the str_replace function
str_pad	Pads a string with another string
str_repeat	Repeats a string
str_replace	Replaces all occurrences of the search string with the replacement string
str_rot13	Performs the rot13 transform on a string
str_shuffle	Shuffles a string randomly
str_split	Converts a string to an array
str_word_count	Returns information about words used in a string
strcasecmp	Performs a binary case-insensitive string comparison
strchr	Alias of the strstr function
strcmp	Performs a binary-safe string comparison
strcoll	Performs a locale-based string comparison
strcspn	Finds the length of the initial segment not matching a mask
strip_tags	Strips HTML and PHP tags from a string
stripcslashes	Unquotes string quoted with addcslashes()
stripos	Finds position of first occurrence of a case-insensitive string
stripslashes	Unquotes string quoted with addslashes()

Table 9-1   The String Functions (*continued*)

Function	Description
stristr	Case-insensitive version of the strstr function
strlen	Gets a string's length
strnatcasecmp	Performs a case-insensitive string comparison
strnatcmp	Performs a string comparison using a "natural order" algorithm
strncasecmp	Performs a binary case-insensitive string comparison of the first n characters
strncmp	Performs a binary-safe string comparison of the first n characters
strpos	Finds the position of first occurrence of a string
strrchr	Finds the last occurrence of a character in a string
strrev	Reverses a string
strripos	Finds the position of last occurrence of a case-insensitive string
strrpos	Finds the position of last occurrence of a character in a string
strspn	Finds the length of initial segment matching mask
strstr	Finds the first occurrence of a string
strtok	Tokenizes a string
strtolower	Converts a string to lowercase
strtoupper	Converts a string to uppercase
strtr	Translates certain characters
substr	Returns part of a string
substr_compare	Performs a binary-safe (optionally case-insensitive) comparison of two strings from an offset
substr_count	Counts the number of substring occurrences
substr_replace	Replaces text within part of a string
trim	Strips whitespace from the beginning and end of a string
ucfirst	Makes a string's first character uppercase
ucwords	Makes the first character of each word in a string uppercase
vprintf	Outputs a formatted string
vsprintf	Returns a formatted string
wordwrap	Wraps a string to a given number of characters

Table 9-1   The String Functions (*continued*)

Another thing that you can do with variables in PHP is interpolate them into strings, as discussed next.

Interpolating Variables into Text Strings

Interpolating variables into text strings means having PHP substitute a variable's value for the name of a variable in a text string. For example, if you have two apples in a variable named $apples, you can display that fact with the echo statement like this:

```
$apples = 2;
echo "I have " . $apples . " apples.";
```

But PHP also allows you to use the following shortcut, where you can simply place a variable in a text string, and the variable's name will be replaced with the value in the variable:

```
$apples = 2;
echo "I have $apples apples.";
```

Variable interpolation happens when you use double quotation (not single!) marks to surround a text string. In such strings, the name of each variable will be replaced by its value. For example, here's what our earlier example variables.php looks like if you use interpolation instead (this is interpolation.php):

```
<head>
    <title>
        Interpolating variables in strings
    </title>
</head>

<body>
    <h1>
        Interpolating variables in strings
    </h1>

    <?php
        echo "I'm setting the number of apples to 2...<br>";

        $apples = 2;

        echo "The current number of apples is $apples.<br>";

        echo "Now I'm adding three more apples...<br>";

        $apples = $apples + 3;

        echo "The number of apples I have now is $apples.<br>";
    ?>

</body>

</html>
```

You can see interpolation.php at work in Figure 9-6. Cool.

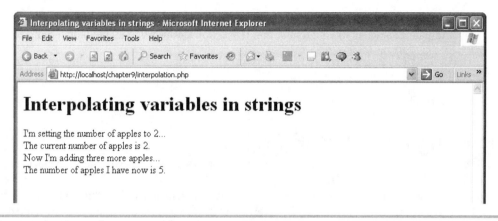

Figure 9-6   Interpolating variables into text strings

But here's a question: can you run a variable name into other text? For example, what if you want to display "I have a hotdog."? You could start by storing the "hot" in "hotdog" in a variable named $data:

```
<?
    $data = "hot";
    .
    .
    .
?>
```

Then, could you put together the word "hotdog" using $data? Would that look like this?

```
<?
    $data = "hot";

    echo "I have a $datadog.<br>";
?>
```

It turns out that this won't work—PHP will want to know what this new variable named $datadog is. Instead, you can surround the name of the variable (but not the leading $) in curly braces to make interpolation work in this case:

```
<?
    $data = "hot";

    echo "I have a ${data}dog. <br>";
?>
```

And that's how to interpolate variables when those variables run up against other nonwhitespace characters in your text string. If you don't want a variable to be interpolated, put a backslash (\) in front of it:

```
echo "I have \$apples.";
```

This will display "I have $apples."

Handling Data in PHP Arrays

The next step up in handling data from variables is arrays, and arrays work in PHP much as they do in JavaScript.

Here's an example, arrays.php, that gives you the fundamentals of working with arrays. In PHP, you can create an array simply by referring to it. Here's how we create an array named $fruit (like other variables, array names in PHP begin with a $) and assign $fruit[0] the string "apples" (as in JavaScript, arrays in PHP are 0-based):

```php
<?php
    $fruit[0] = "apples";
    .
    .
    .
    }
?>
```

We can add other items to the array as well:

```php
<?php
    $fruit[0] = "apples";
    $fruit[1] = "oranges";
    $fruit[2] = "pomegranates";
    .
    .
    .
    }
?>
```

We can overwrite elements in the array simply by assigning another value to that element, like this, where we're overwriting $fruit[2]:

```php
<?php
    $fruit[0] = "apples";
    $fruit[1] = "oranges";
    $fruit[2] = "pomegranates";

    $fruit[2] = "watermelons";
    .
    .
    .
?>
```

In fact, there's a shortcut in PHP to add another element to the end of an array—you can simply omit the index inside the square braces, [and]. For example, here's how we create $fruit[3] and set it to "kumquats":

```php
<?php
    $fruit[0]  =  "apples";
    $fruit[1]  =  "oranges";
    $fruit[2]  =  "pomegranates";

    $fruit[2]  =  "watermelons";

    $fruit[] = "kumquats";
        .
        .
        .
?>
```

Okay, let's print out the array elements in a for loop, which works just like for loops in JavaScript. In PHP, we can determine the number of elements in an array by passing the array to the PHP count function, which returns the number of elements in the array; so, we can loop over all those elements this way:

```php
<?php
    $fruit[0]  =  "apples";
    $fruit[1]  =  "oranges";
    $fruit[2]  =  "pomegranates";

    $fruit[2]  =  "watermelons";

    $fruit[] = "kumquats";

    for ($loopIndex = 0; $loopIndex < count($fruit);
        $loopIndex++){
            .
            .
            .
    }
?>
```

And here's how we display in the browser each element in the array in arrays.php:

```html
<html>
    <head>
        <title>
            Creating PHP Arrays
        </title>
    </head>
```

```
<body>
    <h1>
        Creating PHP Arrays
    </h1>

<?php
    $fruit[0] = "apples";
    $fruit[1] = "oranges";
    $fruit[2] = "pomegranates";

    $fruit[2] = "watermelons";

    $fruit[] = "kumquats";

    for ($loopIndex = 0; $loopIndex < count($fruit);
      $loopIndex++){
        echo "\$fruit[$loopIndex] = $fruit[$loopIndex] <br>";
    }
?>
    </body>
</html>
```

You can see this example at work in Figure 9-7.

You can also use words as array indexes in PHP, like this:

```
$array["fruit"] = "apples";
```

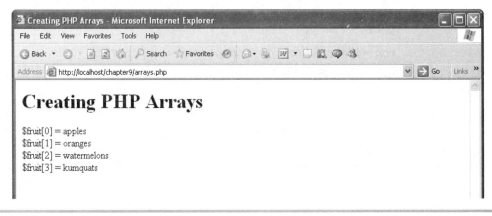

Figure 9-7 Working with arrays

Handling Data with Operators

Just like JavaScript, PHP has a bunch of built-in operators, and here they are, in order of precedence (that is, operators higher up in this list are executed before lower-down operators when used together in the same statement):

- new
- [
- ! ~ ++ --
- * / %
- + - .
- == !=
- &
- |
- &&
- ||
- ? :
- = += -= *= /= .= %= &= |= ^= <<= >>=

Here's an example, operators.php, that puts some operators to work in PHP—specifically, +, -, *, and /:

```
<html>
    <head>
        <title>
            Using PHP Operators
        </title>
    </head>

    <body>
        <h1>
            Using PHP Operators
        </h1>
        <?php
            echo "12 + 3 = ", 12 + 3, "<br>";

            echo "12 - 3 = ", 12 - 3, "<br>";

            echo "12 * 3 = ", 12 * 3, "<br>";

            echo "12 / 3 = ", 12 / 3, "<br>";

        ?>
    </body>
</html>
```

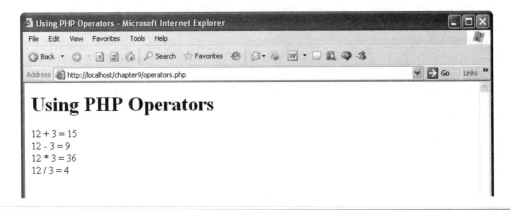

Figure 9-8 Working with PHP operators

The results, shown in Figure 9-8, are the same as you'd expect, based on your knowledge of JavaScript.

Branching with the if Statement

The PHP if statement looks just like the version in JavaScript, except for the addition of optional elseif clauses. Formally, this is what the if statement looks like in PHP (note that *statement* can be a compound statement made up of several lines enclosed in curly braces, { and }):

```
if (condition)
    statement
[elseif(condition)
    statement]
        .

        .

        .
[elseif(condition)
    statement]
else
    statement
```

You already know from your knowledge of JavaScript how the if and else keywords work. The elseif keyword in PHP allows you to test additional conditions and execute code if they're true. Here's an example, elseif.php, that shows how to compare a variable to multiple conditions and execute code corresponding to the first condition that evaluates to true:

```html
<html>
    <head>
        <title>
            Using elseif in PHP
        </title>
    </head>

    <body>
        <h1>
            Using elseif in PHP
        </h1>
        <?
            $temperature = 87;

            if ($temperature < 80){
              echo "Temperature is OK.";
            }
            elseif ($temperature < 85) {
              echo "Pretty warm.";
            }
            elseif ($temperature < 90) {
              echo "Pretty hot.";
            }
            else {
              echo "Too hot!";
            }
        ?>
    </body>
</html>
```

You can see the results in Figure 9-9—pretty hot!

Just as in JavaScript, you can use comparison operators like < and > as well as logical operators like && (the And operator) to express your conditions in code. For example, this if statement checks if the temperature is between 65 and 85, inclusive:

```
<?
    $temperature = 70;

    if (($temperature >= 65) && ($temperature <= 85){
      echo "In the comfort zone.";
    }
?>
```

The PHP comparison operators are summarized in Table 9-2, and the logical operators are summarized in Table 9-3.

Figure 9-9 Working with the elseif keyword

Operator	Operation	Example	Result
==	Equal	$a == $b	True if $a is equal to $b
===	Identical	$a === $b	True if $a is equal to $b, and they are of the same type
!=	Not equal	$a != $b	True if $a is not equal to $b
<>	Not equal	$a <> $b	True if $a is not equal to $b
!==	Not identical	$a !== $b	True if $a is not equal to $b, or they are not of the same type
<	Less than	$a < $b	True if $a is less than $b
>	Greater than	$a > $b	True if $a is greater than $b
<=	Less than or equal to	$a <= $b	True if $a is less than or equal to $b
>=	Greater than or equal to	$a >= $b	True if $a is greater than or equal to $b

Table 9-2 The Comparison Operators

Operator	Operation	Example	Result
and	And	$a and $b	True if both $a and $b are TRUE
or	Or	$a or $b	True if either $a or $b is TRUE
xor	Xor	$a xor $b	True if either $a or $b is TRUE, but not both
!	Not	! $a	True if $a is not TRUE
&&	And	$a && $b	True if both $a and $b are TRUE
||	Or	$a || $b	True if either $a or $b is TRUE

Table 9-3 The Logical Operators

Using for Loops in PHP

The for loop, which repeatedly executes a statement, looks like this in PHP:

```
for (expression1; expression2; expression3)
   statement
```

Here, as in JavaScript, *expression1* lets you initialize your loop, often by initializing a loop counter, also called a loop index, that tracks how many times the loop has executed. The next expression, *expression2*, is the test expression—the loop keeps going while this expression remains true. You usually test the value in your loop counter here. The final expression, *expression3*, is executed after *statement* is executed, each time through the loop. You usually increment your loop counter variable in that expression. Every time through the loop, *statement*, which can be a compound statement consisting of many single statements enclosed in curly braces, is executed.

Here's an example for loop, in for.php, which prints out "I'm going to print this ten times." ten times:

```
<html>
    <head>
        <title>
            Using the PHP for Loop
        </title>
    </head>

    <body>
        <h1>
            Using the PHP for Loop
        </h1>

        <?php
            for ($loopIndex = 0; $loopIndex < 10; $loopIndex++){
               echo "I'm going to print this ten times.<br>";
            }
        ?>
    </body>
</html>
```

And you can see the results in Figure 9-10. Nice.

Looping with the while Loop

The while loop keeps executing its code while its condition remains true. Here's what this loop looks like formally:

```
while (condition)
   statement
```

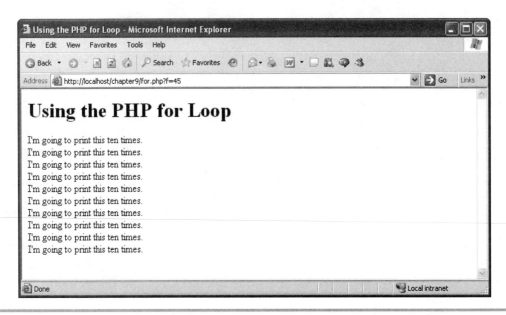

Figure 9-10 Working with the for loop

This loop just keeps executing *statement* (which, of course, can be a compound statement enclosed in curly braces) until *condition* becomes false.

Here's an example, while.php, that keeps displaying the message "I'm going to print this ELEVEN times." First, we set up the while loop and a variable to keep track of the number of times the loop has executed:

```
<html>
    <head>
        <title>
            Using a PHP while Loop
        </title>
    </head>

    <body>
        <h1>
            Using a PHP while Loop
        </h1>
        <?php
            $variable = 0;

            while ($variable < 11){
```

```
            .
            .
            .
        }
    ?>
    </body>
</html>
```

Now we can add the stuffing in the while loop—the part that echoes the message to the browser and increments the variable:

```
<html>
    <head>
        <title>
            Using a PHP while Loop
        </title>
    </head>

    <body>
        <h1>
            Using a PHP while Loop
        </h1>
        <?php
            $variable = 0;

            while ($variable < 11){
                echo "I'm going to print this ELEVEN times.<br>";
                $variable++;
            }
        ?>
    </body>
</html>
```

You can see the results in Figure 9-11—this example did indeed print out the message eleven times. Nice.

Try This Display a Message Multiple Times

Create a PHP example that prints out a message repeatedly for a tenth of a second. You can use the gettimeofday function to get the current time of day; this function returns an array, and the predefined sec constant is the index in that array of the seconds value. So, to keep printing out a message for a tenth of a second, you might do this:

```
<html>
    <head>
        <title>
```

(continued)

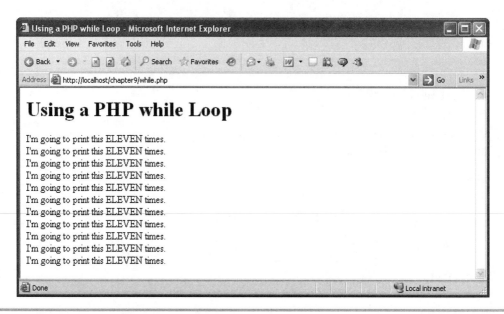

Figure 9-11 Working with the while loop

```
            Using a PHP while Loop
        </title>
    </head>

    <body>
        <h1>
            Using a PHP while Loop
        </h1>
        <?php
          $time = gettimeofday();
          $start = $time[sec];

          $time = gettimeofday();
          $timeNow = $time[sec];

          while ($timeNow < ($start + 0.1)){
            $time = gettimeofday();
            $timeNow = $time[sec];
            echo "I'm going to keep going for a tenth of a second!<br>";
            }
        ?>
    </body>
</html>
```

Looping with the do...while Loop

There's another version of the while loop—the do...while loop. This loop checks its condition at the end of the loop, not at the beginning, which means that the loop's statement is always executed at least once (and that's good if that statement sets the condition you want to test to see if the loop should keep looping). Here's what this loop looks like formally:

```
do
    statement
while (condition)
```

You might have noticed that in the previous Try This example, you had to set the $timeNow variable before starting the while loop—and then again inside the loop every time through the loop. With a do...while loop, we don't have to set the $timeNow variable before starting the loop, because the loop's condition is checked at the end of the loop instead:

```
<html>
    <head>
        <title>
            Using a PHP while Loop
        </title>
    </head>

    <body>
        <h1>
            Using a PHP while Loop
        </h1>
        <?php
          $time = gettimeofday();
          $start = $time[sec];

          do {
            $time = gettimeofday();
            $timeNow = $time[sec];
            echo "I'm going to keep going for a tenth of a second!<br>";
          } while ($timeNow < ($start + 0.1))
        ?>
    </body>
</html>
```

Keep in mind that the body of a do...while loop is always executed at least once.

Looping with the foreach Loop

PHP also has a special loop to loop over all the members of data collections like arrays—the foreach loop. Here's what it looks like:

```
foreach (array as $value)
  statement
```

The foreach loop is a handy one, because each time through the loop, it places the next element from the array into a variable that you can use inside the body of the loop. Here's an example, foreach.php. We start by creating an array of fruits:

```
<html>
    <head>
        <title>Using the PHP foreach Loop</title>
    </head>

    <body>
        <h1>Using the PHP foreach Loop</h1>
            <?php
            $array = array("apples", "oranges", "bananas", "cherries");
            .
            .
            .
            ?>
    </body>
</html>
```

Then we set up a foreach loop that loops over the array, filling a variable we name $fruit with the current element from the array each time through the loop:

```
<html>
    <head>
        <title>Using the PHP foreach Loop</title>
    </head>

    <body>
        <h1>Using the PHP foreach Loop</h1>
            <?php
            $array = array("apples", "oranges", "bananas", "cherries");

            foreach ($array as $fruit) {
            .
            .
            .
            }
            ?>
    </body>
</html>
```

Now we're free to use the $fruit variable in the body of the loop, which we do by printing it out:

```
<html>
    <head>
        <title>Using the PHP foreach Loop</title>
    </head>
```

```
<body>
    <h1>Using the PHP foreach Loop</h1>
        <?php
          $array = array("apples", "oranges", "bananas", "cherries");

          foreach ($array as $fruit) {
              echo "The current fruit: $fruit <br>";
          }
        ?>
    </body>
</html>
```

Great—you can see the results in Figure 9-12.

Note that the foreach loop is an exceptionally useful loop for iterating over arrays. With other loops, you have to set up an array index to iterate through an array (which is hard if your array uses words as index values), and there's always the chance that you'll get the array index off by one when you set up the loop. The foreach loop avoids that problem by looping over all the elements of the array automatically, no array index needed.

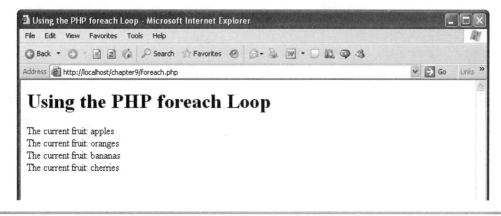

Figure 9-12   Working with the foreach loop

Chapter 10

PHP in Depth

Key Skills & Concepts

- Creating functions

- Passing data to functions

- Creating default arguments

- Returning data from functions

- Working with text fields, checkboxes, and radio buttons

- Handling multiple-selection HTML controls

- Working with image maps

The previous chapter introduced the basics of PHP. In this chapter, you'll get a real working knowledge of the subject. Here, you're going to see how to write functions in JavaScript and how to handle user input in HTML controls like text fields, radio buttons, checkboxes, and more.

Let's start with functions in PHP, which should be somewhat familiar to you from your study of functions in JavaScript.

Introducing PHP Functions

We'll start with PHP functions by jumping right into an example. Say that you have a web page like this:

```
<html>
  <head>
    <title>Using PHP Functions</title>
  </head>

  <body>
    <h1>Using PHP Functions</h1>

    <?php
      echo "<h3>Welcome to my Web page!</h3>";
      echo "<br>";
      echo "Do you like it?";
      echo "<br>";
      echo "<br>";
```

```
          .
          .
          .
    ?>
  </body>
</html>
```

That looks good, but suppose that you don't want anyone to steal anything from your beautiful new page, and thus decide to add a copyright notice. To do that, you plan to call a function named print_copyright_notice, which you can call like this, just as you might in JavaScript:

```
<html>
  <head>
    <title>Using PHP Functions</title>
  </head>

  <body>
    <h1>Using PHP Functions</h1>

    <?php
      echo "<h3>Welcome to my Web page!</h3>";
      echo "<br>";
      echo "Do you like it?";
      echo "<br>";
      echo "<br>";

      print_copyright_notice();
          .
          .
          .

    ?>
  </body>
</html>
```

You can create the print_copyright_notice function just as you can in JavaScript, with the keyword function, the name of the function, and a pair of parentheses:

```
<html>
  <head>
    <title>Using PHP Functions</title>
  </head>

  <body>
    <h1>Using PHP Functions</h1>

    <?php
      echo "<h3>Welcome to my Web page!</h3>";
      echo "<br>";
```

```
      echo "Do you like it?";
      echo "<br>";
      echo "<br>";

      print_copyright_notice();

      function print_copyright_notice()
      {
           .
           .
           .
      }
    ?>
  </body>
</html>
```

Then, you place the code you want to execute when the function is called inside the function's body. In this case, you can display a copyright notice like this (in this example, functions.php):

```
</html>
<html>
  <head>
    <title>Using PHP Functions</title>
  </head>

  <body>
    <h1>Using PHP Functions</h1>

    <?php
      echo "<h3>Welcome to my Web page!</h3>";
      echo "<br>";
      echo "Do you like it?";
      echo "<br>";
      echo "<br>";

      print_copyright_notice();

      function print_copyright_notice()
      {
        echo "<hr>";
        echo "<center>";
        echo "&copy; 2008 PHP Super Wonder Wizards, Inc.";
        echo "</center>";
      }
    ?>
  </body>
</html>
```

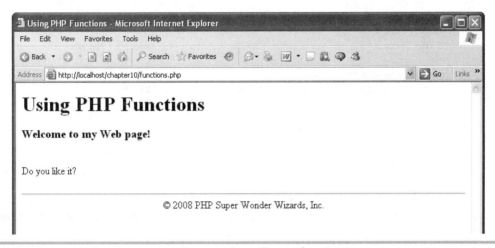

Figure 10-1 Displaying a copyright notice by calling a function

You can see the results in Figure 10-1, where the function has indeed been called, displaying a copyright notice.

Great—but there's a lot more to functions. How about passing data to them?

Passing Data to Functions in PHP

You can also pass data to functions in PHP, just as you can in JavaScript—and the syntax is the same, too. For example, say that you want to pass the copyright text to display to the print_copyright_notice function in a new example, passfunctions.php. You can pass that text like this:

```
<html>
  <head>
    <title>Passing Data to PHP Functions</title>
  </head>

  <body>
    <h1>Passing Data to PHP Functions</h1>

    <?php
      echo "<h3>Welcome to my Web page!</h3>";
      echo "<br>";
```

```
      echo "Do you like it?";
      echo "<br>";
      echo "<br>";

      print_copyright_notice(
        "&copy; 2008 PHP Super Wonder Wizards, Inc.");
            .
            .
            .

  ?>
  </body>
</html>
```

And, just as in JavaScript, you give the passed data a name ($text here) in the argument list of the function, and then you can refer to that data using that name in the body of the function:

```
<html>
  <head>
    <title>Passing Data to PHP Functions</title>
  </head>

  <body>
    <h1>Passing Data to PHP Functions</h1>

    <?php
      echo "<h3>Welcome to my Web page!</h3>";
      echo "<br>";
      echo "Do you like it?";
      echo "<br>";
      echo "<br>";

      print_copyright_notice(
        "&copy; 2008 PHP Super Wonder Wizards, Inc.");

      function print_copyright_notice($text)
      {
        echo "<hr>";
        echo "<center>";
        echo $text;
        echo "</center>";
      }
    ?>
  </body>
</html>
```

The results appear in Figure 10-2—as you can see, the data was passed to the function, which used that data correctly.

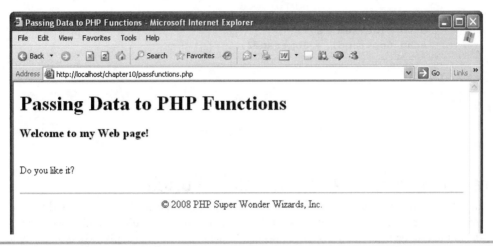

Figure 10-2 Passing data to functions

Try This Pass Multiple Items to a Function

Want to pass multiple items to a function? That also works just the same as in JavaScript. You separate the items in the parameter list with commas. Give this one a try—pass two numbers to a function named adder to add them and display the result. Here's what that looks like:

```
<html>
  <head>
    <title>Passing Data to PHP Functions</title>
  </head>

  <body>
    <h1>Passing Data to PHP Functions</h1>

    <?php
      echo "<h3>Welcome to My Math Page!</h3>";
      echo "<br>";
      echo "How much is 5 + 3?";
      echo "<br>";

      adder(5, 3);

      function adder($operand1, $operand2)
```

(continued)

```
    {
      echo "The sum is ";
      echo $operand1 + $operand2;
    }
  ?>
  </body>
</html>
```

Creating Default Arguments in Functions

In PHP, you can also set up *default* arguments in functions. These defaults are used in case you don't supply a value for a parameter. Here's an example, default.php, that sets some default text to be used in the copyright notice. You can do that by supplying a default value for the $text parameter, which you do with an equal sign in the declaration of the function:

```
function print_copyright_notice($text = "&copy; 2008")
{
  echo "<hr>";
  echo "<center>";
  echo $text;
  echo "</center>";
}
```

Now if you call print_copyright_notice and don't pass any data to the function, $text will be set to "© 2008" by default. Let's test that out by calling the function but not passing any data to it, in a new example, default.php:

```
<html>
  <head>
    <title>Using Default Arguments With PHP Functions</title>
  </head>

  <body>
    <h1>Using Default Arguments With PHP Functions</h1>

    <?php
      echo "<h3>Welcome to my Web page!</h3>";
      echo "<br>";
      echo "Do you like it?";
      echo "<br>";
      echo "<br>";

      print_copyright_notice();

      function print_copyright_notice($text = "&copy; 2008")
```

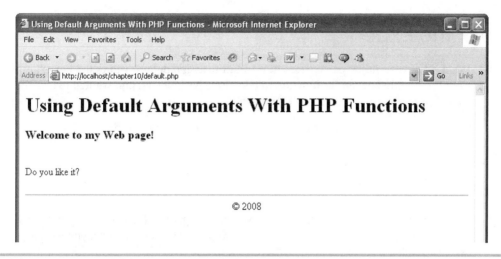

Figure 10-3 Using default arguments with functions

```
    {
        echo "<hr>";
        echo "<center>";
        echo $text;
        echo "</center>";
    }
    ?>
  </body>
</html>
```

You can see the results in Figure 10-3—the default value for the copyright notice was indeed used.

Returning Data from Functions

Because you already know how JavaScript works, you already know how returning data from PHP functions works, for the most part. For example, if you want to build a function named adder that adds two numbers and returns their sum, you can start like this in a new example, returnfunctions.php:

```
<html>
  <head>
    <title>Returning Data From PHP Functions</title>
  </head>

  <body>
    <h1>Returning Data From PHP Functions</h1>
```

Ask the Expert

Q: What if I have multiple parameters that I want to assign default values to? For example, what if I modified the adder function to take three parameters, and wanted to give the second parameter, $operand2, a default value?

```
function adder($operand1, $operand2, $operand3)
{
  echo "The sum is ";
  echo $operand1 + $operand2 + $operand3;
}
```

A: If you give one parameter a default value, you have to give all the parameters to the right of it default values, too. So if you want to give $operand2 a default value, you have to assign a default value to $operand3 also:

```
function adder($operand1, $operand2 = 1, $operand3 = 3)
{
  echo "The sum is ";
  echo $operand1 + $operand2 + $operand3;
}
```

```php
<?php
  echo "<h3>Welcome to My Math Page!</h3>";
  echo "<br>";
  echo "How much is 5 + 3?";
  echo "<br>";

  function adder($operand1, $operand2)
  {
    .
    .
    .
  }
?>
</body>
</html>
```

You can use the return statement to return the sum of the two numbers this way:

```
<html>
  <head>
    <title>Returning Data From PHP Functions</title>
  </head>
```

```
  <body>
    <h1>Returning Data From PHP Functions</h1>

    <?php
      echo "<h3>Welcome to My Math Page!</h3>";
      echo "<br>";
      echo "How much is 5 + 3?";
      echo "<br>";

      function adder($operand1, $operand2)
      {
        return $operand1 + $operand2;
      }
    ?>
  </body>
</html>
```

Now you can call the adder function and, just as in JavaScript, the function's name will be replaced with the value returned by that function:

```
<html>
  <head>
    <title>Returning Data From PHP Functions</title>
  </head>

  <body>
    <h1>Returning Data From PHP Functions</h1>

    <?php
      echo "<h3>Welcome to My Math Page!</h3>";
      echo "<br>";
      echo "How much is 5 + 3?";
      echo "<br>";

      echo "The sum is " . adder(5, 3);

      function adder($operand1, $operand2)
      {
        return $operand1 + $operand2;
      }
    ?>
  </body>
</html>
```

You can see what this looks like in Figure 10-4. Just as you'd expect.

You can also set up PHP functions to return multiple items at the same time. You do that by returning an array, which PHP makes easy to work with in code—here's an example, multiplereturnfunctions.php.

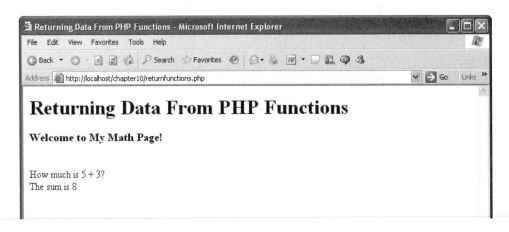

Figure 10-4 Returning data from functions

Start with a function named $fruits that returns an array of fruits, which you create with the built-in PHP array function:

```
<html>
  <head>
    <title>
      Returning Multiple Values From PHP Functions
    </title>
  </head>

  <body>
    <h1>
      Returning Multiple Values From PHP Functions
    </h1>

    <?php
      .
      .
      .
      function fruits()
      {
        $array = array("Apples", "Oranges", "Plums", "Cherries",
          "Strawberries", "Bananas");

        return $array;
      }
    ?>
  </body>
</html>
```

You can handle a function that returns an array with the built-in list function in PHP. That function lets you assign each element in an array to a new variable. Here's how that works, where you're assigning the first element in the returned array to the variable named $first, the second element to the variable named $second, and so on:

```
<html>
  <head>
    <title>
      Returning Multiple Values From PHP Functions
    </title>
  </head>

  <body>
    <h1>
      Returning Multiple Values From PHP Functions
    </h1>

    <?php

      list($first, $second, $third, $fourth, $fifth, $sixth) = fruits();
          .
          .
          .
      function fruits()
      {
        $array = array("Apples", "Oranges", "Plums", "Cherries",
          "Strawberries", "Bananas");

        return $array;
      }
    ?>
  </body>
</html>
```

Finally, you can display the new variables and their values:

```
<html>
  <head>
    <title>
      Returning Multiple Values From PHP Functions
    </title>
  </head>

  <body>
    <h1>
      Returning Multiple Values From PHP Functions
    </h1>
```

```php
<?php

list($first, $second, $third, $fourth, $fifth, $sixth) = fruits();

echo "\$first: $first<br>";
echo "\$second: $second<br>";
echo "\$third: $third<br>";
echo "\$fourth: $fourth<br>";
echo "\$fifth: $fifth<br>";
echo "\$sixth: $sixth<br>";

function fruits()
{
  $array = array("Apples", "Oranges", "Plums", "Cherries",
     "Strawberries", "Bananas");

  return $array;
}
?>
</body>
</html>
```

The results of this example appear in Figure 10-5; as you can see, the fruits function was able to return multiple values.

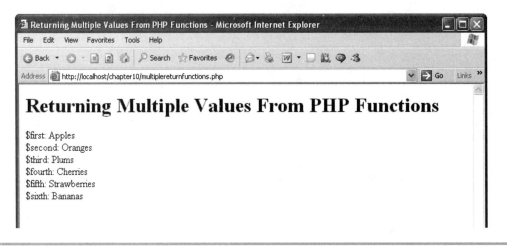

Figure 10-5 Returning multiple data values from functions

Working with HTML Controls in PHP

Much of PHP has to do with reading information entered by the user into HTML controls like text fields, radio buttons, list boxes, and the like, and in this section you'll see how to decode that information in PHP.

To start, you need a <form> element in your web page in which to put your HTML controls. Here are the important attributes of the <form> element:

- **ACTION**   Specifies the URL that will handle the form data. Note that you can omit this attribute, in which case its default is the URL of the current document.

- **METHOD**   Specifies the method or protocol for sending data to the target action URL. If you set it to GET (the default), this method sends all form name/value pair information in an URL that looks like:

   URL?name=value&name=value&name=value

   If you use the POST method, the contents of the form are encoded as with the GET method, but are sent in hidden environment variables.

- **TARGET**   Indicates a named frame for the browser to display the form results in.

Here's an example that uses the <form> element. This example uses the POST method to send its data to the server, and sends its data to a PHP file named responder.php in particular:

```html
<html>
    <head>
        <title>
            Using HTML forms
        </title>
    </head>

    <body>
        <h1>
            Using HTML forms
        </h1>
        <form method="post" action="responder.php">
            .
            .
            .
        </form>
    </body>
</html>
```

Okay, that sets up the <form> element. To actually send the data inside any HTML controls you put in the <form> element, you can use a Submit button, which you create with the <input type="submit"> element:

```
<html>
    <head>
        <title>
            Using HTML forms
        </title>
    </head>

    <body>
        <h1>
            Using HTML forms
        </h1>
        <form method="post" action="responder.php">
            .
            .

            .
            <input type="submit" value="Submit">
        </form>
    </body>
</html>
```

You can also give the user the chance to return the contents of all HTML controls in the form to their default values with a Reset button, which you create with the <input type = "reset"> element:

```
<html>
    <head>
        <title>
            Using HTML forms
        </title>
    </head>

    <body>
        <h1>
            Using HTML forms
        </h1>
        <form method="post" action="responder.php">
            .
            .

            .
            <input type="submit" value="Submit">
            <input type="reset" value="Reset">
        </form>
    </body>
</html>
```

Now that we've set up the <form> element, let's place some HTML controls in the form, starting with text fields, followed by checkboxes, radio buttons, list boxes, and image maps.

Using Text Fields

Text fields let the user enter text in web pages, and you can read that text back on the server with PHP. Here's an example, textfield.html, that shows how to read and display the user's name. We'll start this example with the HTML part, and then write the PHP.

Creating the HTML

We need an HTML form in textfield.html in which to place our new text field, and we need to send the data in the form to textfield.php:

```
<html>
    <head>
        <title>
            Using Text Fields
        </title>
    </head>

    <body>
        <center>

            <h1>
                Using Text Fields
            </h1>

            <form method="post" action="textfield.php">
                .
                .
                .
            </form>

        </center>
    </body>
</html>
```

Next, we can add a prompt to the user to enter their name (you can use HTML inside <form> elements):

```
<html>
    <head>
        <title>
            Using Text Fields
        </title>
    </head>
```

```
<body>
    <center>

        <h1>
            Using Text Fields
        </h1>

        <form method="post" action="textfield.php">
            Please enter your name:
                .
                .
                .
        </form>

    </center>
</body>
</html>
```

And now we'll add the text field itself, which is an <input type="text"> element, giving it the name "name" (because it's supposed to hold the person's name):

```
<html>
    <head>
        <title>
            Using Text Fields
        </title>
    </head>

    <body>
        <center>

            <h1>
                Using Text Fields
            </h1>

            <form method="post" action="textfield.php">
                Please enter your name:

                <input name="name" type="text">
                    .
                    .
                    .
            </form>

        </center>
    </body>
</html>
```

Finally, we can add the needed Submit button:

```html
<html>
    <head>
        <title>
            Using Text Fields
        </title>
    </head>

    <body>
        <center>

            <h1>
                Using Text Fields
            </h1>

            <form method="post" action="textfield.php">
                Please enter your name:

                <input name="name" type="text">

                <br>
                <br>

                <input type="submit" value="Submit">
            </form>

        </center>
    </body>
</html>
```

You can see what textfield.html looks like in Figure 10-6, where the user has entered their name and is clicking the Submit button.

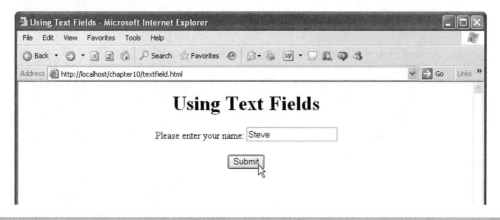

Figure 10-6 Entering text into a text field

So what happens when the user clicks the Submit button? The text in the text field is sent to the PHP script textfield.php, but first we need to write that script.

Creating the PHP

Now we'll write textfield.php. We can place HTML in PHP pages, so we'll start off with a message telling the user that we read their name:

```
<html>
    <head>
        <title>
            Reading text from text fields
        </title>
    </head>

    <body>
        <center>

            <h1>
                Reading text from text fields
            </h1>
            Your name is

                .
                .
                .

        </center>
    </body>
</html>
```

We'll create the PHP part of the script this way:

```
<html>
    <head>
        <title>
            Reading text from text fields
        </title>
    </head>

    <body>
        <center>

            <h1>
                Reading text from text fields
            </h1>
            Your name is
            <?php
                .
                .
                .
            ?>
        </center>
    </body>
</html>
```

To recover data sent from a web page with the GET method, you can use the PHP array $_GET. To recover data sent with the POST method, you can use the PHP array $_POST. You can also read data sent with either GET or POST using the $_REQUEST array, and that's what we'll do here.

So, to read the data from the text field, we only need to pass the name of the text field, which is "name", to the $_REQUEST array. Here's how that works, where we echo the person's name to the web page we send back to the browser:

```
<html>
    <head>
        <title>
            Reading text from text fields
        </title>
    </head>

    <body>
        <center>

            <h1>
                Reading text from text fields
            </h1>
            Your name is
            <?php
                echo $_REQUEST["name"];
            ?>
        </center>
    </body>
</html>
```

You can see the results in Figure 10-7, where we've been successful in reading the user's name from PHP. Cool.

Figure 10-7   Reading the user's name

Using Checkboxes

Another popular HTML control is the checkbox. You handle checkboxes in a slightly different way from text fields, as you're going to see in a new example.

Creating the HTML

This example, checkbox.html, will ask the user if they would like to win the lottery, allowing them to answer Yes or No by checking a box. We start with a form that sends its data to a PHP script named checkbox.php:

```
<html>
    <head>
        <title>Using Checkboxes</title>
    </head>

    <body>
        <center>
        <h1>Using Checkboxes</h1>
        <form method=post action="checkbox.php">
            .
            .
            .
        </form>
        </center>
    </body>
</html>
```

Next we add the prompt to the user and the Yes checkbox, an <input type="checkbox"> element—note the name we give to this control is "check1":

```
<html>
    <head>
        <title>Using Checkboxes</title>
    </head>

    <body>
        <center>
        <h1>Using Checkboxes</h1>
        <form method=post action="checkbox.php">
            Would you like to win the lottery?
            <input name="check1" type="checkbox" value="Yes">
            Yes
            .
            .
            .
        </form>
        </center>
    </body>
</html>
```

We next add the second checkbox, the No checkbox, giving it the name "check2", and add the Submit button:

```
<html>
    <head>
        <title>Using Checkboxes</title>
    </head>

    <body>
        <center>
        <h1>Using Checkboxes</h1>
        <form method=post action="checkbox.php">
            Would you like to win the lottery?
            <input name="check1" type="checkbox" value="Yes">
            Yes
            <input name="check2" Type="checkbox" value="No">
            No
            <br>
            <br>
            <input type="submit" value="Submit">
        </form>
        </center>
    </body>
</html>
```

Great—you can see this new page in Figure 10-8, complete with the checkboxes.

When the user clicks the Submit button, the data in the checkboxes is sent to checkbox .php, and that PHP script is coming up next.

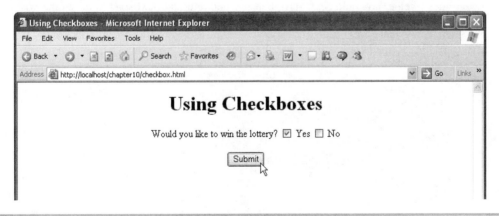

Figure 10-8 A web page complete with checkboxes

Creating the PHP

We named the first checkbox "check1", so can we just examine the setting of check1 and report it like this?

```html
<html>
    <head>
        <title>
            Reading data from checkboxes
        </title>
    </head>

    <body>
        <center>
            <h1>Reading data from checkboxes</h1>

            You checked
            <?php
                echo $_REQUEST["check1"], "<br>";

                .
                .
                .

            ?>
        </center>
    </body>
</html>
```

No, we can't do that. If check1 is not checked, trying to reference $_REQUEST["check1"] will cause an error (because check1 has no value in the $_REQUEST array). So, first we have to determine whether check1 has been checked. We can do this with the isset function, which determines whether array elements have been set and returns true if so (and false otherwise):

```html
<html>
    <head>
        <title>
            Reading data from checkboxes
        </title>
    </head>

    <body>
        <center>
            <h1>Reading data from checkboxes</h1>

            You checked
            <?php
                if (isset($_REQUEST["check1"]))
                    echo $_REQUEST["check1"], "<br>";

                .
                .
                .
```

```
        ?>
    </center>
    </body>
</html>
```

The value of $_REQUEST["check1"] is the value we set for check1 in the checkbox.html web page—that is, "Yes." Similarly, we can evaluate the No checkbox, check2, like this:

```
<html>
    <head>
        <title>
            Reading data from checkboxes
        </title>
    </head>

    <body>
        <center>
            <h1>Reading data from checkboxes</h1>

            You checked
            <?php
                if (isset($_REQUEST["check1"]))
                    echo $_REQUEST["check1"], "<br>";
                if (isset($_REQUEST["check2"]))
                    echo $_REQUEST["check2"], "<br>";
            ?>
        </center>
    </body>
</html>
```

You can see the result in Figure 10-9, where checkbox.php correctly identified the checked checkbox.

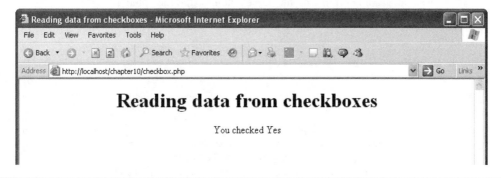

Figure 10-9 Reading data from checkboxes

On the other hand, note that it's perfectly possible for the user to click *both* checkboxes in this example, which would give us the confusing result "You checked Yes No." Since only one answer—Yes *or* No—is possible here, we need to set up two controls so that the user can select only one of them at a time. And that means radio buttons.

Using Radio Buttons

As every web user knows, radio buttons are those round controls in which dots appear when they are clicked (selected). Radio buttons work in concert, meaning only one radio button of a group can be selected at a time.

To get a handle on how radio buttons work with PHP, we'll take a look at an example, radiobutton.html.

Creating the HTML

The radiobutton.html example starts with a form element that will send its data to radiobutton.php:

```
<html>
    <head>
        <title>Using radio buttons</title>
    </head>

    <body>
        <center>
        <h1>Using radio buttons</h1>
        <form method=post action="radiobutton.php">
            .
            .
            .

        </form>
        </center>
    </body>
</html>
```

Next we add a radio button with the name "radio1" and the value Yes:

```
<html>
    <head>
        <title>Using radio buttons</title>
    </head>

    <body>
        <center>
        <h1>Using radio buttons</h1>
        <form method=post action="radiobutton.php">
            Would you like to win the lottery?
            <input name="radio1" type="radio" value="Yes">
            Yes
```

```
            .
            .
            .
        </form>
        </center>
    </body>
</html>
```

For the second radio button, you might think that we are going to name it "radio2", but to make it act together with radio1, we have to give it the same name, radio1 (we also add a Submit button):

```
<html>
    <head>
        <title>Using radio buttons</title>
    </head>

    <body>
        <center>
        <h1>Using radio buttons</h1>
        <form method=post action="radiobutton.php">
            Would you like to win the lottery?
            <input name="radio1" type="radio" value="Yes">
            Yes
            <input name="radio1" Type="radio" value="No">
            No
            <br>
            <br>
            <input type="submit" value="Submit">
        </form>
        </center>
    </body>
</html>
```

You can see radiobutton.html in Figure 10-10.
Next, let's create radiobutton.php.

Creating the PHP
In radiobutton.php, we start with some HTML:

```
<html>
    <head>
        <title>
            Reading data from radio buttons
        </title>
    </head>
```

Figure 10-10 Using radio buttons in radiobutton.html

```
    <body>
        <center>
            <h1>Reading data from radio buttons</h1>

            You selected
                .
                .
                .
        </center>
    </body>
</html>
```

Next, we can use the isset function to check if there's any data waiting for us under the name radio1:

```
<html>
    <head>
        <title>
            Reading data from radio buttons
        </title>
    </head>

    <body>
        <center>
            <h1>Reading data from radio buttons</h1>

            You selected
            <?php
                if (isset($_REQUEST["radio1"]))
```

```
                    .
                    .
                    .
          ?>
       </center>
    </body>
</html>
```

If there is data waiting for us under the name "radio1", that data will be the value of the first radio button ("Yes") or the second radio button ("No"). To display the radio button data, we simply have to echo $_REQUEST["radio1"] this way:

```
<html>
    <head>
        <title>
            Reading data from radio buttons
        </title>
    </head>

    <body>
        <center>
            <h1>Reading data from radio buttons</h1>

            You selected
            <?php
                if (isset($_REQUEST["radio1"]))
                    echo $_REQUEST["radio1"], "<br>";
            ?>
        </center>
    </body>
</html>
```

You can see the results in Figure 10-11—radiobutton.php correctly identified the radio button the user selected.

Figure 10-11   Reading data from radio buttons

Using List Boxes

The next HTML control in our survey is the HTML list box, which lets users select from a list of items. There are two types of list boxes:

- **Single-selection list box**   The user may select only one item. This control works much like the controls we've already reviewed. You name the control in the web page, and get the selection the user made with the $_REQUEST (or $_GET or $_POST) array.

- **Multiple-selection list box**   The user may select from multiple items. You create these list boxes in HTML with the multiple attribute. The way you handle these list boxes is different from how you handle other controls.

The focus of this section is multiple-selection list boxes.

Creating the HTML

This example, listbox.html, will display a list box with a selection of fruits. The user can make multiple selections from the list, which will then be displayed by listbox.php. In listbox.html, we start with a form indicating that listbox.php will be sent the data from the list box:

```
<html>
    <head>
        <title>Using Lists</title>
    </head>

    <body>
        <center>
            <h1>
               Using Lists
            </h1>

            <form method="get" action="listbox.php">
               .
               .
               .
            </form>
        </center>
    </body>
</html>
```

Next, we create a new multiple-selection list box with the <select> element, adding the multiple attribute to make this a multiple-selection list box, and we also add the needed Submit button:

```
<html>
    <head>
        <title>Using Lists</title>
    </head>
```

```
    <body>
        <center>
            <h1>
              Using Lists
            </h1>

            <form method="get" action="listbox.php">

                Select your favorite fruit:
                <br>
                <br>
                <select name="fruit" multiple>
                     .
                     .
                     .
                </select>
                <br>
                <br>
                <input type="submit" value="Submit">
            </form>
        </center>
    </body>
</html>
```

Next, we can stock the list box with fruit, using <option> elements:

```
<html>
    <head>
        <title>Using Lists</title>
    </head>

    <body>
        <center>
            <h1>
              Using Lists
            </h1>

            <form method="get" action="listbox.php">

                Select your favorite fruit:
                <br>
                <br>
                <select name="fruit" multiple>
                    <option>Strawberries</option>
                    <option>Cherries</option>
                    <option>Apples</option>
                    <option>Watermelons</option>
                </select>
                <br>
```

```
                <br>
                <input type="submit" value="Submit">
            </form>
        </center>
    </body>
</html>
```

Here's the key: since this is a multiple-selection list box, the selections the user makes in it won't be sent as a single item to the server, as has happened with the previous HTML examples in this chapter. Instead, the selections the user makes will be sent to the server as an *array*.

How do you tell PHP to expect an array for the fruit list box? When working with PHP, you change the name of the control from a single word, such as fruit, into an array, fruit[]. Here's how it looks in HTML:

```
<html>
    <head>
        <title>Using Lists</title>
    </head>

    <body>
        <center>
            <h1>
              Using Lists
            </h1>

            <form method="get" action="listbox.php">

                Select your favorite fruit:
                <br>
                <br>
                <select name="fruit[]" multiple>
                    <option>Strawberries</option>
                    <option>Cherries</option>
                    <option>Apples</option>
                    <option>Watermelons</option>
                </select>
                <br>
                <br>
                <input type="submit" value="Submit">
            </form>
        </center>
    </body>
</html>
```

Great—you can see this page in Figure 10-12, where the fruits are displayed, and the user has selected two of them (you can use the SHIFT and CTRL keys to make multiple selections in multiple-selection list boxes).

Now it's time to create listbox.php.

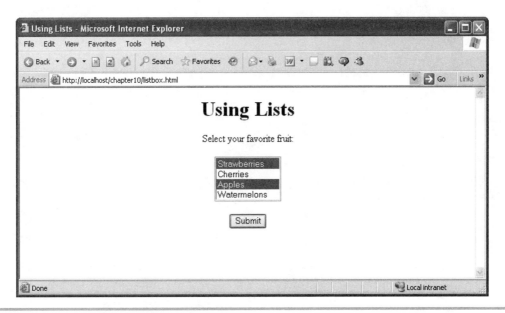

Figure 10-12 A multiple-selection list box

Creating the PHP

We start listbox.php, the script that handles the selections the user made in listbox.html, with some HTML to set the stage:

```html
<html>
    <head>
        <title>Reading Selections From Lists</title>
    </head>

    <body>
        <center>
            <h1>Reading Selections From Lists</h1>
            You selected:
            <br>
            .
            .
            .
        </center>
    </body>
</html>
```

We're going to display the user selections using an HTML unordered list, which uses the
<ul> tag:

```
<html>
    <head>
        <title>Reading Selections From Lists</title>
    </head>

    <body>
        <center>
            <h1>Reading Selections From Lists</h1>
            You selected:
            <br>
            <ul>
                .
                .
                .
            </ul>
        </center>
    </body>
</html>
```

To list the selected fruits, we can use a PHP foreach loop over the fruit[] array, which we
can access as $_REQUEST["fruit"]:

```
<html>
    <head>
        <title>Reading Selections From Lists</title>
    </head>

    <body>
        <center>
            <h1>Reading Selections From Lists</h1>
            You selected:
            <br>
            <ul>
            <?php
            foreach($_REQUEST["fruit"] as $fruit){
                .
                .
                .
            }
            ?>
            </ul>
        </center>
    </body>
</html>
```

Finally, we make every selected fruit into an item in the list with an <li> tag:

```html
<html>
    <head>
        <title>Reading Selections From Lists</title>
    </head>

    <body>
        <center>
            <h1>Reading Selections From Lists</h1>
            You selected:
            <br>
            <ul>
            <?php
            foreach($_REQUEST["fruit"] as $fruit){
                echo "<li> $fruit </li><br>";
            }
            ?>
            </ul>
        </center>
    </body>
</html>
```

You can see the results in Figure 10-13. Cool!

Okay, now let's take a look at the last HTML control covered in this chapter, image maps.

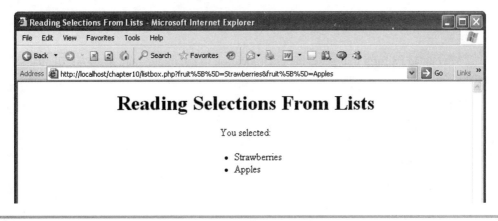

Figure 10-13 Reading data from a multiple-selection list box

Using Image Maps

Image maps are those clickable images that contain "hotspots" that the application responds to when you click them. The way you handle image maps is unlike any other control, because image maps send you two pieces of data—the x and y location where the user clicked the mouse in the image map—and that means you can't just access their data under a single name.

Creating the HTML

In this example, map.html, we start with some HTML to set the stage:

```html
<html>
    <head>
        <title>
            Using Image Maps
        </title>
    </head>

    <body>

        <center>

            <h1>
                Using Image Maps
            </h1>
            .
            .
            .

        </center>

    </body>
</html>
```

We can add a form that posts the click location in the image map to a PHP file named map.php:

```html
<html>
    <head>
        <title>
            Using Image Maps
        </title>
    </head>

    <body>

        <center>

            <h1>
                Using Image Maps
            </h1>
```

```
<form method="post" action="map.php">
    .
    .
    .
</form>

    </center>

    </body>
</html>
```

The image map itself is created with an <input type="image"> element, and we'll name it "map" and use an image file named map.jpg as the image that will appear:

```
<html>
    <head>
        <title>
            Using Image Maps
        </title>
    </head>

    <body>

        <center>

            <h1>
                Using Image Maps
            </h1>

            <form method="post" action="map.php">
                Click anywhere in the image map.

                <br>
                <br>

                <input name="map" type="image" src="map.jpg">

            </form>

        </center>

    </body>
</html>
```

You can see the results in Figure 10-14, where the image map is about to be clicked by the user.

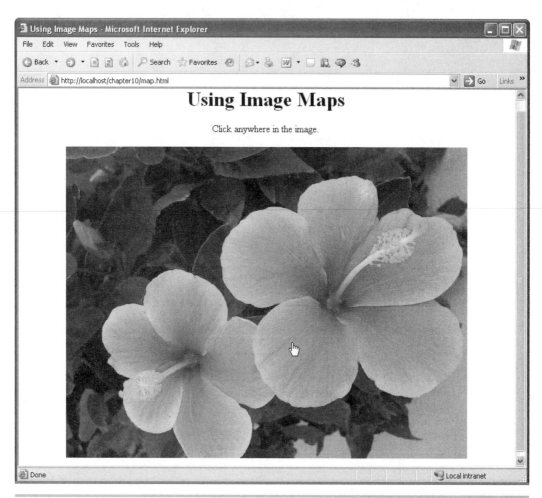

Figure 10-14 An image map

Now let's create the PHP, map.php, that reads and reports the location where the image map was clicked.

Creating the PHP
In map.php, we again start with some HTML:

```
<html>
    <head>
        <title>Reading Image Map Data</title>
    </head>
```

```
<body>

    <center>

        <h1>Reading Image Map Data</h1>

        <br>

        You clicked the image at (
            .
            .
            .
    </center>

    </body>
</html>
```

Now we've got to display the x and y location of the mouse click. The name of the HTML control containing the map was simply "map", and PHP will automatically create map_x to hold the x coordinate and map_y to hold the y coordinate. That means we can display the location at which the user clicked the image map like this, using the $_REQUEST array:

```
<html>
    <head>
        <title>Reading Image Map Data</title>
    </head>

    <body>

        <center>

            <h1>Reading Image Map Data</h1>

            <br>

            You clicked the image at (
            <?php
                echo $_REQUEST["map_x"], ", ", $_REQUEST["map_y"];
            ?>
            ).
        </center>

    </body>
</html>
```

You can see the results in Figure 10-15, which shows the location, in pixel coordinates, where the user clicked the map (note that (0, 0) is at upper left in the image map).

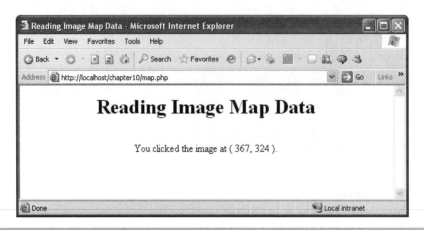

Figure 10-15   Reading data from an image map

Knowing the location at which the mouse was clicked is very important to bring the "hotspots" to life in your web page. Now that you have the mouse location, you know which hotspot was clicked, and can take the appropriate action in your PHP script.

Chapter 11

Validating User Input with Ajax and PHP

Key Skills & Concepts

- Displaying all the data in a form
- Working with the PHP server variables
- Sending form data in arrays
- Creating single-page PHP applications
- Validating numbers
- Validating text

The previous two chapters got you started in the basics of PHP for use with Ajax, and this chapter gives you a good working knowledge of PHP as it's used with Ajax applications today. In this chapter, you're going to pick up skills you need in PHP, including displaying all the data sent to the server in a form, which is terrific for debugging; handling form data in arrays, which is good to do if there's a lot of such data; and creating single-page PHP applications.

Until now, the PHP applications we've created have consisted of an HTML page and a PHP page, but most PHP applications put that all together into a single PHP page, and you'll see how to do that here as well.

This chapter also discusses validating user input—that is, making sure the user fills in required fields and supplies data in the right format. You've seen pages on the Internet that display error messages in red if you omit required data, and we'll see how to do that in our own applications in this chapter.

Here's the framework for validating user input in PHP: You have a function, named, say, check_data, to check the user's input (the checking, done in PHP, is performed on the server). The check_data function stores any errors it finds in an array named $errors, and if that array ends up containing any error entries, you can display the error messages (in red) and then display the "welcome" page again, asking the user to enter their data again. On the other hand, if the user's data is okay, you can call a second function, named, say, process_data, to handle that data. Here's how it looks:

```
check_data();

if(count($errors) != 0){
  display_errors();
  display_welcome();
}
else {
  process_data();
}
```

You'll see this skeleton code fleshed out near the end of this chapter. Let's start with an essential PHP skill: seeing what data your HTML form is actually sending to the server.

Displaying All the Data in an HTML Form

When you're creating an Ajax application, knowing what data your web page is sending to your PHP on the server can be important, for debugging purposes. What does the data your PHP script is getting actually look like? Let's take a look at an example, datadumper.html, that dumps all the data a form sends to it.

Creating the HTML

We can start datadumper.html with a form that will send its data to datadumper.php:

```
<html>
  <head>
    <title>Displaying All Form Data</title>
  </head>

  <body>
    <center>
      <h1>Displaying All Form Data</h1>

      <form method="post" action="datadumper.php">
        .
        .
        .
      </form>

    </center>
  </body>
</html>
```

And we can add some controls so that data will in fact be sent to datadumper.php, starting with a text field:

```
<html>
  <head>
    <title>Displaying All Form Data</title>
  </head>

  <body>
    <center>
      <h1>Displaying All Form Data</h1>

      <form method="post" action="datadumper.php">

        Please enter your name:
        <input name="name" type="text">
```

```
        <br>
        <br>
         .
         .
         .
      </form>
    </center>
  </body>
</html>
```

We might also send some data that will be sent as an array—say, fruit[]—using a list box, as well as add the Submit button:

```
<html>
  <head>
    <title>Displaying All Form Data</title>
  </head>

  <body>
    <center>
      <h1>Displaying All Form Data</h1>

      <form method="post" action="datadumper.php">

        Please enter your name:
        <input name="name" type="text">

        <br>
        <br>
        Select your favorite fruit:
        <br>
        <br>
        <select name="fruit[]" multiple>
          <option>Bananas</option>
          <option>Strawberries</option>
          <option>Apples</option>
          <option>Watermelons</option>
        </select>

        <br>
        <br>

        <input type="submit" value="Submit">
      </form>
    </center>
  </body>
</html>
```

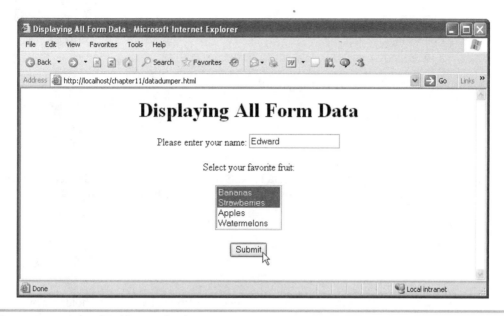

Figure 11-1   The datadumper.html page

That finishes datadumper.html, which you can see in Figure 11-1.

Now it's time to write datadumper.php, the PHP all-purpose script that will display all the data sent to it, which is very handy for debugging purposes.

Creating the PHP

Our goal in datadumper.php is to create an all-purpose PHP script that displays the form data sent to it, no matter which page sends that form data. That means we need to recover the form data from the $_REQUEST array, which can handle data sent with either GET or POST, not just the $_GET or $_POST arrays.

Let's start with some HTML to set the scene, and a PHP section:

```
<html>
  <head>
    <title>
      Displaying All Form Data
    </title>
  </head>

  <body>
    <center>
      <h1>Displaying All Form Data</h1>
```

```
      Here is the form's data I got:
      <br>
      <?php
          .

          .

          .

      ?>
      </center>
  </body>
</html>
```

Now we want to loop over all the data in the $_REQUEST array, and to do that, we'll use a foreach loop. You've already seen the first form of the foreach loop in Chapter 9:

```
foreach ($array as $value){
    .

    .

    .

}
```

Here, we're looping over $array, and each time through the loop, $value holds a new element from the array. The second form of the foreach loop looks like this:

```
foreach ($array as $index => $value){
    .

    .

    .

}
```

Here, $index is the index of $value in the array—and $index can be a number or a string (note especially that you need the => operator in this form of the foreach loop). The second form of the foreach loop is what we want to use here, because, in addition to displaying the data values we got in datadumper.php, we want to display the name of each data item. So here's how we loop over the $_REQUEST array:

```
<html>
  <head>
    <title>
      Displaying All Form Data
    </title>
  </head>

  <body>
    <center>
      <h1>Displaying All Form Data</h1>

      Here is the form's data I got:
```

```
        <br>
        <?php
          foreach($_REQUEST as $index => $value){
            .


            .


            .
          }
        ?>
        </center>
      </body>
</html>
```

The first time through the loop, $index will hold the name of the text field, which is just "name", and $value will hold the name the user entered into the text field. The second time through the loop, $index will hold the name of the list box's data array, "fruit", and $value will hold the actual $fruit array.

In other words, we have to handle both single-item data and array data in datadumper.php. To check if $value is an array, we can use the PHP function is_array:

```
<html>
  <head>
    <title>
      Displaying All Form Data
    </title>
  </head>

  <body>
    <center>
      <h1>Displaying All Form Data</h1>

      Here is the form's data I got:
      <br>
      <?php
        foreach($_REQUEST as $index => $value){
          if(is_array($value)){
            .


            .


            .
          }
        }
      ?>
      </center>
  </body>
</html>
```

If $value is an array, we can loop over it with another foreach loop:

```html
<html>
  <head>
    <title>
      Displaying All Form Data
    </title>
  </head>

  <body>
    <center>
      <h1>Displaying All Form Data</h1>

      Here is the form's data I got:
      <br>
      <?php
        foreach($_REQUEST as $index => $value){
          if(is_array($value)){
            foreach($value as $number => $item){
              .
              .
              .
            }
          }
        }
      ?>
    </center>
  </body>
</html>
```

Inside this new loop, we're looping over the array in the $value variable; $number will hold the index number of the items in the array, and $item will hold the name of the item itself. That means that we can echo the array name, the index of the current item, and the item name itself like this:

```html
<html>
  <head>
    <title>
      Displaying All Form Data
    </title>
  </head>

  <body>
    <center>
      <h1>Displaying All Form Data</h1>

      Here is the form's data I got:
      <br>
```

```php
<?php
  foreach($_REQUEST as $index => $value){
    if(is_array($value)){
      foreach($value as $number => $item){
        echo "${index}[${number}] => $item <br>";
      }
    }
  }
?>
</center>
</body>
</html>
```

Whew. Okay, but what if $value is not an array—what if it's only a single data item? In that case, we just need to display the name of the item, and its value:

```php
<html>
  <head>
    <title>
      Displaying All Form Data
    </title>
  </head>

  <body>
    <center>
      <h1>Displaying All Form Data</h1>

      Here is the form's data I got:
      <br>
      <?php
        foreach($_REQUEST as $index => $value){
          if(is_array($value)){
            foreach($value as $number => $item){
              echo "${index}[${number}] => $item <br>";
            }
          }
          else {
            echo $index, " => ", $value, "<br>";
          }
        }
      ?>
    </center>
  </body>
</html>
```

Great, that completes datadumper.php. In Figure 11-2, you can see it in action after the user enters some data in datadumper.html and clicks the Submit button. Note that datadumper .php has indeed correctly identified the data sent to it—both single items and arrays. Not bad.

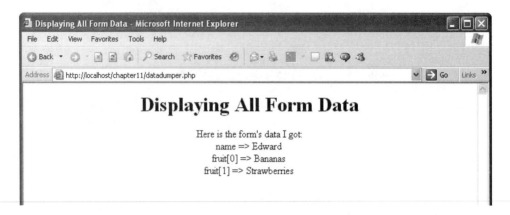

Figure 11-2 Displaying the form data sent to datadumper.php

Working with PHP Server Variables

PHP also has a number of useful built-in variables that you can access in your PHP code, called server variables. You can find the list of PHP server variables in Table 11-1.

Server Variable	Description
AUTH_TYPE	When running under the Apache web server and doing HTTP authentication, holds the authentication type (such as password authentication).
DOCUMENT_ROOT	Contains the document root directory where the script is.
GATEWAY_INTERFACE	Contains the version of the CGI (Common Gateway Interface—how servers communicate with browsers) specification the server is using.
HTTP_ACCEPT	Contains the text in the Accept: header from the current request.
HTTP_ACCEPT_CHARSET	Contains the text in the Accept-Charset: header from the current request.
HTTP_ACCEPT_ENCODING	Contains the text in the Accept-Encoding: header from the current request.
HTTP_ACCEPT_LANGUAGE	Contains the text in the Accept-Language: header from the current request.
HTTP_CONNECTION	Contains the text in the Connection: header from the current request.
HTTP_HOST	Contains the text in the Host: header from the current request.

Table 11-1 PHP Server Variables

Server Variable	Description
HTTP_REFERER	Contains the address of the page (if any) that referred the user agent to the current page. Set by the browser.
HTTP_USER_AGENT	Contains the text in the User-Agent: header from the current request.
PATH_TRANSLATED	Specifies the file-system-based path to the script.
PHP_AUTH_PW	When running under the Apache web server and doing HTTP authentication, holds the password provided by the user.
PHP_AUTH_USER	When running under the Apache web server and doing HTTP authentication, holds the username provided by the user.
PHP_SELF	Contains the filename of the currently executing script, relative to the document root.
QUERY_STRING	Contains the query string, if there is one.
REMOTE_ADDR	Contains the IP address from which the user is viewing the current page.
REMOTE_HOST	Contains the hostname from which the user is viewing the current page.
REMOTE_PORT	Contains the port being used on the user's machine to communicate with the web server.
REQUEST_METHOD	Specifies which request method was used to access the page, such as 'GET', 'HEAD', 'POST', 'PUT'.
REQUEST_URI	Specifies the URI that was given to access this page, such as '/index.html'.
SCRIPT_FILENAME	Specifies the absolute pathname of the currently executing script.
SCRIPT_NAME	Contains the current script's path. This is useful for pages that need to point to themselves.
SERVER_ADMIN	Contains the value given to the SERVER_ADMIN directive in the web server configuration file.
SERVER_NAME	Contains the name of the server host under which the script is executing.
SERVER_PORT	Contains the port on the server machine being used by the web server for communication.
SERVER_PROTOCOL	Contains the name and revision of the information protocol via which the page was requested.
SERVER_SIGNATURE	Contains the server version and virtual hostname.
SERVER_SOFTWARE	Contains the server identification string.

Table 11-1   PHP Server Variables (*continued*)

The PHP server variables can be very useful to you as an Ajax programmer. For example, HTTP_USER_AGENT holds the name of the browser the user is using. Since you interact with the user exclusively through the browser, it's good to know which browser they are using, because different browsers have different capabilities. For example, say that you want to display the user's name in a <marquee> element, which scrolls across the page—but is available only in Internet Explorer. You can use the HTTP_USER_AGENT server variable to determine whether or not the user has Internet Explorer. Let's see this in action in a new example, servervariables.html.

Creating the HTML

This HTML page will send its data to servervariables.php, which will display the user's name in a <marquee> element—if the user has Internet Explorer. Here's servervariables.html, which starts with a form that sends its data to servervariables.php:

```html
<html>
  <head>
    <title>
      Using Server Variables
    </title>
  </head>

  <body>
    <center>

      <h1>Using Server Variables</h1>

      <form method="post" action="servervariables.php">
        .
        .
        .
      </form>

    </center>
  </body>
</html>
```

And here are the text field and Submit button in this example:

```html
<html>
  <head>
    <title>
      Using Server Variables
    </title>
  </head>

  <body>
    <center>
```

```
    <h1>Using Server Variables</h1>

    <form method="post" action="servervariables.php">
      Please enter your name:
      <input type="text" name="name">
      <br>
      <br>
      <input type="submit" value="Submit">

    </form>

  </center>
  </body>
</html>
```

And that's all we need—you can see the results in Figure 11-3.

Creating the PHP

In servervariables.php, we first have to determine if the user has Internet Explorer; if so, we display their name in a <marquee> element, and if not, we display their name as normal text. We start servervariables.php with some HTML:

```
<html>
  <head>
    <title>Using Server Variables</title>
  </head>

  <body>
    <center>
        <h1>Using Server Variables</h1>
```

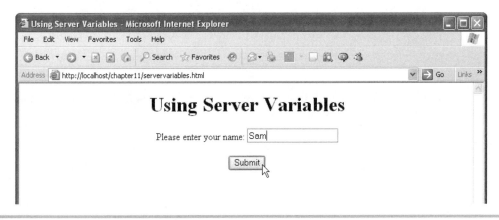

Figure 11-3   servervariables.html in action

```
            <br>
            <?php
              .
              .
              .
            ?>

        </center>
    </body>
</html>
```

Then we check the HTTP_USER_AGENT server variable to see if it contains the text "MSIE", which it will if the user's browser is Internet Explorer. We access the HTTP_USER_AGENT server variable using the PHP $_SERVER array, and we can use the strpos PHP string function to find "MSIE"—if there is no "MSIE" in the string, strpos will return false:

```
<html>
  <head>
    <title>Using Server Variables</title>
  </head>

  <body>
    <center>
        <h1>Using Server Variables</h1>

        <br>
        <?php
          if(strpos($_SERVER["HTTP_USER_AGENT"], "MSIE")){
            .
            .
            .
          }
        ?>

    </center>
  </body>
</html>
```

If we are indeed dealing with Internet Explorer, we can recover the person's name and display it in a <marquee> element like this:

```
<html>
  <head>
    <title>Using Server Variables</title>
  </head>

  <body>
    <center>
        <h1>Using Server Variables</h1>
```

```
      <br>
      <?php

        $name = $_REQUEST["name"];

        if(strpos($_SERVER["HTTP_USER_AGENT"], "MSIE")){
          echo("<marquee><h1>Welcome to my page,
            ${name}!</h1></marquee>");
        }
          .
          .
          .

      ?>

    </center>
  </body>
</html>
```

If, on the other hand, we're not dealing with Internet Explorer, we can display the person's name in a simple <h1> header:

```
<html>
  <head>
    <title>Using Server Variables</title>
  </head>

  <body>
    <center>
        <h1>Using Server Variables</h1>

        <br>
        <?php

          $name = $_REQUEST["name"];

          if(strpos($_SERVER["HTTP_USER_AGENT"], "MSIE")){
            echo("<marquee><h1>Welcome to my page,
              ${name}!</h1></marquee>");
          }
          else {
              echo("<h1>Welcome to my page, ${name}!</h1>");
          }
        ?>

    </center>
  </body>
</html>
```

Figure 11-4 Displaying a <marquee> element in Internet Explorer

The result appears in Figure 11-4 in Internet Explorer, where the second line is a <marquee> element that scrolls across the screen. Cool.

On the other hand, the same text appears as a static <h1> header in Firefox, as shown in Figure 11-5.

Figure 11-5 Displaying static text in Firefox

Getting Your Data in Array Format

PHP supports a convenient way to organize the data you send to it from HTML forms. You can store such data in arrays, which is great if you have a lot of data to send, especially if your HTML page includes several forms. Organizing your form data in arrays means such data items are less likely to interfere with each other.

Creating the HTML

Using form arrays is simple. Just use the array and index name as the name of the variable you want to store data under. For example, here's what storing the user's name in an array named $data under the index "name" looks like in formarrays.html:

```
<html>
  <head>
    <title>
      Sending Arrays of Form Data
    </title>
  </head>

  <body>
    <center>
      <h1>
        Sending Arrays of Form Data
      </h1>

      <form method="post" action="formarrays.php">

        Enter your name:
        <input name="data[name]" type="text">
          .
          .
          .
      </form>

    </center>
  </body>
</html>
```

Giving the name of the text field as data[name] means that you can access the user's name in your PHP script as $data["name"] (note that you omit the quotation marks when naming the variable in your HTML page). Here's how we might ask the user's height in inches and store that information as $data["height"]:

```
<html>
  <head>
    <title>
      Sending Arrays of Form Data
    </title>
  </head>
```

```
<body>
  <center>
    <h1>
      Sending Arrays of Form Data
    </h1>

    <form method="post" action="formarrays.php">

      Enter your name:
      <input name="data[name]" type="text">

      <br>
      <br>
      Enter your height in inches:
      <input name="data[height]" type="text">

      <br>
      <br>
      <input type="submit" value="Submit">
    </form>

  </center>
</body>
</html>
```

You can see what this page, formarrays.html, looks like in Figure 11-6, where the user has entered some information and is just about to click the Submit button.

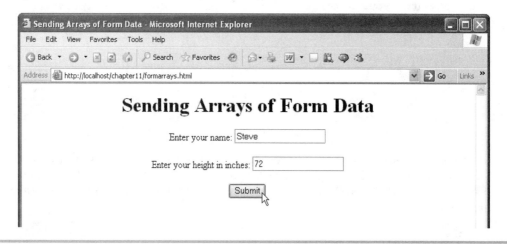

Figure 11-6 Preparing to send form data in arrays to PHP

Creating the PHP

In the PHP script, formarrays.php, you can recover the array containing the form data and name it $data:

```html
<html>
  <head>
    <title>
      Receiving Arrays of Form Data
    </title>
  </head>

  <body>
    <center>
      <h1>
        Receiving Arrays of Form Data
      </h1>

      Your name is
      <?php
        $data = $_REQUEST['data'];
          .
          .
          .
      </center>

  </body>
</html>
```

And you can recover the user's name by referencing it as $data['name']:

```html
<html>
  <head>
    <title>
      Receiving Arrays of Form Data
    </title>
  </head>

  <body>
    <center>
      <h1>
        Receiving Arrays of Form Data
      </h1>

      Your name is
      <?php
```

```
    $data = $_REQUEST['data'];
    echo $data['name'], "<br>";
  ?>
      .

      .

      .

  </center>

</body>
</html>
```

You can also display the user's height in inches like this:

```
<html>
  <head>
    <title>
      Receiving Arrays of Form Data
    </title>
  </head>

  <body>
    <center>
      <h1>
        Receiving Arrays of Form Data
      </h1>

      Your name is
      <?php
        $data = $_REQUEST['data'];
        echo $data['name'], "<br>";
       ?>

      Your height in inches is
      <?php
        $data = $_REQUEST['data'];
        echo $data['height'], "<br>";
      ?>
    </center>

  </body>
</html>
```

You can see the results in Figure 11-7. Nice.

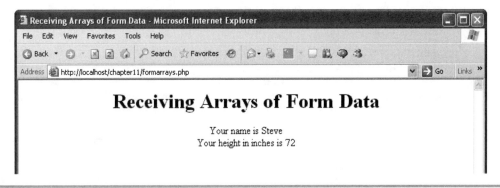

Figure 11-7   Displaying form array data

Wrapping Applications into a Single PHP Page

Most PHP applications that you see don't start with an HTML page and then go to a PHP page, as ours have been doing. In most PHP applications, everything is wrapped up into a single PHP page, and displaying everything in a PHP page means returning at least two different pages to the browser: a welcome page, where you ask the user to enter their data, and a results page, where you process the data they've sent and return the results to them.

So how do such applications do that? How do they know which page to return? The usual way is to check whether there's any data waiting to be processed—if not, the application displays the welcome page; if so, the application processes that data and sends back the results page.

Here's how that looks in a new, single-page example, singlepage.php. In the welcome page, we'll ask the user for their name and display that name in the results page. So how do we know if we've got data (that is, the user's name) to process? We can check if there is any data in the $_REQUEST array under "name":

```
<html>
    <head>
        <title>
          A PHP Application in a Single Page
        </title>
    </head>

    <body>
        <center>
          <h1>A PHP Application in a Single Page</h1>
          <?php
            if(isset($_REQUEST["name"])){
          ?>
            .
            .
            .
        </center>
    </body>
</html>
```

If the name data is waiting for us, we can echo it back to the browser:

```
<html>
    <head>
        <title>
            A PHP Application in a Single Page
        </title>
    </head>

    <body>
        <center>
            <h1>A PHP Application in a Single Page</h1>
            <?php
                if(isset($_REQUEST["name"])){
            ?>
                Your name is
            <?php
                echo $_REQUEST["name"];
                }
                    .
                    .
                    .
            ?>
        </center>
    </body>
</html>
```

On the other hand, if there is no name data waiting for us, we can display the welcome page, which asks the user for their name by using a text field in a new form that will send its data back to the same page, singlepage.php:

```
<html>
    <head>
        <title>
            A PHP Application in a Single Page
        </title>
    </head>

    <body>
        <center>
            <h1>A PHP Application in a Single Page</h1>
            <?php
                if(isset($_REQUEST["name"])){
            ?>
                Your name is
            <?php
                echo $_REQUEST["name"];
                }
```

```
      else {
   ?>
     <form method="post" action="singlepage.php">
        Please enter your name:

        <input name="name" type="text">
        <br>
        <br>
        <input type="submit" value="Submit">
     </form>
   <?php
     }
   ?>
   </center>
  </body>
</html>
```

Note that in single-page PHP applications, you can omit the action attribute in the <form> element, because the default action is to send the form's data back to the same page. That means you could also write singlepage.php like this:

```
<html>
  <head>
    <title>
      A PHP Application in a Single Page
    </title>
  </head>

  <body>
    <center>
      <h1>A PHP Application in a Single Page</h1>
      <?php
        if(isset($_REQUEST["name"])) {
      ?>
        Your name is
      <?php
        echo $_REQUEST["name"];
        }
        else {
      ?>
        <form method="post">
          Please enter your name:

          <input name="name" type="text">
          <br>
          <br>
```

Figure 11-8 Displaying form array data: welcome page

```
            <input type="submit" value="Submit">
        </form>
    <?php
        }
    ?>
        </center>
    </body>
</html>
```

Okay, let's take a look at what we've done in a browser. You can see the welcome page in Figure 11-8, where the user has entered their name and is just about to click Submit.

The results page, which reports the user's name, appears in Figure 11-9. Very cool.

Placing all the code for a PHP application in a single page is a new and powerful skill. Next, you'll see another way to test if the welcome page has already been displayed—by setting a hidden control in the web page.

Figure 11-9 Displaying form array data: results page

Validating Input from the User

As the last topic in this chapter, we'll take a look at how to validate data that the user entered into a web page. Did they enter their name? Is what they typed for their age a number? Those are the kinds of questions we'll take up now.

Here's an overview of the PHP code that you first saw at the beginning of this chapter, indicating how we check for errors and display them as needed:

```
check_data();

if(count($errors) != 0){
  display_errors();
  display_welcome();
}
else {
  process_data();
}
```

Let's put this example, checkdata.php, together. In this example, the user will be asked to enter their name. If they don't enter it but click the Submit button, that'll be considered an error and handled on the server in PHP. That means that if the welcome page has already been displayed, we don't need to check whether the text field contains any data, because the welcome page would not be displayed if the text field didn't contain data.

Instead, we'll use an <"input type=hidden"> control named welcome_already_displayed to keep track of whether or not the welcome page has been displayed. This technique may be even better than checking whether a text field has any data, because in some cases you may want to allow the user to leave a text field blank.

Here's how we check if the welcome page has already been shown, in checkdata.php:

```
<html>
  <head>
    <title>
      Validating User Data
    </title>
  </head>

  <body>
    <center>

      <h1>Validating User Data</h1>
      <?php

        if(isset($_REQUEST["welcome_already_displayed"])){
          .
          .
          .
        ?>

    </center>
  </body>
</html>
```

If there is data waiting for us, we can check that data in a new function, check_data, which will fill an array named $errors with any errors that were found:

```html
<html>
  <head>
    <title>
      Validating User Data
    </title>
  </head>

  <body>
    <center>

      <h1>Validating User Data</h1>
      <?php
        $errors = array();

        if(isset($_REQUEST["welcome_already_displayed"])){

          check_data();
            .
            .
            .

        ?>

    </center>
  </body>
</html>
```

In the check_data function, we start by indicating that the $errors array is a global array, not restricted to the check_data function:

```html
<html>
  <head>
    <title>
      Validating User Data
    </title>
  </head>

  <body>
    <center>

      <h1>Validating User Data</h1>
      <?php
        $errors = array();
```

```php
    if(isset($_REQUEST["welcome_already_displayed"])){

      check_data();
      .
      .
      .

    function check_data()
    {
      global $errors;
      .
      .
      .
    }
  ?>

  </center>
  </body>
</html>
```

Now we're free to check if the user entered any text in the text field—and if they did not, we store an error message ("Please enter your name") in the $errors array:

```php
<html>
  <head>
    <title>
      Validating User Data
    </title>
  </head>

  <body>
    <center>

      <h1>Validating User Data</h1>
      <?php
        $errors = array();

        if(isset($_REQUEST["welcome_already_displayed"])){

          check_data();
          .
          .
          .

        function check_data()
        {
          global $errors;

          if($_REQUEST["name"] == "") {
```

```
              $errors[] = "<font color='red'>Please enter your name</font>";
          }
      }
  ?>

      </center>
    </body>
  </html>
```

Back in the main part of the code, just after the call to check_data, we see if any errors were stored in the $errors array. If so, we display the error(s) with a function named display_errors, and then display the rest of the welcome page—so that the user can try again—with a function named display_welcome:

```
<html>
  <head>
    <title>
      Validating User Data
    </title>
  </head>

  <body>
    <center>

        <h1>Validating User Data</h1>
        <?php
          $errors = array();

          if(isset($_REQUEST["welcome_already_displayed"])){

            check_data();

            if(count($errors) != 0){
              display_errors();
              display_welcome();
            }
            .
            .
            .
        ?>

      </center>
    </body>
  </html>
```

In the display_errors function, we send the current error message(s) back to the browser:

```
<html>
  <head>
```

```
      <title>
        Validating User Data
      </title>
    </head>

  <body>
    <center>

      <h1>Validating User Data</h1>
      <?php
        $errors = array();

        if(isset($_REQUEST["welcome_already_displayed"])){

          check_data();

          if(count($errors) != 0){
            display_errors();
            display_welcome();
          }
          .
          .
          .
        function display_errors()
        {
          global $errors;

          foreach ($errors as $error){
            echo $error, "<br>";
          }
        }
      ?>

    </center>
  </body>
</html>
```

Next, in the display_welcome function, we display the welcome part of the page, which includes the text field and the prompt to the user to enter their name. Note that the display_welcome function also creates the hidden control named welcome_already_displayed (so we'll know on the server that the welcome page has already been shown).

```
<html>
  <head>
    <title>
      Validating User Data
    </title>
  </head>
```

```php
<body>
  <center>

    <h1>Validating User Data</h1>
    <?php
      $errors = array();

      if(isset($_REQUEST["welcome_already_displayed"])){

        check_data();

        if(count($errors) != 0){
          display_errors();
          display_welcome();
        }
        .
        .
        .
      function display_errors()
      {
        global $errors;

        foreach ($errors as $error){
          echo $error, "<br>";
        }
      }

      function display_welcome()
      {
        echo "<form method='post' action='checkdata.php'>";
        echo "Please enter your name";
        echo "<br>";
        echo "<input name='name' type='text'>";
        echo "<br>";
        echo "<br>";
        echo "<input type='submit' value='Submit'>";
        echo "<input type='hidden'
          name='welcome_already_displayed' value='data'>";
        echo "</form>";
      }
    ?>

  </center>
  </body>
</html>
```

On the other hand, if there were no errors, we call a function named process_data to handle the data the user entered:

```html
<html>
  <head>
    <title>
      Validating User Data
    </title>
  </head>

  <body>
    <center>

      <h1>Validating User Data</h1>
      <?php
        $errors = array();

        if(isset($_REQUEST["welcome_already_displayed"])){

          check_data();

          if(count($errors) != 0){
            display_errors();
            display_welcome();
          }
          else {
            process_data();
          }
        }
        .

        .

        .
      ?>

    </center>
  </body>
</html>
```

In the process_data function in this example, we just fetch the name the user entered and display it:

```html
<html>
  <head>
    <title>
      Validating User Data
    </title>
  </head>
```

```
<body>
  <center>

    <h1>Validating User Data</h1>
    <?php
      $errors = array();

      if(isset($_REQUEST["welcome_already_displayed"])){

        check_data();

        if(count($errors) != 0){
          display_errors();
          display_welcome();
        }
        else {
          process_data();
        }
      }
      .
      .
      .
      function process_data()
      {
        echo "Thank you. Your name is ";
        echo $_REQUEST["name"];
      }
    ?>

  </center>
</body>
</html>
```

Whew. That handles the case where the welcome page has already appeared. But what if the welcome page hasn't already been shown (that is, if the hidden control was not found), and we have to display the welcome page? Here's what that looks like in code:

```
<html>
  <head>
    <title>
      Validating User Data
    </title>
  </head>

  <body>
    <center>

      <h1>Validating User Data</h1>
      <?php
        $errors = array();
```

```
        if(isset($_REQUEST["welcome_already_displayed"])){

          check_data();

          if(count($errors) != 0){
            display_errors();
            display_welcome();
          }
          else {
            process_data();
          }
        }
        else {
         display_welcome();
        }
        .
        .
        .

      ?>

    </center>
  </body>
</html>
```

That completes the code—here's the whole thing for your reference, checkdata.php:

```
<html>
  <head>
    <title>
      Validating User Data
    </title>
  </head>

  <body>
    <center>

      <h1>Validating User Data</h1>
      <?php
        $errors = array();

        if(isset($_REQUEST["welcome_already_displayed"])){

          check_data();

          if(count($errors) != 0){
            display_errors();
            display_welcome();
          }
          else {
            process_data();
          }
        }
```

```
     else {
      display_welcome();
     }

     function check_data()
     {
       global $errors;

       if($_REQUEST["name"] == "") {
       $errors[] = "<font color='red'>Please enter your name</font>";
       }
     }

     function display_errors()
     {
       global $errors;

       foreach ($errors as $error){
         echo $error, "<br>";
       }
     }

     function process_data()
     {
       echo "Thank you. Your name is ";
       echo $_REQUEST["name"];
     }

     function display_welcome()
     {
        echo "<form method='post' action='checkdata.php'>";
        echo "Please enter your name";
        echo "<br>";
        echo "<input name='name' type='text'>";
        echo "<br>";
        echo "<br>";
        echo "<input type='submit' value='Submit'>";
        echo "<input type='hidden'
          name='welcome_already_displayed' value='data'>";
        echo "</form>";
     }
    ?>

  </center>
 </body>
</html>
```

Okay, but does it work? Take a look at checkdata.php in Figure 11-10.

If the user doesn't enter their name before clicking Submit, they see the result shown in Figure 11-11, where an error message asks them to enter their name.

If they now enter their name, say, Steve, and click Submit, that name will appear in the results page, as you see in Figure 11-12. Not bad.

Figure 11-10   Displaying the welcome page

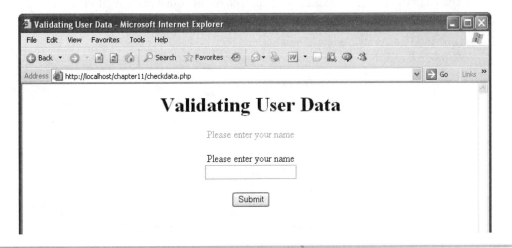

Figure 11-11   Displaying an error

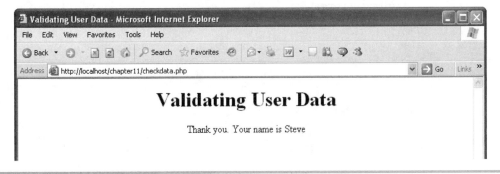

Figure 11-12   Displaying the results page

Validating Integers

What if you want to validate the actual format of the entered data? For example, what if you want to insist that a number be an integer?

Here's a new example, checkdatainteger.php, that asks the user to enter their age, and objects if it's not an integer. How does it check if the data entered is an integer? The code uses the PHP intval function to turn the entered text into an integer and then converts it back to a string using the PHP strval function. If the result is the same as what was originally typed, then the entered data was an integer. If not, the data wasn't in integer form and we have to add an error message to the $errors array:

```
if(strcmp($_REQUEST["number"],
   strval(intval($_REQUEST["number"]))))  {
     $errors[] = "<font color='red'>Please enter an integer</font>";
}
```

Here's the whole of checkdatainteger.php, with the lines that make it different from checkdata.php highlighted:

```
<html>
  <head>
    <title>
      Validating User Data: Integers
    </title>
  </head>

  <body>
    <center>

      <h1>Validating User Data: Integers</h1>
      <?php
        $errors = array();

        if(isset($_REQUEST["welcome_already_displayed"])){

          check_data();

          if(count($errors) != 0){
            display_errors();
            display_welcome();
          }
          else {
            process_data();
          }
        }
        else {
         display_welcome();
        }

        function check_data()
```

```
    {
      global $errors;

      if($_REQUEST["number"] == "") {
      $errors[] = "<font color='red'>Please enter your age</font>";
      }
      if(strcmp($_REQUEST["number"],
        strval(intval($_REQUEST["number"])))) {
        $errors[] = "<font color='red'>Please enter an integer</font>";
      }
    }

    function display_errors()
    {
      global $errors;

      foreach ($errors as $error){
        echo $error, "<br>";
      }
    }

    function process_data()
    {
      echo "Thank you. Your age is ";
      echo $_REQUEST["number"];
    }

    function display_welcome()
    {
        echo "<form method='post' action='checkdatainteger.php'>";
        echo "Please enter your age";
        echo "<br>";
        echo "<input name='number' type='text'>";
        echo "<br>";
        echo "<br>";
        echo "<input type='submit' value='Submit'>";
        echo "<input type='hidden'
          name='welcome_already_displayed' value='data'>";
        echo "</form>";
    }
    ?>

    </center>
  </body>
</html>
```

As you can see, the code is substantially the same as that for checkdata.php, indicating that you can readily modify our PHP validation technique to check for the kinds of errors you want. The checkdatainteger.php application appears in Figure 11-13.

If the data you enter is not an integer, you'll get an error, as you see in Figure 11-14. Beautiful.

Figure 11-13 Displaying the welcome page

Figure 11-14 Displaying an error

Validating Text

You can even check to make sure text entries are in the right format with PHP's regular expression checking. Regular expressions let you examine the format of text to make sure it matches a template you supply—see http://perldoc.perl.org/perlre.html for all the details.

Say, for example, that you want to make sure that the user enters their social security number, which in digit terms is xxx-xx-xxxx. You can do that with PHP's preg_match function, which, using the fact that digits are represented by \d in regular expressions, would make your validate_data function look like this:

```
function validate_data()
{
  global $errors;

  if(!preg_match('/^\d\d\d-\d\d-\d\d\d\d$/', $_REQUEST["data"])){
    $errors[] =
    "<font color='red'>Please enter a social security number" </font>";
  }
}
```

Chapter 12

Using the HTML DOM and Ajax

Key Skills & Concepts

- Introducing the DOM

- Appending elements using the DOM

- Replacing elements using the DOM

- Handling Ajax timeouts

Web pages can be viewed as collections of objects using the HTML DOM (Document Object Model), which gives you the power to access everything in a page. In Ajax, knowing how to update your web pages with newly downloaded data is essential. You've already seen that the basic model is to use a <div> or <span> element and to simply replace the contents of that element with the new data:

```
function getData(dataSource, divID)
{
  if(XMLHttpRequestObject) {
    var obj = document.getElementById(divID);
    XMLHttpRequestObject.open("GET", dataSource);

    XMLHttpRequestObject.onreadystatechange = function()
    {
      if (XMLHttpRequestObject.readyState == 4 &&
        XMLHttpRequestObject.status == 200) {
          obj.innerHTML = XMLHttpRequestObject.responseText;
      }
    }
  }
```

Beyond the basic model, another option is to use dynamic HTML, as you saw in Chapter 8. There, you found new ways of inserting new data into web pages, such as using the insertAdjacentHTML method:

```
<html>
  <head>
    <title>
      Updating a Page With insertAdjacentHTML
    </title>

    <script language="JavaScript">
      function addHTML()
      {
        targetDiv.insertAdjacentHTML("AfterEnd",
        "<p><input type=text value='Hello there.'> See? A new text
          field.</p>");
      }
```

```
    </script>
  </head>
      .
      .
      .
```

It turns out that there are additional techniques that you can use to modify a web page without refreshing that web page, and those techniques are wrapped up into the HTML DOM. The DOM provides a way of looking at the contents of a web page as a collection of objects, complete with built-in methods and properties, all available for you to use in your Ajax applications.

Getting to Know the DOM

As mentioned, the DOM treats a web page as a collection of objects. The easiest way to explain this is through an example, so let's start with a likely looking HTML web page:

```
<html>
  <head>
    <title>
       The Report
    </title>
  </head>

  <body>
    <h1>
        All quiet on the Western front.
    </h1>
  </body>
<html>
```

This is just a plain web page with a title that will appear in the browser's title bar and some text that will appear in an <h1> header. But looked at in DOM terms, the elements of this simple web page make up a collection of objects, arranged into a tree structure. Here's what this web page looks like in DOM terms, as a tree of nodes:

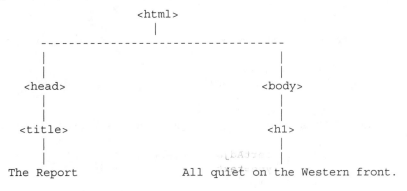

JavaScript has the following built-in properties that you can use to work with the DOM nodes in web documents like this one:

Property	Description
attributes	Attributes of this node
childNodes	Array of child nodes
documentElement	Document element
firstChild	First child node
lastChild	Last child node
localName	Local name of the node
name	Name of the node
nextSibling	Next sibling node
nodeName	Name of the node
nodeType	Node type
nodeValue	Value of the node
previousSibling	Previous sibling node

These JavaScript properties are coming up in this chapter. Note the nodeType property, which in HTML can have these values (in XML, there are nine more possible values):

- 1   Element
- 2   Attribute
- 3   Text node

In terms of DOM node types, here's what our page looks like:

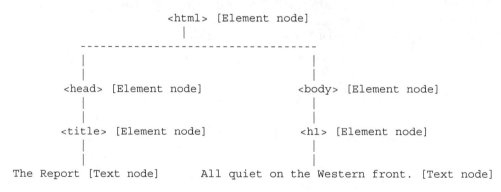

Besides the properties listed in the previous table, nodes support these methods in JavaScript:

Method	Description
replaceNode(a, b)	Replaces node b with node a
insertBefore(a, b)	Inserts node a before node b
appendChild(a)	Appends a child, a, to the node that you call this method on

Okay, that's the overview. Time to put the DOM to work.

Appending New Elements to a Web Page Using the DOM and Ajax

The first use we'll make of the DOM is to append new element nodes to the tree of nodes in a web page. In other words, we'll download data using Ajax and display that data by actually creating a new element and appending that element to the DOM node tree that makes up the web page.

This page starts with a button that the user can click to download data using Ajax:

```
<body>

  <h1>Appending Elements With the DOM and Ajax</h1>

  <form>
    <input type = "button" value = "Download the message"
      onclick = "getData()">
  </form>
       .
       .
       .
</body>
```

We also add a <div> element that we'll insert the downloaded data into:

```
<body>

  <h1>Appending Elements With the DOM and Ajax</h1>

  <form>
    <input type = "button" value = "Download the message"
      onclick = "getData()">
  </form>
```

```
<div id="targetDiv" width =100 height=100>
  <p id="text"></p>
</div>

</body>
```

When the button is clicked, we're supposed to download and display a file, data1.txt, which has these contents:

```
This text was appended using the DOM.
```

This download and display will take place in a function named getData:

```
<html>
  <head>

    <title>Appending Elements With the DOM and Ajax</title>

    <script language = "javascript">

      function getData()
      {
        .
        .
        .
      }

    </script>
  </head>
    .
    :
    .
</html>
```

In the getData function, we start by creating an XMLHttpRequest object:

```
<script language = "javascript">

  function getData()
  {
    var XMLHttpRequestObject = false;

    if (window.XMLHttpRequest) {
      XMLHttpRequestObject = new XMLHttpRequest();
    } else if (window.ActiveXObject) {
      XMLHttpRequestObject = new ActiveXObject("Microsoft.XMLHTTP");
    }
      .
      .
      .
  }

</script>
```

Then we check if that XMLHttpRequest object was in fact created:

```
<script language = "javascript">

  function getData()
  {
    var XMLHttpRequestObject = false;

    if (window.XMLHttpRequest) {
      XMLHttpRequestObject = new XMLHttpRequest();
    } else if (window.ActiveXObject) {
      XMLHttpRequestObject = new ActiveXObject("Microsoft.XMLHTTP");
    }

    if(XMLHttpRequestObject) {
      .
      .
      .
    }
  }

</script>
```

If the XMLHttpRequest object exists, we can configure it to download data1.txt by opening it:

```
<script language = "javascript">

  function getData()
  {
    var XMLHttpRequestObject = false;

    if (window.XMLHttpRequest) {
      XMLHttpRequestObject = new XMLHttpRequest();
    } else if (window.ActiveXObject) {
      XMLHttpRequestObject = new ActiveXObject("Microsoft.XMLHTTP");
    }

    if(XMLHttpRequestObject) {

      XMLHttpRequestObject.open("GET", "data1.txt");
      .
      .
      .
    }
  }

</script>
```

And we can attach an anonymous function to the object's onreadystatechange property to monitor the download of the data:

```
<script language = "javascript">

  function getData()
  {
    var XMLHttpRequestObject = false;

    if (window.XMLHttpRequest) {
      XMLHttpRequestObject = new XMLHttpRequest();
    } else if (window.ActiveXObject) {
      XMLHttpRequestObject = new ActiveXObject("Microsoft.XMLHTTP");
    }

    if(XMLHttpRequestObject) {

      XMLHttpRequestObject.open("GET", "data1.txt");

      XMLHttpRequestObject.onreadystatechange = function()
      {
        if (XMLHttpRequestObject.readyState == 4 &&
          XMLHttpRequestObject.status == 200) {
          .
          .
          .
        }
      }
    }
  }

</script>
```

After we download the data from the file, data1.txt, we'll create a new <p> element to hold that data, and append the <p> element to the <div> element already in our web page (beneath the button). Here's how we use the createElement method to create a new <p> element:

```
<script language = "javascript">

  function getData()
  {
    var XMLHttpRequestObject = false;

    if (window.XMLHttpRequest) {
      XMLHttpRequestObject = new XMLHttpRequest();
    } else if (window.ActiveXObject) {
      XMLHttpRequestObject = new ActiveXObject("Microsoft.XMLHTTP");
    }

    if(XMLHttpRequestObject) {
```

```
      XMLHttpRequestObject.open("GET", "data1.txt");

      XMLHttpRequestObject.onreadystatechange = function()
      {
        if (XMLHttpRequestObject.readyState == 4 &&
          XMLHttpRequestObject.status == 200) {
          var newPElement = document.createElement("p");
            .
            .
            .

        }
      }

    }
  }

</script>
```

You can't just insert text into a <p> element, or any HTML element—you have to insert that text into a text node first. So we begin inserting the text by creating a new text node (note that we place the downloaded data, XMLHttpRequestObject.responseText, in the text node):

```
<script language = "javascript">

  function getData()
  {
    var XMLHttpRequestObject = false;

    if (window.XMLHttpRequest) {
      XMLHttpRequestObject = new XMLHttpRequest();
    } else if (window.ActiveXObject) {
      XMLHttpRequestObject = new ActiveXObject("Microsoft.XMLHTTP");
    }

    if(XMLHttpRequestObject) {

      XMLHttpRequestObject.open("GET", "data1.txt");

      XMLHttpRequestObject.onreadystatechange = function()
      {
        if (XMLHttpRequestObject.readyState == 4 &&
          XMLHttpRequestObject.status == 200) {
          var newPElement = document.createElement("p");
          var newText =
            document.createTextNode(XMLHttpRequestObject.responseText);
            .
            .
            .

        }
      }
```

```
          XMLHttpRequestObject.send(null);
      }
  }

</script>
```

Now we have to place the new text node into the <p> element, and we can do that with the appendChild method this way:

```
<script language = "javascript">

  function getData()
  {
    var XMLHttpRequestObject = false;

    if (window.XMLHttpRequest) {
      XMLHttpRequestObject = new XMLHttpRequest();
    } else if (window.ActiveXObject) {
      XMLHttpRequestObject = new ActiveXObject("Microsoft.XMLHTTP");
    }

    if(XMLHttpRequestObject) {

      XMLHttpRequestObject.open("GET", "data1.txt");

      XMLHttpRequestObject.onreadystatechange = function()
      {
        if (XMLHttpRequestObject.readyState == 4 &&
          XMLHttpRequestObject.status == 200) {
          var newPElement = document.createElement("p");
          var newText =
            document.createTextNode(XMLHttpRequestObject.responseText);
          newPElement.appendChild(newText);
          .
          .
          .

        }
      }

      XMLHttpRequestObject.send(null);
    }
  }

</script>
```

Great, that places the downloaded data into the <p> element. The final step is to insert the <p> element into the web page using DOM methods. We can do that by getting an object corresponding to the target <div> element, and using the appendChild method to insert the <p> element into the web page:

```
<script language = "javascript">

  function getData()
  {
    var XMLHttpRequestObject = false;

    if (window.XMLHttpRequest) {
      XMLHttpRequestObject = new XMLHttpRequest();
    } else if (window.ActiveXObject) {
      XMLHttpRequestObject = new ActiveXObject("Microsoft.XMLHTTP");
    }

    if(XMLHttpRequestObject) {

      XMLHttpRequestObject.open("GET", "data1.txt");

      XMLHttpRequestObject.onreadystatechange = function()
      {
        if (XMLHttpRequestObject.readyState == 4 &&
          XMLHttpRequestObject.status == 200) {
          var newPElement = document.createElement("p");
          var newText =
            document.createTextNode(XMLHttpRequestObject.responseText);
          newPElement.appendChild(newText);
          var divElement = document.getElementById("targetDiv");
          divElement.appendChild(newPElement);
        }
      }

      XMLHttpRequestObject.send(null);
    }
  }

</script>
```

Here's the whole page, appender.html:

```
<html>
  <head>

    <title>Appending Elements With the DOM and Ajax</title>

    <script language = "javascript">

      function getData()
      {
        var XMLHttpRequestObject = false;

        if (window.XMLHttpRequest) {
          XMLHttpRequestObject = new XMLHttpRequest();
```

```
    } else if (window.ActiveXObject) {
      XMLHttpRequestObject = new ActiveXObject("Microsoft.XMLHTTP");
    }

    if(XMLHttpRequestObject) {

      XMLHttpRequestObject.open("GET", "data1.txt");

      XMLHttpRequestObject.onreadystatechange = function()
      {
        if (XMLHttpRequestObject.readyState == 4 &&
          XMLHttpRequestObject.status == 200) {
          var newPElement = document.createElement("p");
          var newText =
             document.createTextNode(XMLHttpRequestObject.responseText);
          newPElement.appendChild(newText);
          var divElement = document.getElementById("targetDiv");
          divElement.appendChild(newPElement);
        }
      }

      XMLHttpRequestObject.send(null);
    }
  }

  </script>
</head>

<body>

  <h1>Appending Elements With the DOM and Ajax</h1>

  <form>
    <input type = "button" value = "Download the message"
      onclick = "getData()">
  </form>

  <div id="targetDiv" width =100 height=100>
    <p id="text"></p>
  </div>

</body>

</html>
```

You can see how this works in Figure 12-1, in which the user clicked the download button, the data was downloaded and inserted into a new <p> element, and the <p> element was subsequently inserted into the page using DOM methods. Very nice.

Besides appending elements using the DOM, you can also replace them.

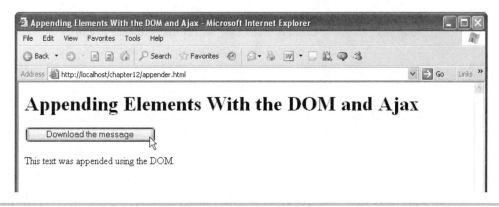

Figure 12-1   Appending new elements using the DOM

Replacing Elements Using the DOM

As you saw in the previous section, you can use the appendChild method to append child nodes using the DOM. You can also replace child nodes entirely using the replaceChild method, and we'll take a look at how that works now, in a new example, replacer.html. This example will have a <div> element with the ID "targetDiv":

```
<body>

    <h1>Replacing Elements With the DOM</h1>
        .
        .
        .
    <div id="targetDiv" width =100 height=100>
        .
        .
        .
    </div>

</body>
```

And that's the <div> element whose child we'll be replacing. In order to make that happen, we have to give it a child to start with, so let's enclose a <p> element with the ID "text" in the <div> element like this:

```
<body>

    <h1>Replacing Elements With the DOM</h1>
        .
        .
        .
```

```
<div id="targetDiv" width =100 height=100>
  <p id="text">The fetched message will appear here.</p>
</div>

</body>
```

So that's the element we'll work on replacing—the <p> element with the ID "text".

We'll also need a button that, when clicked, will download new text using Ajax and replace the <p> element. That new text will be in a file named replace1.txt, and here's the button that downloads this file:

```
<body>

  <h1>Replacing Elements With the DOM</h1>

  <form>
    <input type = "button" value = "Download message 1"
      onclick = "getData('1')">
      .
      .
      .
  </form>

  <div id="targetDiv" width =100 height=100>
    <p id="text">The fetched message will appear here.</p>
  </div>

</body>
```

That is, to download the file replace1.txt, you simply have to pass "1" to the JavaScript function getData.

Let's add a second button to download a different file, replace2.txt. When you download replace2.txt, the text in that file will replace the <p> element. Here's what the second button looks like:

```
<body>

  <h1>Replacing Elements With the DOM</h1>

  <form>
    <input type = "button" value = "Download message 1"
      onclick = "getData('1')">
    <input type = "button" value = "Download message 2"
      onclick = "getData('2')">
  </form>

  <div id="targetDiv" width =100 height=100>
    <p id="text">The fetched message will appear here.</p>
  </div>

</body>
```

Okay, we're ready to write the JavaScript to download replace1.txt and replace2.txt. Here's the text in replace1.txt:

```
This text replaced the earlier text using the DOM.
```

And here's the text in replace2.txt:

```
This text also replaced the earlier text using the DOM.
```

Now it's time to write the getData function that will do the actual downloading and replacing:

```
<script language = "javascript">

    function getData(number)
    {
      .
      .
      .
    }

</script>
```

First, we'll create a new XMLHttpRequest object:

```
<script language = "javascript">

  function getData(number)
  {
    var XMLHttpRequestObject = false;

    if (window.XMLHttpRequest) {
      XMLHttpRequestObject = new XMLHttpRequest();
    } else if (window.ActiveXObject) {
      XMLHttpRequestObject = new ActiveXObject("Microsoft.XMLHTTP");
    }
    .
    .
    .
  }

</script>
```

Then we check if the XMLHttpRequest object was actually created:

```
<script language = "javascript">

  function getData(number)
  {
    var XMLHttpRequestObject = false;

    if (window.XMLHttpRequest) {
      XMLHttpRequestObject = new XMLHttpRequest();
    } else if (window.ActiveXObject) {
      XMLHttpRequestObject = new ActiveXObject("Microsoft.XMLHTTP");
    }
```

```
      if(XMLHttpRequestObject) {
        .
        .
        .
      }
    }

</script>
```

If the XMLHttpRequest object was indeed created, we can configure it to download replace1.txt or replace2.txt, depending on whether "1" or "2" was passed to the getData function:

```
<script language = "javascript">

  function getData(number)
  {
    var XMLHttpRequestObject = false;

    if (window.XMLHttpRequest) {
      XMLHttpRequestObject = new XMLHttpRequest();
    } else if (window.ActiveXObject) {
      XMLHttpRequestObject = new ActiveXObject("Microsoft.XMLHTTP");
    }

    if(XMLHttpRequestObject) {

      XMLHttpRequestObject.open("GET", "replace" + number +  ".txt");
      .
      .
      .
    }
  }

</script>
```

Next, we attach an anonymous inner function to the onreadystatechange property:

```
<script language = "javascript">

  function getData(number)
  {
    var XMLHttpRequestObject = false;

    if (window.XMLHttpRequest) {
      XMLHttpRequestObject = new XMLHttpRequest();
    } else if (window.ActiveXObject) {
      XMLHttpRequestObject = new ActiveXObject("Microsoft.XMLHTTP");
    }
```

```
      if(XMLHttpRequestObject) {

        XMLHttpRequestObject.open("GET", "replace" + number +  ".txt");

        XMLHttpRequestObject.onreadystatechange = function()
        {
          .
          .
          .
        }

      }
    }

  </script>
```

And we can check when the download is complete with the status and readyState properties:

```
  <script language = "javascript">

    function getData(number)
    {
      var XMLHttpRequestObject = false;

      if (window.XMLHttpRequest) {
        XMLHttpRequestObject = new XMLHttpRequest();
      } else if (window.ActiveXObject) {
        XMLHttpRequestObject = new ActiveXObject("Microsoft.XMLHTTP");
      }

      if(XMLHttpRequestObject) {

        XMLHttpRequestObject.open("GET", "replace" + number +  ".txt");

        XMLHttpRequestObject.onreadystatechange = function()
        {
          if (XMLHttpRequestObject.readyState == 4 &&
            XMLHttpRequestObject.status == 200) {
            .
            .
            .
          }
        }

      }
    }

  </script>
```

Now that we've downloaded the new text, it's time to create our new <p> element, which we'll use to replace the existing <p> element. Here's how we use the createElement method to create the new <p> element:

```
<script language = "javascript">

  function getData(number)
  {
    var XMLHttpRequestObject = false;

    if (window.XMLHttpRequest) {
      XMLHttpRequestObject = new XMLHttpRequest();
    } else if (window.ActiveXObject) {
      XMLHttpRequestObject = new ActiveXObject("Microsoft.XMLHTTP");
    }

    if(XMLHttpRequestObject) {

      XMLHttpRequestObject.open("GET", "replace" + number +  ".txt");

      XMLHttpRequestObject.onreadystatechange = function()
      {
        if (XMLHttpRequestObject.readyState == 4 &&
          XMLHttpRequestObject.status == 200) {
          var newPElement = document.createElement("p");
          .
          .
          .
        }
      }

    }
  }

</script>
```

Note that the current <p> element—the one about to be replaced—has an ID of "text". We'll also give the new <p> element the same ID so that it can be replaced in turn (by a later button click):

```
<script language = "javascript">

  function getData(number)
  {
    var XMLHttpRequestObject = false;

    if (window.XMLHttpRequest) {
      XMLHttpRequestObject = new XMLHttpRequest();
    } else if (window.ActiveXObject) {
```

```
    XMLHttpRequestObject = new ActiveXObject("Microsoft.XMLHTTP");
  }

  if(XMLHttpRequestObject) {

    XMLHttpRequestObject.open("GET", "replace" + number +  ".txt");

    XMLHttpRequestObject.onreadystatechange = function()
    {
      if (XMLHttpRequestObject.readyState == 4 &&
        XMLHttpRequestObject.status == 200) {
        var newPElement = document.createElement("p");
        newPElement.setAttribute("id", "text");
          .
          .
          .
      }
    }

  }
}

</script>
```

We'll need to place the newly downloaded text, XMLHttpRequestObject.responseText, into its own text node before placing it in the <p> element, and we create the new text node this way:

```
<script language = "javascript">

  function getData(number)
  {
    var XMLHttpRequestObject = false;

    if (window.XMLHttpRequest) {
      XMLHttpRequestObject = new XMLHttpRequest();
    } else if (window.ActiveXObject) {
      XMLHttpRequestObject = new ActiveXObject("Microsoft.XMLHTTP");
    }

    if(XMLHttpRequestObject) {

      XMLHttpRequestObject.open("GET", "replace" + number +  ".txt");

      XMLHttpRequestObject.onreadystatechange = function()
      {
        if (XMLHttpRequestObject.readyState == 4 &&
          XMLHttpRequestObject.status == 200) {
          var newPElement = document.createElement("p");
          newPElement.setAttribute("id", "text");
```

```
          var newText = document.createTextNode(XMLHttpRequestObject
            .responseText);
              .
              .
              .
        }
      }

    }
  }

</script>
```

We append the new text node to the new <p> element like this:

```
<script language = "javascript">

  function getData(number)
  {
    var XMLHttpRequestObject = false;

    if (window.XMLHttpRequest) {
      XMLHttpRequestObject = new XMLHttpRequest();
    } else if (window.ActiveXObject) {
      XMLHttpRequestObject = new ActiveXObject("Microsoft.XMLHTTP");
    }

    if(XMLHttpRequestObject) {

      XMLHttpRequestObject.open("GET", "replace" + number +  ".txt");

      XMLHttpRequestObject.onreadystatechange = function()
      {
        if (XMLHttpRequestObject.readyState == 4 &&
          XMLHttpRequestObject.status == 200) {
          var newPElement = document.createElement("p");
          newPElement.setAttribute("id", "text");
          var newText = document.createTextNode(XMLHttpRequestObject
            .responseText);
          newPElement.appendChild(newText);
              .
              .
              .
        }
      }

    }
  }

</script>
```

Next, we get an object corresponding to the <div> element:

```
<script language = "javascript">

  function getData(number)
  {
    var XMLHttpRequestObject = false;

    if (window.XMLHttpRequest) {
      XMLHttpRequestObject = new XMLHttpRequest();
    } else if (window.ActiveXObject) {
      XMLHttpRequestObject = new ActiveXObject("Microsoft.XMLHTTP");
    }

    if(XMLHttpRequestObject) {

      XMLHttpRequestObject.open("GET", "replace" + number +  ".txt");

      XMLHttpRequestObject.onreadystatechange = function()
      {
        if (XMLHttpRequestObject.readyState == 4 &&
          XMLHttpRequestObject.status == 200) {
          var newPElement = document.createElement("p");
          newPElement.setAttribute("id", "text");
          var newText = document.createTextNode(XMLHttpRequestObject
            .responseText);
          newPElement.appendChild(newText);
          var divElement = document.getElementById("targetDiv");
            .
            .
            .
        }
      }

    }
  }

</script>
```

We also get an object corresponding to the <p> element we want to replace:

```
<script language = "javascript">

  function getData(number)
  {
    var XMLHttpRequestObject = false;

    if (window.XMLHttpRequest) {
      XMLHttpRequestObject = new XMLHttpRequest();
    } else if (window.ActiveXObject) {
      XMLHttpRequestObject = new ActiveXObject("Microsoft.XMLHTTP");
    }
```

```
    if(XMLHttpRequestObject) {

      XMLHttpRequestObject.open("GET", "replace" + number +  ".txt");

      XMLHttpRequestObject.onreadystatechange = function()
      {
        if (XMLHttpRequestObject.readyState == 4 &&
          XMLHttpRequestObject.status == 200) {
          var newPElement = document.createElement("p");
          newPElement.setAttribute("id", "text");
          var newText = document.createTextNode(XMLHttpRequestObject
            .responseText);
          newPElement.appendChild(newText);
          var divElement = document.getElementById("targetDiv");
          var oldPElement = document.getElementById("text");
          .
          .
          .
        }
      }

      XMLHttpRequestObject.send(null);
    }
  }

</script>
```

And now we're ready to replace the old <p> element with the new <p> element, using replaceChild. We pass the new element and the old element, in that order, to replaceChild this way:

```
<script language = "javascript">

  function getData(number)
  {
    var XMLHttpRequestObject = false;

    if (window.XMLHttpRequest) {
      XMLHttpRequestObject = new XMLHttpRequest();
    } else if (window.ActiveXObject) {
      XMLHttpRequestObject = new ActiveXObject("Microsoft.XMLHTTP");
    }

    if(XMLHttpRequestObject) {

      XMLHttpRequestObject.open("GET", "replace" + number +  ".txt");

      XMLHttpRequestObject.onreadystatechange = function()
      {
        if (XMLHttpRequestObject.readyState == 4 &&
          XMLHttpRequestObject.status == 200) {
          var newPElement = document.createElement("p");
```

```
         newPElement.setAttribute("id", "text");
         var newText = document.createTextNode(XMLHttpRequestObject
            .responseText);
         newPElement.appendChild(newText);
         var divElement = document.getElementById("targetDiv");
         var oldPElement = document.getElementById("text");
         divElement.replaceChild(newPElement, oldPElement);
       }
     }

   }
 }

</script>
```

And that does the trick. All that's left is to connect to the server using the send method:

```
<script language = "javascript">

   function getData(number)
   {
     var XMLHttpRequestObject = false;

     if (window.XMLHttpRequest) {
       XMLHttpRequestObject = new XMLHttpRequest();
     } else if (window.ActiveXObject) {
       XMLHttpRequestObject = new ActiveXObject("Microsoft.XMLHTTP");
     }

     if(XMLHttpRequestObject) {

       XMLHttpRequestObject.open("GET", "replace" + number +  ".txt");

       XMLHttpRequestObject.onreadystatechange = function()
       {
         if (XMLHttpRequestObject.readyState == 4 &&
           XMLHttpRequestObject.status == 200) {
           var newPElement = document.createElement("p");
           newPElement.setAttribute("id", "text");
           var newText = document.createTextNode(XMLHttpRequestObject
              .responseText);
           newPElement.appendChild(newText);
           var divElement = document.getElementById("targetDiv");
           var oldPElement = document.getElementById("text");
           divElement.replaceChild(newPElement, oldPElement);
         }
       }

       XMLHttpRequestObject.send(null);
     }
   }

</script>
```

Great—here's replacer.html in full for reference:

```html
<html>
  <head>

    <title>Replacing Elements With the DOM</title>

    <script language = "javascript">

      function getData(number)
      {
        var XMLHttpRequestObject = false;

        if (window.XMLHttpRequest) {
          XMLHttpRequestObject = new XMLHttpRequest();
        } else if (window.ActiveXObject) {
          XMLHttpRequestObject = new ActiveXObject("Microsoft.XMLHTTP");
        }

        if(XMLHttpRequestObject) {

          XMLHttpRequestObject.open("GET", "replace" + number +  ".txt");

          XMLHttpRequestObject.onreadystatechange = function()
          {
            if (XMLHttpRequestObject.readyState == 4 &&
              XMLHttpRequestObject.status == 200) {
              var newPElement = document.createElement("p");
              newPElement.setAttribute("id", "text");
              var newText = document.createTextNode(XMLHttpRequestObject
                .responseText);
              newPElement.appendChild(newText);
              var divElement = document.getElementById("targetDiv");
              var oldPElement = document.getElementById("text");
              divElement.replaceChild(newPElement, oldPElement);
            }
          }

          XMLHttpRequestObject.send(null);
        }
      }

    </script>
  </head>

  <body>

    <h1>Replacing Elements With the DOM</h1>

    <form>
      <input type = "button" value = "Download message 1"
```

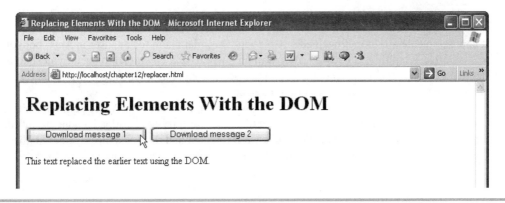

Figure 12-2 Appending new elements using the DOM—first message

```
      onclick = "getData('1')">
    <input type = "button" value = "Download message 2"
      onclick = "getData('2')">
  </form>

  <div id="targetDiv" width =100 height=100>
    <p id="text">The fetched message will appear here.</p>
  </div>

 </body>

</html>
```

You can see the results in Figure 12-2—when the user clicks button 1, the first message is downloaded and displayed.

And, as you can see in Figure 12-3, when the user clicks button 2, the second message is downloaded and displayed.

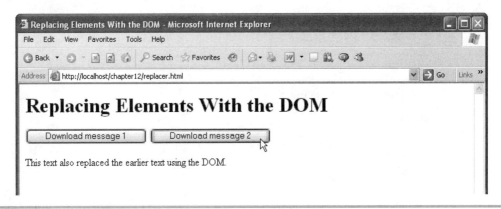

Figure 12-3 Appending new elements using the DOM—second message

Handling Timeouts in Ajax

Suppose you are all set to download a requested file or data item for the user in Ajax, but you can't find it. What should you do? After waiting a while for a download to occur, you should let the user know the operation timed out. Otherwise, your Ajax application will just keep waiting for a nonexistent resource or a broken connection.

Here's an example, timeout.html, that shows how to time out if an Ajax operation isn't successful after a certain amount of time. In this case, we'll try to download a nonexistent file, data.txt, and then, when the operation fails, we'll time out and display a message box to the user. We start timeout.html with a button that the user can click to attempt to download data.txt in a function named getData:

```
<body>

  <H1>Handling Ajax Timeouts</H1>

  <form>
    <input type = "button" value = "Download Message"
      onclick = "getData('data.txt', 'targetDiv')">
  </form>
      .
      .
      .
</body>
```

We'll add a <div> element to display the results in:

```
<body>

  <H1>Handling Ajax Timeouts</H1>

  <form>
    <input type = "button" value = "Download Message"
      onclick = "getData('data.txt', 'targetDiv')">
  </form>

  <div id="targetDiv">
    <p>The fetched data will go here.</p>
  </div>

</body>
```

Next, we'll create the getData function:

```
<script language = "javascript">

  function getData(dataSource, divID)
  {
      .
      .
      .
  }

</script>
```

And we'll need an XMLHttpRequest object:

```
<script language = "javascript">

  function getData(dataSource, divID)
  {
    var XMLHttpRequestObject = false;

    if (window.XMLHttpRequest) {
      XMLHttpRequestObject = new XMLHttpRequest();
    } else if (window.ActiveXObject) {
      XMLHttpRequestObject = new ActiveXObject("Microsoft.XMLHTTP");
    }
      .
      .
      .

  }
</script>
```

We'll use the JavaScript setTimeout function to set the timeout. The idea is that if the data hasn't been downloaded in a second (1000 ms), we stop the download attempt and display an error message in a message box. We start the process by configuring the XMLHttpRequest object:

```
<script language = "javascript">
  function getData(dataSource, divID)
  {
    var XMLHttpRequestObject = false;

    if (window.XMLHttpRequest) {
      XMLHttpRequestObject = new XMLHttpRequest();
    } else if (window.ActiveXObject) {
      XMLHttpRequestObject = new ActiveXObject("Microsoft.XMLHTTP");
    }

    if(XMLHttpRequestObject) {

      XMLHttpRequestObject.open("GET", dataSource);
        .
        .
        .

    }
  }
</script>
```

Now we'll attach the anonymous function that will monitor the download:

```
<script language = "javascript">
  function getData(dataSource, divID)
  {
    var XMLHttpRequestObject = false;

    if (window.XMLHttpRequest) {
      XMLHttpRequestObject = new XMLHttpRequest();
    } else if (window.ActiveXObject) {
```

```
        XMLHttpRequestObject = new ActiveXObject("Microsoft.XMLHTTP");
      }

      if(XMLHttpRequestObject) {

        XMLHttpRequestObject.open("GET", dataSource);

        XMLHttpRequestObject.onreadystatechange = function()
        {
          .
          .
          .
        }

      }
    }
</script>
```

When the download starts, the readyState property will contain a value of 1, and we want to set our timeout clock ticking at that point, by setting the timeout. We don't want to set the timeout if it's already been set (which would reset it to 0), so we'll introduce a variable named timeoutIsSet and check if the timeout has already been set, this way:

```
<script language = "javascript">
  function getData(dataSource, divID)
  {
    var XMLHttpRequestObject = false;

    if (window.XMLHttpRequest) {
      XMLHttpRequestObject = new XMLHttpRequest();
    } else if (window.ActiveXObject) {
      XMLHttpRequestObject = new ActiveXObject("Microsoft.XMLHTTP");
    }

    if(XMLHttpRequestObject) {

      XMLHttpRequestObject.open("GET", dataSource);

      var timeoutIsSet = false;

      XMLHttpRequestObject.onreadystatechange = function()
      {
        if (XMLHttpRequestObject.readyState == 1) {
          if(!timeoutIsSet){
            .
            .
            .
          }
        }
      }

    }
  }
</script>
```

To set the timeout, we will use the setTimeout function to call another anonymous function in 1000 ms:

```
<script language = "javascript">
  function getData(dataSource, divID)
  {
    var XMLHttpRequestObject = false;

    if (window.XMLHttpRequest) {
      XMLHttpRequestObject = new XMLHttpRequest();
    } else if (window.ActiveXObject) {
      XMLHttpRequestObject = new ActiveXObject("Microsoft.XMLHTTP");
    }

    if(XMLHttpRequestObject) {
      var obj = document.getElementById(divID);
      XMLHttpRequestObject.open("GET", dataSource);

      var timeoutIsSet = false;
      var downloadWentOK = false;

      XMLHttpRequestObject.onreadystatechange = function()
      {
        if (XMLHttpRequestObject.readyState == 1) {
          if(!timeoutIsSet){
            window.setTimeout(function(){
              .
              .
              .
            },
            1000);
            timeoutIsSet = true;
          }
        }

        .
        .
        .

      }
    }
  }
</script>
```

In the anonymous function, we will check if the download went okay by checking the value of a variable named downloadWentOK:

```
<script language = "javascript">
  function getData(dataSource, divID)
  {
    var XMLHttpRequestObject = false;

    if (window.XMLHttpRequest) {
      XMLHttpRequestObject = new XMLHttpRequest();
```

```
      } else if (window.ActiveXObject) {
      XMLHttpRequestObject = new ActiveXObject("Microsoft.XMLHTTP");
      }

      if(XMLHttpRequestObject) {
        var obj = document.getElementById(divID);
        XMLHttpRequestObject.open("GET", dataSource);

        var timeoutIsSet = false;
        var downloadWentOK = false;

        XMLHttpRequestObject.onreadystatechange = function()
        {
          if (XMLHttpRequestObject.readyState == 1) {
              if(!timeoutIsSet){
                window.setTimeout(function(){
                  if(!downloadWentOK){
                     .
                     .
                     .
                  }
                },
                1000);
                timeoutIsSet = true;
              }
          }

        }
      }
    }
  </script>
```

And if the data was not downloaded by the time the operation timed out, we can display an
error and abort the Ajax operation with the XMLHttpRequest object's abort method:

```
  <script language = "javascript">
    function getData(dataSource, divID)
    {
      var XMLHttpRequestObject = false;

      if (window.XMLHttpRequest) {
        XMLHttpRequestObject = new XMLHttpRequest();
      } else if (window.ActiveXObject) {
        XMLHttpRequestObject = new ActiveXObject("Microsoft.XMLHTTP");
      }

      if(XMLHttpRequestObject) {
        var obj = document.getElementById(divID);
        XMLHttpRequestObject.open("GET", dataSource);

        var timeoutIsSet = false;
        var downloadWentOK = false;
```

```
  XMLHttpRequestObject.onreadystatechange = function()
  {
    if (XMLHttpRequestObject.readyState == 1) {
      if(!timeoutIsSet){
        window.setTimeout(function(){
          if(!downloadWentOK){
            alert("Sorry, but I timed out.");
            XMLHttpRequestObject.abort();
          }
        },
        1000);
        timeoutIsSet = true;
      }
    }

  }

  }
  }
</script>
```

On the other hand, if the download operation did go okay, we can display the data and set the downloadWentOK variable to true:

```
<script language = "javascript">
  function getData(dataSource, divID)
  {
    var XMLHttpRequestObject = false;

    if (window.XMLHttpRequest) {
      XMLHttpRequestObject = new XMLHttpRequest();
    } else if (window.ActiveXObject) {
      XMLHttpRequestObject = new ActiveXObject("Microsoft.XMLHTTP");
    }

    if(XMLHttpRequestObject) {
      var obj = document.getElementById(divID);
      XMLHttpRequestObject.open("GET", dataSource);

      var timeoutIsSet = false;
      var downloadWentOK = false;

      XMLHttpRequestObject.onreadystatechange = function()
      {
        if (XMLHttpRequestObject.readyState == 1) {
          if(!timeoutIsSet){
            window.setTimeout(function(){
              if(!downloadWentOK){
                alert("Sorry, but I timed out.");
                XMLHttpRequestObject.abort();
              }
            },
```

```
           1000);
           timeoutIsSet = true;
        }
      }

      if (XMLHttpRequestObject.readyState == 4 &&
        XMLHttpRequestObject.status == 200) {
          downloadWentOK = true;
          obj.innerHTML = XMLHttpRequestObject.responseText;
      }
    }

    XMLHttpRequestObject.send(null);
  }
}
</script>
```

Note that at the end of the preceding code, we use the XMLHttpRequest object's send method to attempt to download the data. Here's the whole example, timeout.html:

```
<html>
  <head>
    <title>Handling Ajax Timeouts</title>

    <script language = "javascript">
      function getData(dataSource, divID)
      {
        var XMLHttpRequestObject = false;

        if (window.XMLHttpRequest) {
          XMLHttpRequestObject = new XMLHttpRequest();
        } else if (window.ActiveXObject) {
          XMLHttpRequestObject = new ActiveXObject("Microsoft.XMLHTTP");
        }

        if(XMLHttpRequestObject) {
          var obj = document.getElementById(divID);
          XMLHttpRequestObject.open("GET", dataSource);

          var timeoutIsSet = false;
          var downloadWentOK = false;

          XMLHttpRequestObject.onreadystatechange = function()
          {
            if (XMLHttpRequestObject.readyState == 1) {
              if(!timeoutIsSet){
                window.setTimeout(function(){
                  if(!downloadWentOK){
```

```
                    alert("Sorry, but I timed out.");
                    XMLHttpRequestObject.abort();
                }
            },
            1000);
            timeoutIsSet = true;
        }
    }

        if (XMLHttpRequestObject.readyState == 4 &&
          XMLHttpRequestObject.status == 200) {
            downloadWentOK = true;
            obj.innerHTML = XMLHttpRequestObject.responseText;
        }
    }

        XMLHttpRequestObject.send(null);
    }
    }
    </script>
</head>

<body>

    <H1>Handling Ajax Timeouts</H1>

    <form>
      <input type = "button" value = "Download Message"
        onclick = "getData('data.txt', 'targetDiv')">
    </form>

    <div id="targetDiv">
      <p>The fetched data will go here.</p>
    </div>

</body>
</html>
```

Because the file this example tries to download, data.txt, doesn't exist, the Ajax operation times out in this case, as you can see in the message box in Figure 12-4. Cool.

Figure 12-4   Timing out in an Ajax application

Downloading Images with Ajax

We'll take a look at one last example in this chapter, showing how to download images using Ajax. "What's that?" you ask. "Downloading *images*? Can't you download only text-based data with Ajax?"

That's right, you can download only text. But that text can be the name of the image file you want to download, and if you use that image's filename to create an HTML <img> element, then the browser—through the magic of dynamic HTML—will download the image immediately, no page refresh needed.

Here's an example, images.html, that shows this in action. First, we can add to the page two buttons that let the user download either of two images, image 1 or image 2, as well as a <div> element to display the new images in:

```
<body>

  <H1>Downloading Images With Ajax</H1>

  <form>
    <input type = "button" value = "Show image 1"
      onclick =
        "getData('imageName1.txt', callback)">
    <input type = "button" value = "Show image 2"
      onclick =
        "getData('imageName2.txt', callback)">
  </form>

  <div id="targetDiv">
    <p>The fetched image will appear here.</p>
  </div>

</body>
```

Note that the getData function is being asked to download imageName1.txt or imageName2.txt, which are the files that contain the name of the image to download using dynamic HTML. Here's what's in imageName1.txt:

```
Image1.jpg
```

And here's what's in imageName2.txt:

```
Image2.jpg
```

So what we're actually downloading using Ajax is the name of the image file. After that's been downloaded, we can pass that name to a new function named, say, callback, to create the new <img> element:

```
<script language = "javascript">

  function getData(imageName, callback)
```

```
    {
      var XMLHttpRequestObject = false;

      if (window.XMLHttpRequest) {
        XMLHttpRequestObject = new XMLHttpRequest();
      } else if (window.ActiveXObject) {
        XMLHttpRequestObject = new
          ActiveXObject("Microsoft.XMLHTTP");
      }

      if(XMLHttpRequestObject) {
        XMLHttpRequestObject.open("GET", imageName);

        XMLHttpRequestObject.onreadystatechange = function()
        {
          if (XMLHttpRequestObject.readyState == 4 &&
            XMLHttpRequestObject.status == 200) {
              callback(XMLHttpRequestObject.responseText);
              delete XMLHttpRequestObject;
              XMLHttpRequestObject = null;
          }
        }

        XMLHttpRequestObject.send(null);
      }
    }
        .
        .
        .

  </script>
```

In the callback function, we use the name of the image to create a new <img> element, which we place in the target <div> element like this:

```
  <script language = "javascript">

    function getData(imageName, callback)
    {
      var XMLHttpRequestObject = false;

      if (window.XMLHttpRequest) {
        XMLHttpRequestObject = new XMLHttpRequest();
      } else if (window.ActiveXObject) {
        XMLHttpRequestObject = new
          ActiveXObject("Microsoft.XMLHTTP");
      }

      if(XMLHttpRequestObject) {
        XMLHttpRequestObject.open("GET", imageName);
```

```
      XMLHttpRequestObject.onreadystatechange = function()
      {
        if (XMLHttpRequestObject.readyState == 4 &&
          XMLHttpRequestObject.status == 200) {
            callback(XMLHttpRequestObject.responseText);
            delete XMLHttpRequestObject;
            XMLHttpRequestObject = null;
        }
      }

      XMLHttpRequestObject.send(null);
    }
  }


  function callback(imageName)
  {
    document.getElementById("targetDiv").innerHTML =
      "<img border='1' src= " + imageName + ">";
  }

</script>
```

And that's it—now we've downloaded the name of the image the user wants to see, and displayed that image. Here's the whole application, images.html:

```
<html>
  <head>
    <title>Downloading Images With Ajax</title>

    <script language = "javascript">

      function getData(imageName, callback)
      {
        var XMLHttpRequestObject = false;

        if (window.XMLHttpRequest) {
          XMLHttpRequestObject = new XMLHttpRequest();
        } else if (window.ActiveXObject) {
          XMLHttpRequestObject = new
            ActiveXObject("Microsoft.XMLHTTP");
        }

        if(XMLHttpRequestObject) {
          XMLHttpRequestObject.open("GET", imageName);

          XMLHttpRequestObject.onreadystatechange = function()
          {
```

```
            if (XMLHttpRequestObject.readyState == 4 &&
               XMLHttpRequestObject.status == 200) {
                callback(XMLHttpRequestObject.responseText);
                delete XMLHttpRequestObject;
                XMLHttpRequestObject = null;
            }
          }

          XMLHttpRequestObject.send(null);
        }
      }

      function callback(imageName)
      {
        document.getElementById("targetDiv").innerHTML =
          "<img border='1' src= " + imageName + ">";
      }

    </script>
  </head>

  <body>

    <H1>Downloading Images With Ajax</H1>

    <form>
      <input type = "button" value = "Show image 1"
        onclick =
          "getData('imageName1.txt', callback)">
      <input type = "button" value = "Show image 2"
        onclick =
          "getData('imageName2.txt', callback)">
    </form>

    <div id="targetDiv">
      <p>The fetched image will appear here.</p>
    </div>

  </body>
</html>
```

You can see the results in Figure 12-5, where the user has clicked button 1 and downloaded image 1—no browser window refresh needed.

And in Figure 12-6, you can see how the user can download image 2 by clicking button 2. Cool.

Of course, this was just an example—the real power of this technique becomes apparent when the images sent from the server vary depending on the data sent to the server.

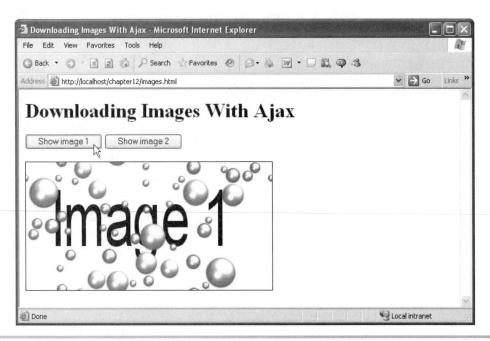

Figure 12-5 Downloading image 1

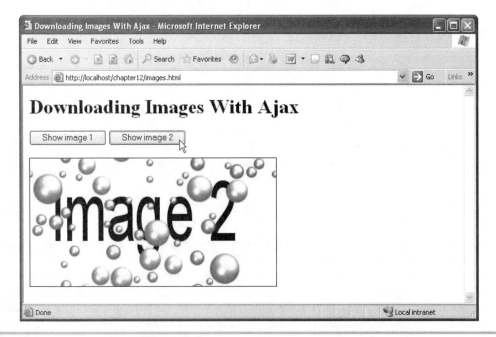

Figure 12-6 Downloading image 2

Index

D

T